Complete Technical BIM

Project using

Autodesk® Revit®

Architecture - Structure - MEP

Mohammad Imtaar

Available from Amazon.com, CreateSpace.com, and other retail outlets

Acknowledgments

In writing this book, I have consulted many of my colleagues in the Department of Building Engineering, University of Dammam, who gave me very helpful suggestions. I am thankful to Engr. Mohammad Fouad, Dr. Essam Shaawat, Dr. Mohammed Moonis Zaheer and Engr. Rehan Jamil for guiding me on different topics. Thanks to Engr. Abdullah Maqsud of Saudi Oger Ltd. for consultations on different topics. Thanks to Dr. Othman AlShamrani, Department Chairman for very helpful support. Thanks to all of you and I hope that you will guide me more to improve this book.

I am also thankful to my students who asked me such questions whose answers were very helpful to make this book more useful.

Introduction

Suppose you want to make architectural, structural, mechanical, electrical and plumbing models of a building using Autodesk® Revit® but you don't have any practical experience of using Revit, then this book is for you. You will start from scratch and the book will guide you in step by step procedures to develop the models. I have tried to include all the information needed to develop the models in the book. I hope you will not be stuck at any point and waste your time in searching Help, Internet or other books to work on the topics.

The book doesn't teach you lessons to remember or doesn't ask you questions to answer. From Chapter 1, you start your model and by the end of each chapter, you will see that a part of the model is complete.

The book has three parts, Architecture, Structure and MEP. You start with making architectural model. When it is complete, you will use it to extract information for Structural model. In the last part, you will add services (air-conditioning, lighting, electrical and plumbing) to your architectural model (used as linked model).

Starting Point:

To work on each part, you will need a starting project. These projects can found in the download folder as explained below.

If you want to work on Architectural model only, start from Chapter 1.

If you want to work on Structural model only, start from Chapter 2 and jump to Chapter 12.

If you want to work on AC Design only, start from Chapter 17.

If you want to work on Lighting and Electrical Design only, start from Chapter 22.

If you want to work on Plumbing Design only, start from Chapter 24.

Download Folder:

You download the required files from BimBook folder at
http://www.keepandshare.com/doc20/show.php?i=2635007&cat=2
and save them on your hard disk.

- Keep all files in the same folder.
- Unzip Join32.zip. Run Join32.exe.
- One by one, open all *.rvt files in Revit and save them again.
- Delete all 001, 002 etc. files.

E-mail for Suggestions:

bimbooktech@gmail.com

What you accomplish in each chapter:

Part 1 . Architecture

Chapter 1

You setup levels, make grids and set the angle of true north.

Chapter 2

You make structural columns and shear walls.

Chapter 3

You work on the Ground Floor level. You make walls, floor, rooms, doors, windows, stairs and ceilings.

Chapter 4

You work on Pavement level. You make stairs and ramp at entrance. You also make pavement floor.

Chapter 5

You work on First Floor level. You copy walls, doors and windows from Ground Floor level and edit them according to the plan.

Chapter 6

You work on the Roof level. You make walls and roof.

Chapter 7

You work on the Sit plan. You make Boundary Wall, Pavement Curb, Roads and add planting, Parking Spaces, vehicles and other site components.

Chapter 8

You extract building information from the model in form of schedules. You make door and room schedules in different forms.

Chapter 9

You will present the model in the form of sheets. You make a title block. On this title block, you make sheets for ground floor plan, first floor plan, site plan and schedules.

Chapter 10

You make a callout from a section view. You add material tags showing structure of floor and wall. You present this information on a sheet.

Part 2 . Structure

Chapter 11

You start a new structural project and copy levels, grids, columns, shear walls and stairs from the architectural model.

Chapter 12

You work on Foundation level. You make isolated foundations under the columns and wall foundations under the shear walls.

Chapter 13

You work on Ground Floor level. You make ground beams, slab on grade and slab edges.

Chapter 14

You work on First Floor level. You copy beams from Ground Floor level and edit them to make drop beams and hourdi beams. You make one-way and two-way hourdi slabs. In some part, you make solid slab.

Chapter 15

You work on Roof level. You copy drop beams from First Floor level. In one part of the roof, you add pre-cast hollow core slabs. In another part, you make waffle slab.

Chapter 16

You present the structural plans in the form of sheets.

Part 3 . MEP

Chapter 17

You start a new MEP project. You link it with the architectural model and prepare it to add services.

Chapter 18

You divide the model in spaces and zones. You set energy analysis properties of zones.

Chapter 19

You make energy analysis of the model to calculate heating and cooling load of spaces, zones and the whole building. On the base of this calculation, you add air terminals on the ceiling and adjust their air flow.

Chapter 20

You add VAV boxes and make secondary air supply system by automatically connecting VAV boxes and air terminals with ducts. You run a primary duct connecting VAV boxes with the air conditioner. You make automatic duct sizing and repair any problems in the ductwork.

Chapter 21

You present the duct layout plans and 3D views of AC system on sheets.

Chapter 22

You make lighting analysis of the building and add lighting fixtures in different spaces according to the lighting requirement.

Chapter 23

You place distribution panel boards in mechanical/electrical rooms. You add lighting switches and power receptacles in different rooms. You make electrical wiring for lighting systems and power receptacles. You present the wiring diagrams on sheets.

Chapter 24

You copy plumbing fixtures from architectural model. You add more plumbing fixtures and fittings. You make pipe work for sanitary, vent, cold water and hot water systems. You make automatic pipe sizing. You present different plumbing systems (in plans and 3D views) on sheets.

Contents at a Glance

Contents

Part 1 . Architecture

1　New Architectural Project

Before starting a new Architectural Project, you need to get familiar with Revit environment. You will know where different components are stored. You will explore different parts of the user interface. Then you will start your project by defining levels of your building (in an elevation view) and grid layout (in a floor plan view).

1.1 Revit Options

After you install Revit, sometimes you may need to setup the places where libraries for components (or blocks), templates and other elements are saved. It saves time when you want to find different elements.

Normally these places are setup by the install process. But you may change them if you need.

1. Install Autodesk Revit Software with US Metric content.
2. If Revit Content is not downloaded then
   - Download US Metric Library.
   - Copy it in C:\ProgramData\Autodesk\RVT 201?\Libraries\. (You can copy it at any other place on your computer and set file locations properly).
3. Open Revit Program.
4. Click on 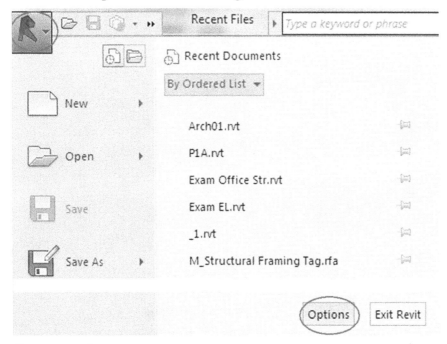 (Revit Button).
5. Click on Options as shown in Fig 1.1.

Fig. 1.1　– Revit Button

6. Check that File Locations for User Files and Family Template Files are set properly (Fig. 1.2).
7. Check that Places for Metric Library and Metric Detail Library are set properly.

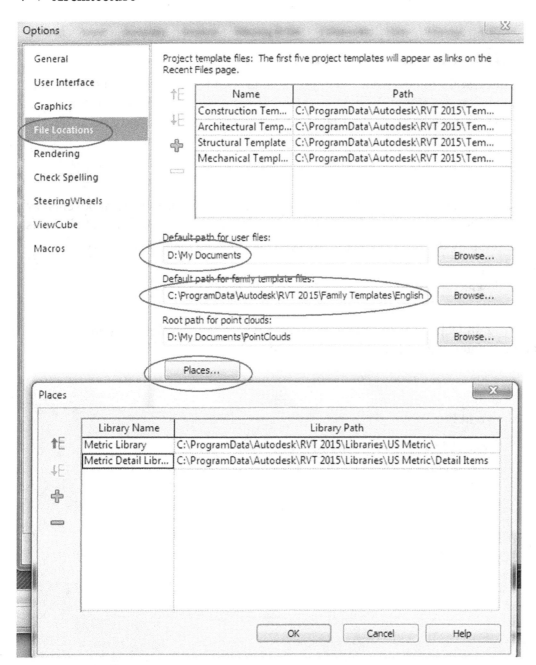

Fig. 1.2 – Setting File Locations

1.2 The Revit Project

What you make in Revit is a Project. A Revit Project consists of many Views (Plans, Elevations, Sections etc.), Schedules (Tables), Drawing Sheets etc. These elements are arranged in a tree view called the Project Browser (Fig. 1.3).

Each element has different properties. These properties are shown in Properties Palette (Fig. 1.3).

Any change in an element in one view or schedule revises all other views or schedules instantly. That is why the name **Revit** (**Rev**ise **i**nstantly). Different views can have different visibility settings.

1.3 The User Interface

When you start the Revit program, what you see on the desktop is the user interface. Different tools are arranged in the form of a Ribbon. The default user interface shows the Ribbon, Palettes and a large drawing area where you draw different elements of your Revit project. In a plan view, you can see the four elevation symbols.

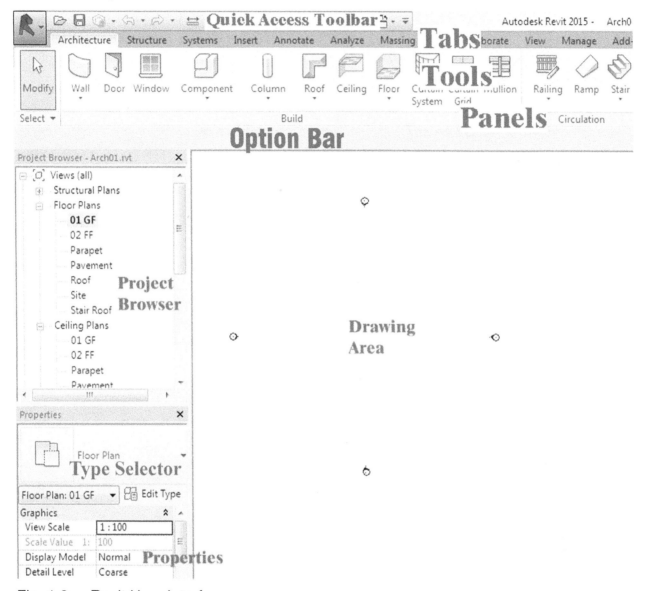

Fig. 1.3 – Revit User Interface

1. The Ribbon consists of Tabs, Panels, Tools etc.
2. Each **TAB** (Architecture, Structure, System, Insert ...) represents a particular topic.
3. When you press a tab, all panels change according to the topic of the tab.
4. Each panel contains tools to do a particular job.
5. A **contextual tab** appears to show tools to edit/modify a particular object. When job is done, the contextual tab disappears.
6. The Option Bar contains textboxes, checkboxes, radiobuttons etc. to gather information about the object under work.
7. In the drawing area, you sketch/modify different Revit elements.

8. You can put frequently used tools on QAT (Quick Access Toolbar). Right-click any tool and select Add to QAT. On far right of QAT, there is dropdown box which controls the visibility of the tools on QAT.

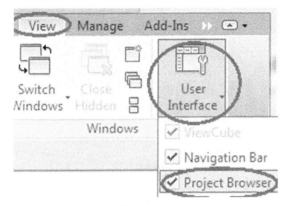

Fig. 1.4 – Visibility settings for Revit User Interface components

9. If you do not see the Project Browser, then on View tab → Windows panel → User Interface dropdown → Select Project Browser (Fig. 1.4).
10. If you do not see the Properties palette, then on View tab → Windows panel → User Interface dropdown → Select Properties.
11. On lower part of the Revit window, you see the View Control bar, which contains tools to control the view. Bring cursor on any tool to see its description (Fig. 1.5).

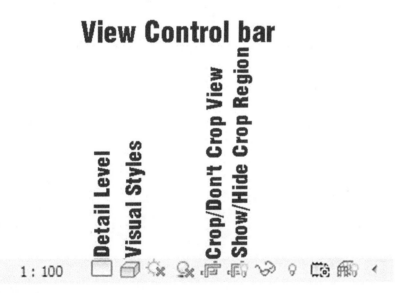

Fig. 1.5 – View Control Bar Tools

1.4 Initial Setup

Before you start sketching the elements of your Revit project, you need some preparations.

1.4.1 Starting a New Architectural Project

You will start your work with a project ArchProject.rvt. You will download this file from Download Folder (page v).

1. Open Revit → Projects → Open (Fig. 1.6).

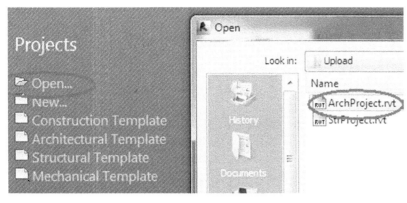

Fig. 1.6 – Opening a new project

2. Select **arch_project.rvt** → Open
3. Save Project As **Arch01**

1.4.2 Enter Project Information

At the start of a new project, you will enter some information about your project. This information will be used in different places. (You can enter or revise this information at some later time also.)

1. Manage Tab (Fig. 1.7).
2. Settings Panel.
3. Click Project Information.

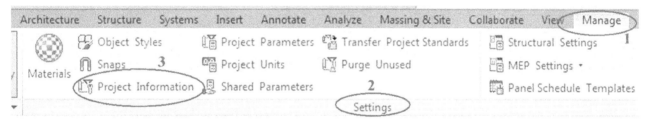

Fig. 1.7 – Project Information tool

4. Enter all the information (Fig. 1.8).

Parameter	Value
Identity Data	
Organization Name	My Organization
Organization Description	Building Material Traders
Building Name	Sales Office
Author	My Name
Energy Analysis	
Energy Settings	Edit...
Other	
Project Issue Date	01/01/2015
Project Status	Under Construction
Client Name	My Client
Project Address	Edit...
Project Name	My Project
Project Number	PRJ - 123

Fig. 1.8 – Project Information table

1.4.3 Set Project Units

You can set project units as millimeters, meters etc.

1. Manage Tab
2. Settings Panel
3. Click Project Units
4. Set Project Units = Meters with rounding up to 2 decimal places as shown in Fig 1.9.

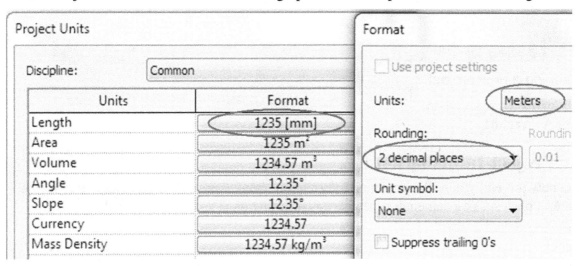

Fig. 1.9 – Project Units

1.5 Project Levels

First thing you add to a technical project are levels. By default, 2 levels (Level 1 and Level 2) and their Floor Plan and Ceiling Plan views are present. You can add more levels in an Elevation or Section view.

1.5.1 Plan Views

Each level has associated plan views e.g. Floor Plan view, Structural Plan view, Ceiling Plan view. Different plan views are grouped in the Project Browser. When you create a new level, you can decide which plan views you want to create with it. Any plan view can be created or deleted later on.

1. If a level is deleted, all of its associated plan views are also deleted.
2. If a plan view is not created or it is deleted, it can be created again with all the elements present in it.

1.5.2 Add Levels

You will add more levels showing their associated plan views in the project browser.

1. In Project Browser, under Elevations, double-click South (Fig. 1.10). You will see that 01 Level and 02 Level are already present.
2. Architecture Tab
3. Datum Panel → Click Level.
4. In Type selector, select Level : 8mm Head (Fig. 1.11).
5. On Option bar click Plan View Types → Select Floor Plan (Fig. 1.11).

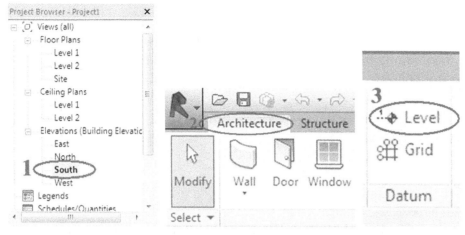

Fig. 1.10 – Level tool to draw new levels

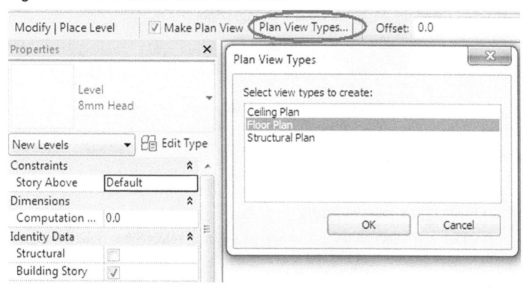

Fig. 1.11 – Selecting Plan View Types for new levels

6. Draw three levels below 01 Level and three levels above 02 Level. (Draw at any height. Level names and level heights will be adjusted later). To draw a level:

- Bring cursor to left side. When you see dashed aligning line, click.
- Bring cursor to right side. When you see dashed aligning line, click. New level is created.

Fig. 1.12 – Selecting Plan View Types for new levels

7. All new levels appear in Project Browser, under Floor Plans node.

1.5.3 Change Levels Symbols

The level symbols you see in the project are circles. Sometimes you want to change them to triangles. First you will load the triangle symbol family from the library. Then you will make a new level type. You will edit type and change the symbol.

1. Insert Tab.
2. Load From Library Panel → Click Load Family.
3. Annotations → M_Level Head - Triangle Spot.rfa.
4. In Project Browser, under Elevations, double-click South.
5. Select a Level.
6. On Properties Palette , click Edit Type (Fig. 1.12).
7. Type Properties dialog box will appear.
8. In Type Properties dialog box, click Duplicate button → Enter Name = 8mm Head Triangle Spot → OK.
9. Under Graphics group, select Symbol = M_Level Head - Triangle Spot → OK.
10. New type of level is created.

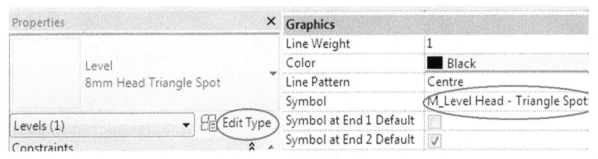

Fig. 1.12 – Selecting Plan View Types for new levels

11. Select other levels (press CTRL and select all levels) → In type selector, select 8mm Head Triangle Spot. Level Symbols will change as shown in Fig. 1.13.

1.5.4 Adjust Levels

The levels you just added have different names and elevations as seen on the Level Symbol. You need to change both name and elevation for each level.

1. Click on a Level.
2. In Properties, change Name (or click (slowly) twice on Name and change).
3. "Would you like to rename corresponding views?" **Yes**
4. In Properties, change Elevation (or click (slowly) twice on Elevation and change).
5. Adjust all levels as shown in Fig 1.13.

1.5.5 Make Elbow in Level Line

Some level lines are very close and the information overlaps. You can bend the level line by making an elbow or kink.

1. Click on a Level.
2. You will see a Break Control on the Level Line (Fig. 1.15).
3. Click on the Break Control.
4. The Level Line will bend.
5. Adjust the bend points.
6. Align bend points of all levels (Fig. 1.15).

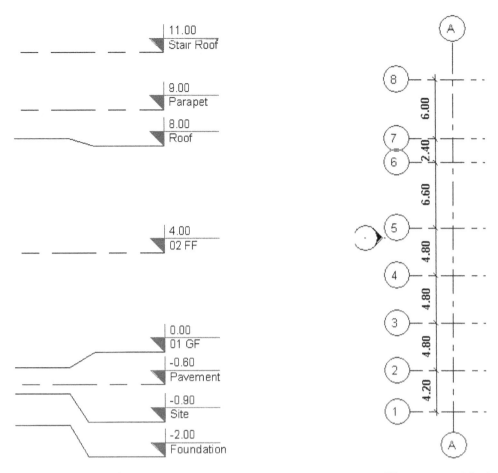

Fig. 1.13 – Project levels

Fig. 1.14 – Horizontal Grid Lines

Fig. 1.15 – Elbow in Level Line

1.6 Grids

After the levels, the next thing in a technical project is Grid Lines. The grid lines are drawn according to module. Most of the building elements (columns, walls, foundations etc.) are drawn on grids.

1.6.1 Horizontal Grids

You will draw grids on a module of 0.6m.

1. Project Browser → Floor Plans → double-click 01 GF.
2. On Architecture tab → Datum panel → Click Grid.
3. In Type selector, select Type = 6.5mm Bubble.
4. Near the South Elevation, click left then click right to draw a grid line between West and East Elevations (Fig. 1.16).

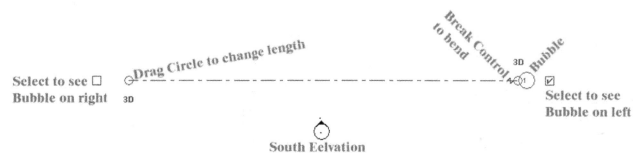

Fig. 1.16 – Horizontal Grid Line

5. See that the number inside the Bubble is 1. (If not, then click on number 2 times and change it to 1).
6. Architecture Tab → Datum Panel → Click Grid.
7. You will see Contextual Tab of Modify | Place Grid.
8. Click on Pick Lines (Fig. 1.17).
9. Offset = 4.2
10. Hover over the Grid 1.
11. You will see a dashed blue line above or below the Grid 1 (depending on where you place the mouse pointer).

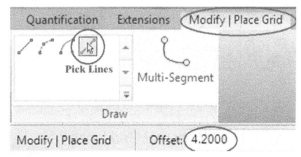

Fig. 1.17 – Pick Lines tool on Modify | Place Grid Contextual Tab

12. When you see the dashed blue line above the Grid 1(Fig. 1.18), click.
13. You will see the Grid 2.
14. In this way draw other horizontal Grid lines at offset distances 4.8, 4.8, 4.8, 6.6, 2.4, 6.0 as shown in Fig. 1.14.

Fig. 1.18 – Grid Line Offset.

15. The grids can be drawn in the following ways also:

- Draw all the grids by clicking left and right (Fig. 1.16) and the adjust distances from Grid 2 upwards.
- Install Grid Generator utility and use it.

1.6.2 Vertical Grids

1. Now draw a vertical grid line from down to up near the west elevation.
2. Change its number (in the bubble) to A as shown in Fig. 1.19.
3. Now Pick Lines for other grid lines at Offset = 5.4, 2.4, 6.6, 4.8, 4.8, 4.8, 4.2

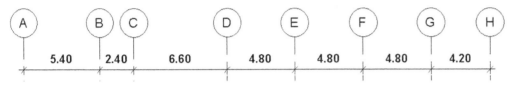

Fig. 1.19 – Vertical Grid Lines

1.6.3 Position Grids

1. Select a horizontal grid and drag its Drag Circles to adjust its length from left and right
2. Similarly adjust length of vertical grid
3. Select all the grid lines by dragging a window from top-right to lower-left
4. Bring mouse pointer on any line. A four-sided arrow will appear
5. Drag to bring all the grids approximately in the middle of the Elevations.

1.6.4 Change Grid Length

If we select a Grid and drag the circle near the Head or Bubble, length of all locked Grids change. To change the length of one Grid, we must unlock it.

1. Click on Grid 5. A lock appears
2. Click on lock to unlock it as shown in Fig. 1.20.

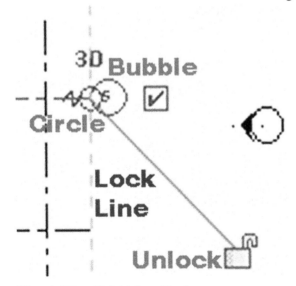

Fig. 1.20 – Grid Line End

3. Drag the Circle on right side to bring it near Grid C.
4. In this way change the length of other Grid lines as shown in Fig. 1.21.

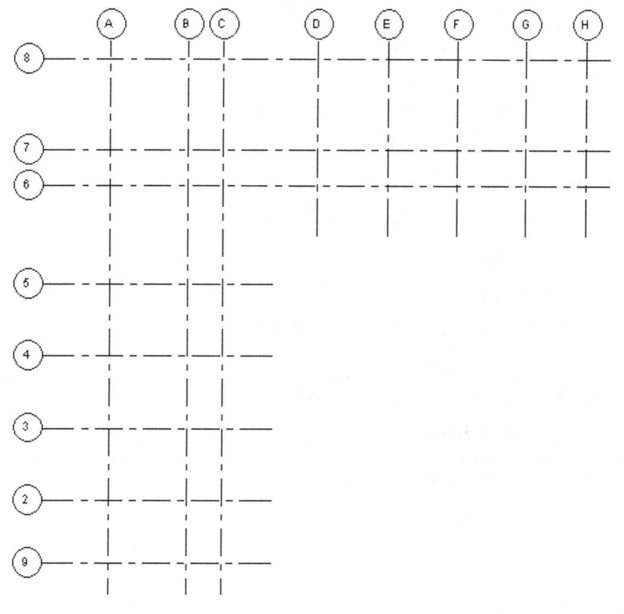

Fig. 1.21 – Project Grid

1.7 True North

1. Project Browser → under Floor Plans → double-click Site.
2. Press VG (on keyboard) to show the Visibility/Graphics dialog Box.
3. On Model Categories tab, expand Site and select Project Base Point → OK (Fig. 1.22).
4. You will see the Project Base Point in the view.
5. Click in the center of Project Base Point.
6. In Properties palette, change Angle to True North = 120° (Fig. 1.23).

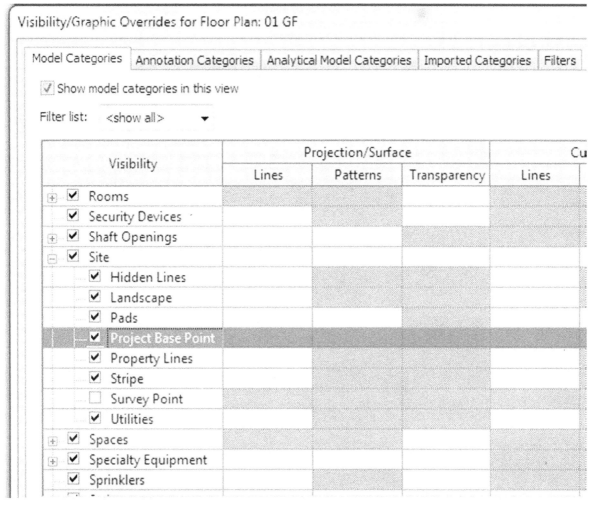

Fig. 1.22 – Visibility/Graphics Overrides

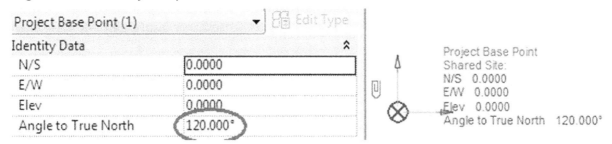

Fig. 1.23 – Setting True North

7. Click ![save icon] to Save Projet As **Arch01**.

2 Structural Elements

Now you can start drawing the building elements or components. You will draw structural components such as columns and shear walls. If a component family is not loaded in the project, then you will load it from the component library or folder.

Sometimes you need to place an element whose properties (width, height etc.) are different from those found in the library. You can select an element, duplicate and rename it. Then you can change its properties as needed.

2.1 Columns

Rectangular concrete columns will be placed on grid intersections. Each column will have base level at Foundation and top level at Roof.

2.1.1 Add New Concrete Columns at Foundation Level

You will add concrete columns 400 x 600 mm going from Foundation level to Roof level. This type of column is not available in the library but 450 x 600 mm is available. You will use this type to make a new type.

1. Open Project **Arch01.**
2. Save Project As **Arch02.**
3. Floor Plans → Foundation.
4. Structure Tab → Structure Panel → Click on Column Tool.
5. Mode Panel → Load Family.
6. You should see subfolders in US Metric folder. If not, then make settings as shown in Fig. 1.2.
7. Structural Columns → Concrete → M_Concrete-Rectangular-Column.rfa.
8. In Properties palette → Type selector → select Type = M_Concrete- Rectangular -Column : 450 x 600 mm (Fig. 2.1).

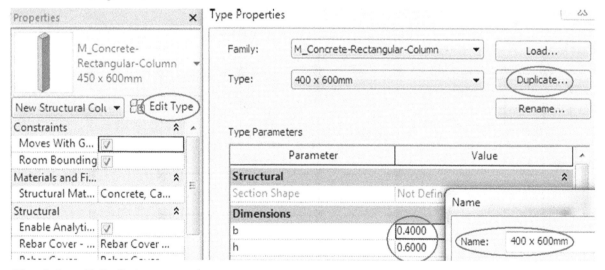

Fig. 2.1 – Edit Column type

9. In Properties palette , click Edit Type.
10. Click Duplicate → Name = 400 x 600 mm.
11. b = 0.4, h = 0.6
12. Placement Panel → select Vertical Column (Blue).
13. On Option bar, set Height = Roof.

14. Multiple Panel → At Grids (Fig. 2.2).

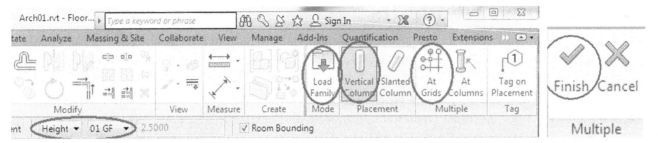

Fig. 2.2 – Column placement   Fig. 2.3 – Finish

15. Draw a selection box (Right to Left) around all the grids → Click Finish (Fig. 2.3).

2.1.2 Delete Extra Columns

Columns are placed on all grid intersections. Some columns need to be deleted.

1. Draw a selection box (Left to Right) around the grid B from Grids 3 to 7 to select columns at B2, B3, B4, B5, B6, B7 → Press Delete.
2. Select C6, (press Ctrl) C7, F7 → Press Delete.

2.1.3 Add a Column manually

If a column is not on a grid intersection, it will not be drawn. You can draw this column manually.

1. Structure Tab → Structure Panel → Click on Column Tool.
2. Height = Roof (Fig. 2.2).
3. In Properties palette → Type selector → select Type = M_Concrete- Rectangular -Column : 400 x 600 mm.
4. Add a column anywhere on grid C between grid 7 and grid 8 (Fig 2.4).

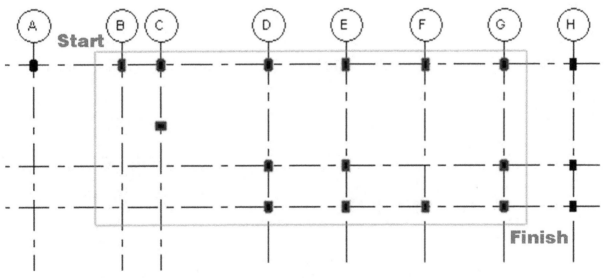

Fig. 2.4 – Selection box for Columns

5. Select this column. Temporary dimensions appear. Adjust its distance = 3.6m from grid 8.
6. If the temporary dimension is not showing distance from grid 8, drag the witness line control (blue dot) to grid 8. The dimension will show distance of column from grid 8 (Fig 2.5).
7. Click on number in temporary dimension → change → press Enter.

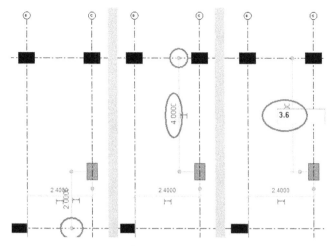

Fig. 2.5 – Selection box for Columns

2.1.4 Rotate Selected Columns

Some columns need to be rotated along the wall. This can be done by just pressing Space bar.

1. Draw a selection box (Left to Right) around columns (close to columns) at the intersection of grids B-G and 6-8.
2. Click on Filter → Click Check None → Select Structural Columns (Fig. 2.5).

3. Press Space bar. All selected columns will be rotated by 90 °.

2.1.4 Change Appearance of Columns

In Foundation plan, the columns are shown with concrete pattern. You can change the appearance to Solid Black by editing the Structural Material.

1. Draw a selection box (Right to Left) to select all.
2. Click on Filter → Click Check None → Select Structural Columns (Fig. 2.5).

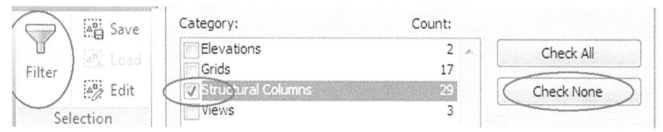

Fig. 2.5 – Filter for Columns

3. Properties Palette → Structural Material (Concrete, Cast-in-Place gray). Click on ⋯ (Fig. 2.6).
4. In Materials Palette, Duplicate the Selected Material (right-click on material → Duplicate).
5. Rename it as Concrete, Cast-in-Place gray col (right-click on material → Rename).
6. Select Cut Pattern = Solid Fill, Color = RGB 0, 0, 0 (Black) (Fig. 2.7).

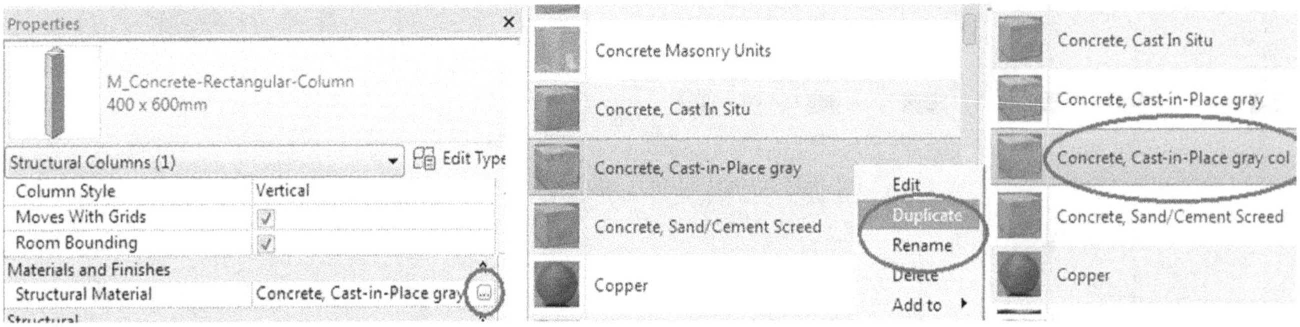

Fig. 2.6 – Material for Columns

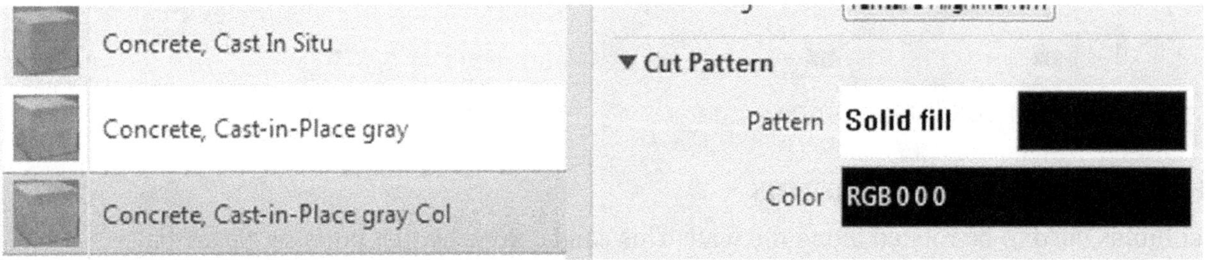

Fig. 2.7 – Cut Pattern for Material

7. The Foundation Plan view looks as shown in Fig 2.9.
8. See 3D View.

    - Click on 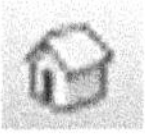 on Quick Access Toolbar.
    - Project Browser → 3D Views → click on {3D}.

9. You will see the 3D View.

2.1.5 Room Bounding

1. Floor Plans → 01 GF.
2. Select all → Filter → Check None → Select Structural Columns only.
3. In Properties palette, set Room Bounding = ☐ False (Fig. 2.8).

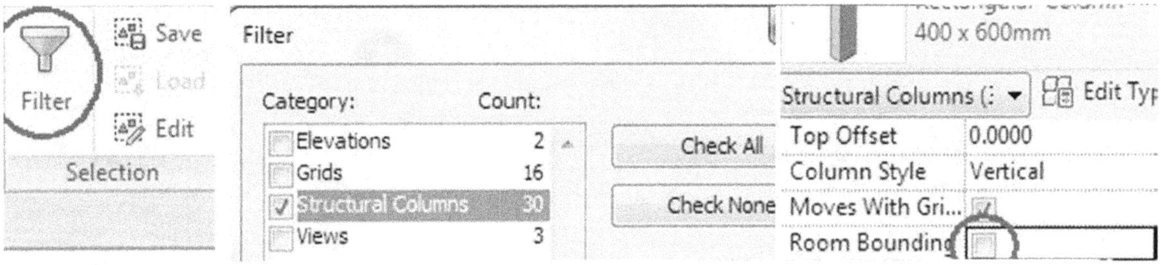

Fig. 2.8 – Remove Room Bounding property

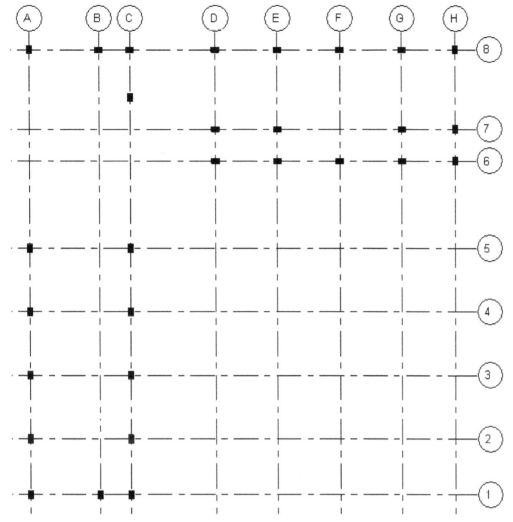

Fig. 2.9 – Foundation Plan

2.2 Shear Walls

Shear walls are structural load bearing walls. They are constructed around stairs or elevators. Shear walls are continuous from Foundation level to Roof level. You will make a 250 mm thick wall for this purpose (245 mm concrete, 5 mm Plaster).

1. Floor Plans → Foundation
2. Structure Tab → Structure Panel → Wall → Wall : Structural Wall (Fig. 2.10).
3. Height = Roof
4. In Properties palette → Type selector → select type = Basic Wall : Retaining - 300mm Concrete
5. Click on Edit Type
6. In Type Properties, click on Duplicate → Name = Shear - 250mm Concrete
7. Under Type Parameters → Construction group → Structure → click Edit.
8. Under Layers, change thickness of layer 2 to 0.248 (Fig. 2.11).
9. Bring cursor on layer 1 and click (You will see a small arrow on left side).
10. Press Insert.
11. A new layer will be added above Core Boundary layer.

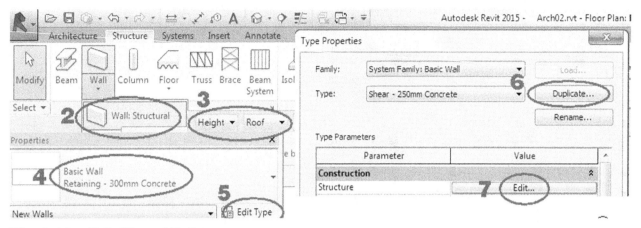

Fig. 2.10 – Edit Shear Wall type

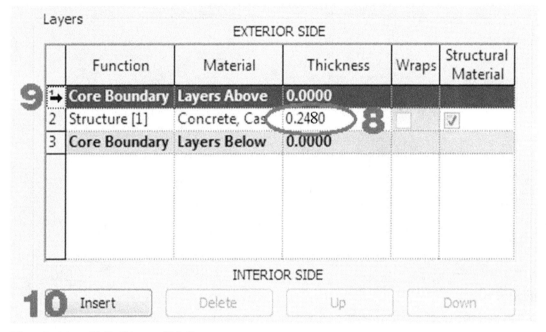

Fig. 2.11 – Edit Shear Wall structure

12. Change Function to Finish 1 [4] (Fig. 2.12).
13. Change thickness to 0.002. Wraps ☑

14. Under Material, click on ⌄. Material Browser will open.
15. Check if Library Panel is visible. If not, click on square in upper right corner.
16. In Library Panel, click on Autodesk Materials.
17. In materials list, click on Plaster then click on Up arrow.
18. Click OK → OK. New material (Plaster) will be added. Click OK → OK (Material for layer 1 will be Plaster).

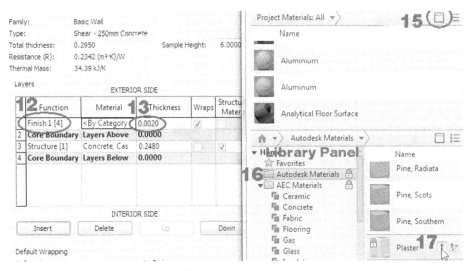

Fig. 2.12 – Edit Shear Wall material

19. Edit Type → Under Type Parameters → Graphics group → Coarse Scale Fill Pattern = Solid Fill.
20. On Modify | Place Structural Wall contextual tab → Draw panel → select Line tool.
21. Set properties: Base Constraint = Foundation, Top Constraint = Up to level: Roof

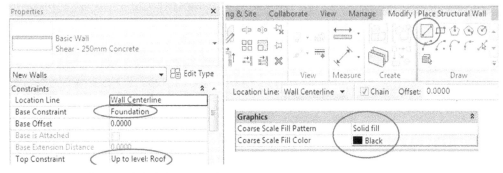

Fig. 2.13 – Shear Wall Properties

22. Now draw the shear wall as shown in Fig. 2.14.

- Click on A (intersection B7) – B (intersection A7) – C (Anywhere on grid A) – D (Anywhere on grid B) – E (intersection B6) – F (intersection A6) – Esc.
- Click on G (mid point of EF) – H (mid point of CD) – Esc.
- Select CD. Temporary dimensions appear. Click on number and change distance = 2.00 from grid 6. Press Enter.

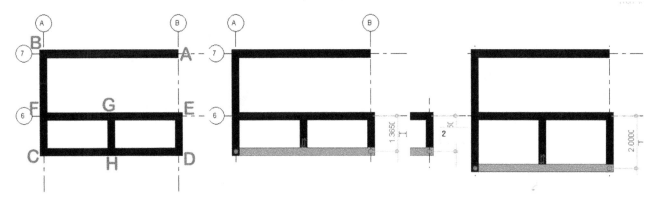

Fig. 2.14 – Shear Wall placement

23. Make sure that the plaster is on outer side. To do this, click to select each shear wall. You will see a double arrow. It should be on the outer side. If it is not, then click on the double-arrow (or press space bar) to bring it on the outer side.

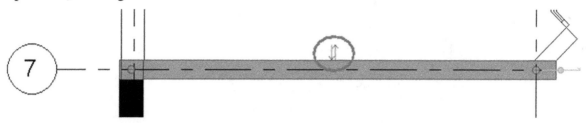

Fig. 2.15 – Shear Wall outer side

24. Select the shear wall on grid A.
25. Click on Edit Type
26. In Type Properties, click on Duplicate → Name = Shear - 300mm Concrete
27. Under Type Parameters → Construction group → Structure → click Edit
28. Change thickness of layer 3 (Structure [1]) to 0.298.

	Function	Material	Thickness	Wraps	Structural Material
1	Finish 1 [4]	Plaster	0.0020	✓	
2	**Core Boundary**	**Layers Above**	**0.0000**		
3	Structure [1]	Concrete, Cas	0.2980		✓
4	**Core Boundary**	**Layers Below**	**0.0000**		

Fig. 2.16 – Shear Wall structure

29. Click OK → OK.
30. See 3D View as explained in step 8 of § 2.1.4. (On View Control Bar at the bottom, change Visual Style = Shaded)

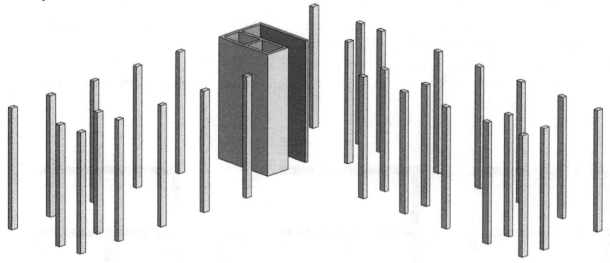

Fig. 2.17 – 3D view (Shaded)

31. Click 🖫 to Save Project As **Arch02**.

3 The Ground Floor Level

On the Ground Floor Level, you will add architectural elements such as Walls, Floor, Doors, Windows etc. You will adjust the structure of different elements where needed.

3.1 Materials

A wall or floor consists of many layers. Each layer has its own material and thickness. Before you make walls or floors, you need to prepare the materials to be used in different layers. Many materials are present in Autodesk Materials Library. You can add them to Project Materials list and change their appearance and properties.

3.1.1 Material with Pattern (Cement Block)

1. Open Project **Arch02**
2. Save Project As **Arch03a**
3. Manage Tab → Settings Panel → Materials
4. In Library Panel, click on Autodesk Materials (Fig. 3.1).
5. In materials list, click on Concrete Masonry Units then click on Up arrow. (If this material already exists in Project Materials, then click on Cancel).
6. In Project Materials, right-click on Concrete Masonry Units and select Duplicate.

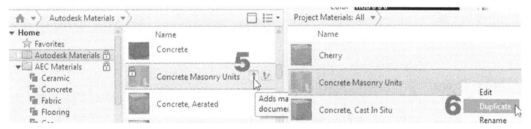

Fig. 3.1 – New Project Material

7. Rename the duplicated material as Cement Block
8. In Project Materials, select Cement Block and change Patterns as shown in Fig. 3.2

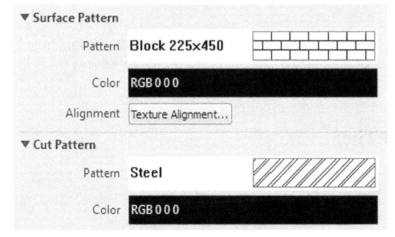

Fig. 3.2 – Change Material Patterns

3.1.2 Material with Color (Paint)

1. From Autodesk Materials, add Plastic, Opaque Black to Project Materials

2. Duplicate and rename it to Paint (Fig. 3.3).
3. On Appearance tab, adjust color.
4. Click on Duplicate Asset.

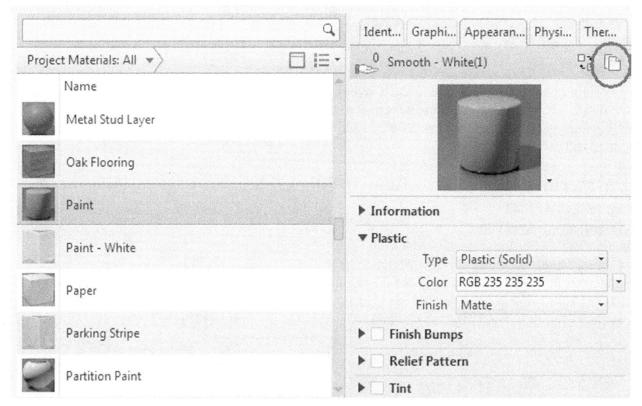

Fig. 3.3 – Change Material Color

3.1.3 Material with Image (Stone Floor)

1. From Autodesk Materials, add Stone to Project Materials (Fig 3.4).
2. Duplicate and rename it to Stone Floor.
3. Click on Appearance.
4. Click on Duplicate Asset.
5. Click on Image.
6. Click on Source and select Masonry.Stone.Marble.Square.Stacked.Polished.White-Brown.jpg from C:\Program Files (x86)\Common Files\Autodesk Shared\Materials\Textures\3\Mats folder.
7. Adjust other parameters.
8. Press OK.

3.1.4 Material with Image (Wall Tile)

1. Select Stone
2. Duplicate and rename it to Tile Wall.
3. Click on Appearance.
4. Click on Duplicate Asset.
5. Click on Image.
6. Click on Source and select Finishes.Wall Covering.Stripes.Vertical.Multi-colored.jpg from C:\Program Files (x86)\Common Files\Autodesk Shared\Materials\Textures\3\Mats folder.
7. Adjust other parameters.
8. Press OK.

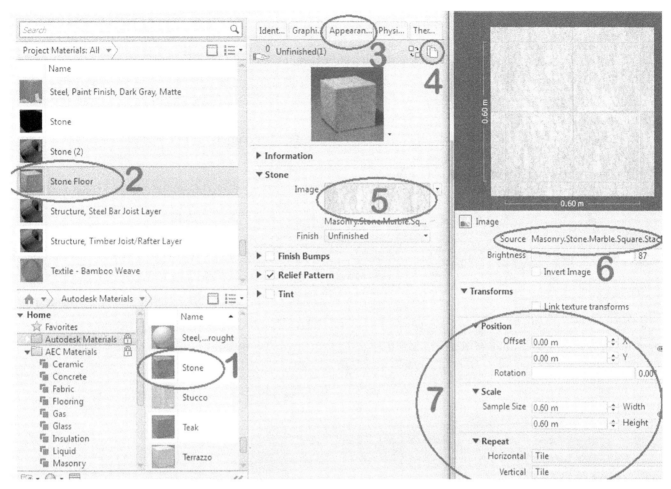

Fig. 3.4 – Change Material Appearance

3.1.5 Material with Image (Restroom Tile)

1. Select Stone
2. Duplicate and rename it to Tile Restroom.
3. Click on Appearance.
4. Click on Duplicate Asset.
5. Click on Image.
6. Click on Source and select Finishes.Flooring.Tile.Diamond.Red.png from C:\Program Files (x86)\Common Files\Autodesk Shared\Materials\Textures\3\Mats folder.
7. Under the image → Scale → Sample Size → change width = 0.30 m and height = 0.30 m.
8. Press OK.

3.2 Exterior Walls

An exterior wall consists of many layers for different purposes. Exterior layer is made of stone, marble, tile etc. for weather protection. Some middle layers are for energy efficiency and damp-proofing. Structural support is given by layers made of Structural Materials such as concrete, cement blocks, bricks etc. Interior layers are for paint or decoration.

3.2.1 Adjust the Structure of Exterior Walls

You will start the architectural model by adding an exterior wall. There are many types of walls present in Revit library, but you may want to add an exterior wall whose structure is of your choice. Therefore you will start with an existing wall and change its structure.

1. Floor Plans → 01 GF
2. On Architecture tab → Build panel → click Wall tool.
3. In Properties Palette , click on Type Selector (Fig. 3.5).
4. Select Basic Wall : Exterior - Block on Mtl. Stud. (You can select any other wall).
5. Click on Edit Type.
6. On Type Properties box, click on Duplicate.
7. Change Name = Exterior - 300mm → OK

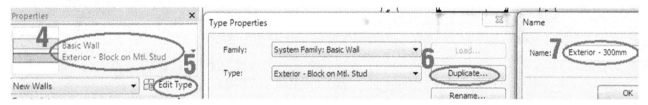

Fig. 3.5 – Edit Wall Type

8. On Type Properties dialog box → Construction group → Structure parameter → click on Edit (Fig. 3.6).

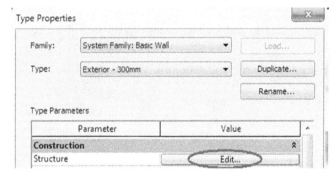

Fig. 3.6 – Edit Wall Structure

9. In the Edit Assembly dialogue box, use Insert, Delete, Up, Down buttons to add and position wall layers as shown.
10. Select Functions and Materials of layers. Write thickness of each layer select Wraps and Structural Material (Fig. 3.7).

Layers

EXTERIOR SIDE

	Function	Material	Thickness	Wraps	Stru Ma
1	Finish 1 [4]	Tile Wall	0.0120	✓	
2	Thermal/Air Laye	Thermal Barriers - External Wall Insulation	0.0400	✓	
3	Membrane Layer	Damp-proofing	0.0000	✓	
4	**Core Boundary**	**Layers Above Wrap**	**0.0000**		
5	Structure [1]	Cement Block	0.2100		✓
6	Thermal/Air Laye	Air	0.0250		
7	**Core Boundary**	**Layers Below Wrap**	**0.0000**		
8	Substrate [2]	Gypsum Wall Board	0.0120	✓	
9	Finish 2 [5]	Paint	0.0010	✓	

Fig. 3.7 – Wall Layers

3.2.2 Add Parapet Cap

You will add a Parapet Cap on top of the wall. It is present in component library under wall profiles.

1. Architecture Tab → Build Panel → Wall
2. Select Basic Wall : Exterior - 300mm.
3. Click on Edit Type.
4. On Type Properties dialog box → Construction group → Structure parameter → click on Edit.
5. Click on Preview to see the graphical display of structure (Fig. 3.8).
6. For View, select Section.
7. Click on Sweeps

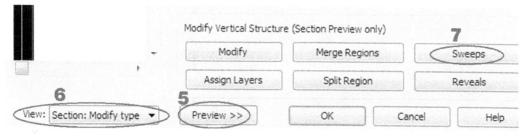

Fig. 3.8 – Add Wall Sweep

8. Click Load Profile.
9. Navigate to US Metric → Profiles → Wall → M_Parapet Cap-Precast.rfa → Open.
10. Click Add.
11. Make following settings as shown (Fig. 3.9).

- Profile : M_Parapet Cap-Precast : 450mm
- Material : Concrete, Precast
- From : Top
- Offset : 0.07
- Cuts Walls : ☑

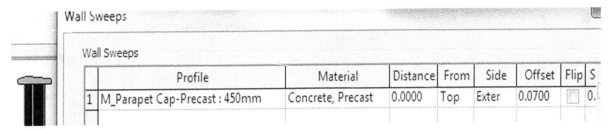

	Profile	Material	Distance	From	Side	Offset	Flip	S
1	M_Parapet Cap-Precast : 450mm	Concrete, Precast	0.0000	Top	Exter	0.0700	☐	0.

Fig. 3.9 – Load Wall Sweep Profile

3.2.3 Draw Exterior Walls

Exterior walls go from Pavement Level to Parapet Level. You will draw them so that Center line of the wall is on Grids.

1. Floor Plans → 01 GF
2. Architecture Tab → Build Panel → Wall tool.
3. Select Basic Wall : Exterior - 300mm.
4. On Modify | Place Wall contextual tab → select Height = Parapet
5. In Properties palette (Fig. 3.11), Constraints group (or on Modify | Place Wall contextual tab) → select

   - Location Line = Wall Centerline
   - Base Constraint = Pavement
   - Base Offsets = 0.0
   - Top Constraint = Parapet
   - Top Offsets = 0.0

6. Start drawing the wall from A7 to A8 to H8 to H6 to middle of C6 and D6 (Fig. 3.10).

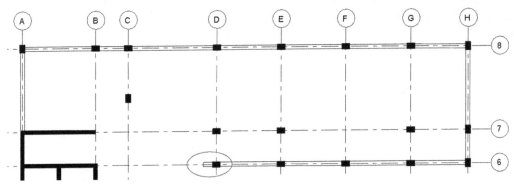

Fig. 3.10 – Draw Wall

7. Zoom to area near D6.
8. Click on Wall. Temporary dimensions appear.

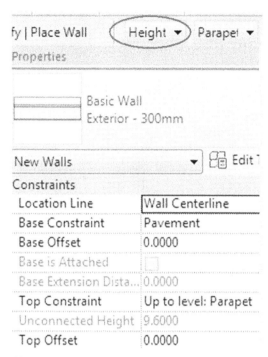

Fig. 3.11 – Wall Properties

9. Look at the Horizontal dimension from edge of the wall. One end of the dimension is on the edge of the wall. The other end of the dimension should be on grid D. If it is not then drag the witness line control (small blue dot) to grid D.
10. Click on the measurement. The measurement appears in a textbox. Write 1 and press Enter.
11. The edge of the wall is now 1 meter from the grid D.

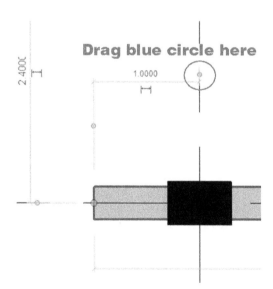

Fig. 3.12 – Adjust Wall Length

12. Do the same near C5.
13. The 3D view looks as shown in Fig 3.13.

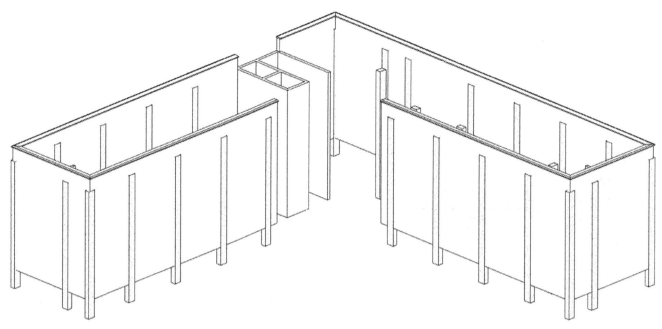

Fig. 3.13 – 3D View : Exterior Walls

3.2.4 Exterior Side

You have set the construction of Exterior walls so that the Tile layer is on Exterior side of the building and Paint layer is on the interior side. While drawing the wall, its sides may flip by mistake. You should check the sides and adjust them correctly.

1. Floor Plans → 01 GF
2. Click on a wall. You should see a double arrow on the exterior side (Fig. 3.14).

Fig. 3.14 – Exterior side of Wall

3. If the arrow is on interior side it means that the exterior side of the wall is on the interior side of the building.
4. To flip the selected wall, press space bar (in 3D view) or click on the arrow (in Plan view). The arrow will move to the exterior side.
5. Click on all the exterior walls to check that their exterior side is on the outer side of the building.

3.2.5 Align Walls

The shear wall on west side you added before is 300mm thick and the exterior wall is 300mm thick. You have drawn the two walls so that the center line is on the grid A. If the two walls are not aligned, you can align the walls as follows.

1. Floor Plans → 01 GF
2. Zoom to shear wall on grid A.
3. Modify Tab → Modify Panel → Click on Align →
4. First click on left side of exterior wall. (Align to) (Fig. 3.15).
5. Then click on left side of shear wall. (Align this)

6. Exterior sides of the two walls get aligned.

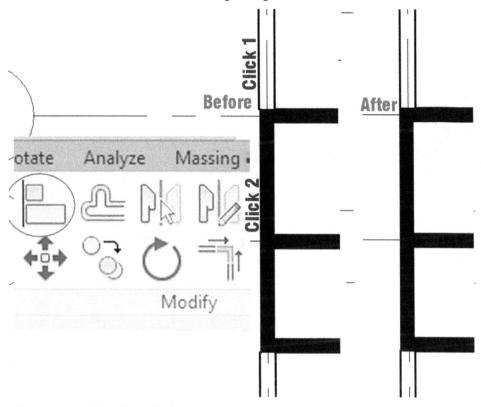

Fig. 3.15 – Aligning Walls

3.2.6 Push Columns inside the Wall

In the 3D view, the columns are seen extruded outside the exterior wall. You will align them with the structural layer of the wall so that the columns are concealed in the finishing layers.

1. Floor Plans → 01 GF
2. Make Detail Level = Fine (Fig. 3.16).

Fig. 3.16 – Set Detail Level of a view

3. Zoom to column B8 on north side.
4. Modify Tab → Modify Panel → Click on Align
5. Bring cursor on the outer line of structural layer and press Tab (Fig. 3.17).
6. The outer line of structural layer is highlighted. (If not, press Tab again).
7. Click to select it.
8. Then click on the outer side of the column.
9. The column will align with the outer side of structural layer.

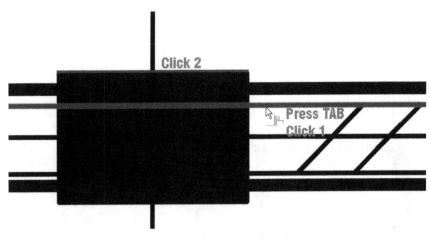

Fig. 3.17 – Align Columns with Structural Layer

10. In this way align all columns. (or align C8 with B8 → D8 with C8 → E8 with D8 etc).
11. 3D view will be shown as in Fig. 3.18.

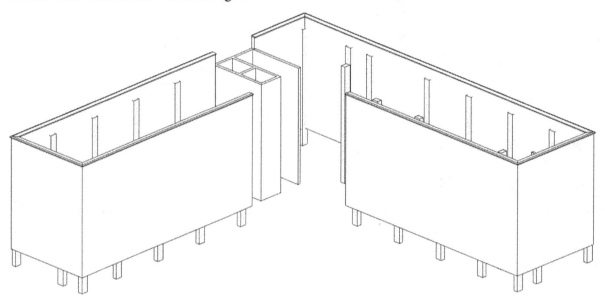

Fig. 3.18 – 3D view : Align Columns

12. Change Visual Style to Realistic to see the materials also (Fig. 3.19).

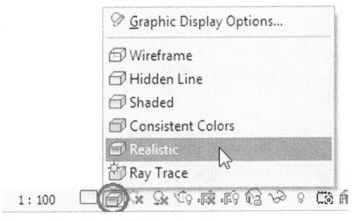

Fig. 3.19 – Visual Styles of a view

3.3 Interior Walls

An interior wall consists of many layers for different purposes. Outer layers are for paint or decoration. Inner layers are for structural support given by Materials such as concrete, cement blocks, bricks etc.

3.3.1 Adjust the Structure of Interior Walls

You will start with an existing wall and change its structure with steps similar to those explained in § 3.2.1.

1. Floor Plans → 01 GF
2. On View Control Bar:
   - Set Detail Level = Coarse.
   - Set Visual Style = Hidden Line.
3. Architecture Tab → Build Panel → Wall
4. In Properties Palette , click on Element Dropdown.
5. Select Basic Wall : Generic - 200mm.
6. Click on Edit Type.
7. On Type Properties box, click on Duplicate.
8. Change Name = Interior - 200mm → OK
9. On Type Properties box, Construction group, Structure parameter, click on Edit.
10. In the Edit Assembly dialogue box, use Insert, Delete, Up, Down buttons to add and position wall layers as shown in Fig. 3.20.

Layers

EXTERIOR SIDE

	Function	Material	Thickness	Wraps	Stru· Ma·
1	Finish 1 [4]	Paint	0.0010	✓	
2	**Core Boundary**	**Layers Above**	**0.0000**		
3	Structure [1]	Cement Block	0.1980		✓
4	**Core Boundary**	**Layers Below**	**0.0000**		
5	Finish 1 [4]	Paint	0.0010	✓	

INTERIOR SIDE

Fig. 3.20 – Interior Wall Structure

3.3.2 Draw Interior Walls

Interior walls may go from the Associated Level to Upper Level. If there is False Ceiling in the room, then interior walls are partition walls. Partition walls go from the Associated Level to a height little above False Ceiling. You will draw them so that Center line of the wall is on Grids.

1. Floor Plans → 01 GF
2. Architecture Tab → Build Panel → Wall tool.

3. Select Basic Wall : Interior - 200mm.
4. On Modify | Place Wall contextual tab → select Height = Unconnected
5. In Properties palette , Constraints group (or on Modify | Place Wall contextual tab) → select (Fig. 3.21)

- Location Line = Wall Centerline
- Base Constraint = 01 GF
- Base Offsets = 0.0
- Top Constraint = Unconnected
- Unconnected Height = 2.8

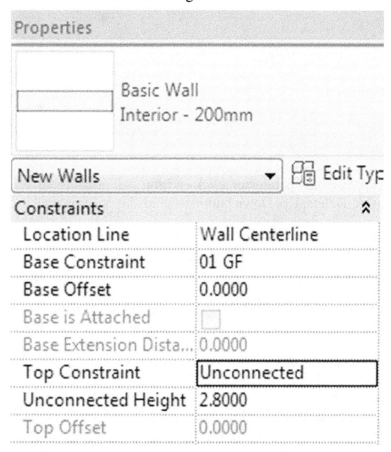

Fig. 3.21 – Interior Wall Properties

6. Draw interior walls as shown in Fig. 3.22.
7. Walls between grids G and H (or 1 and 2) are drawn anywhere. Their distances will be adjusted later.
8. All walls are on grids except some.
9. A wall starting at B7 goes to column on grid C and then to grid D.
10. Walls between grids G and H need adjustment.
11. Click on wall near grid H. Temporary dimensions appear.
12. Click on number (showing measurement from grid H), write 0.75 and press Enter (Fig 3.23).
13. Similarly make distance = 1.2 for wall near grid G
14. Do the same for walls between grids 1 and 2.

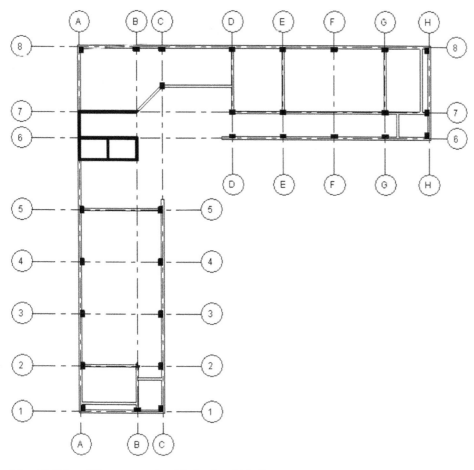

Fig. 3.22 – Placement of Interior Walls

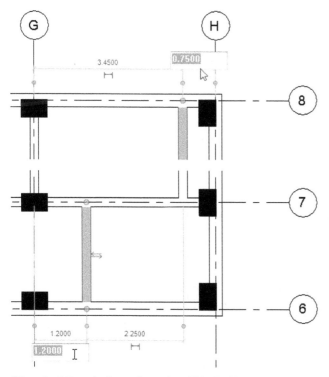

Fig. 3.23 – Adjust Interior Wall distances

3.3.3 Wall Height Adjustment

The walls around shafts should be continuous from 01 GF level to Parapet level.

1. Floor Plans → 01 GF
2. Zoom to area between grids 7 and 8 near grid H. Select columns H7 and H8. Press HH to hide them temporarily (Fig. 3.24).
3. Select the wall on grid 7. You will see a blue circle at the east end of the wall.
4. Drag this blue circle to the wall on west side.
5. Draw a new wall (Basic wall - Interior 200mm) on grid 7.
6. Select 2 walls shown in Fig. 3.24. In Properties palette, make:

    - Top Constraint = Up to Level: Parapet.
    - Top Offset = 0.000.

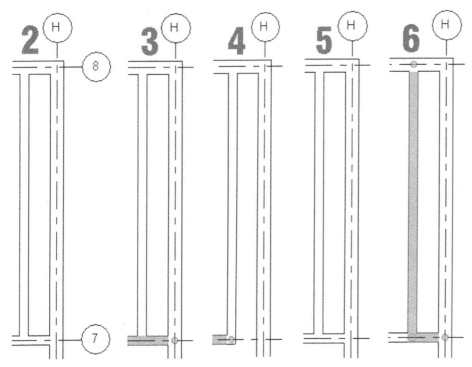

Fig. 3.24 – Adjust Interior Wall Height in shafts

7. Do the same for wall between grids A and B near grid 1.
8. Press HR to unhide the temporarily hidden elements.

3.3.4 Wall Joint

The wall joint between shear wall and the interior wall at B7 does not look nice. You can adjust the wall joint in many shapes.

1. Floor Plans → 01 GF
2. Zoom around B7.
3. On Modify tab → Geometry panel → click Wall Joints tool.
4. Click on the wall joint shown in Fig. 3.25.
5. On Option Bar, select Square Off.
6. The wall joint will change.

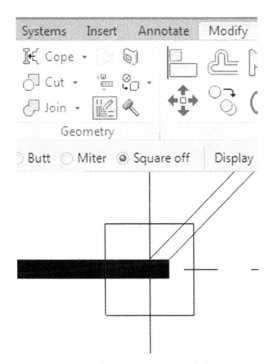

Fig. 3.25 – Change Wall Joints

3.3.5 Draw Curtain Wall

A curtain wall consists of panels and mullions. A simple curtain wall is drawn just like any other wall. A panel has many types such as glazed, glass, solid, empty etc. You can also select a mullion type.

1. Floor Plans → 01 GF
2. Architecture Tab → Build Panel → Wall tool.
3. In Properties palette , wall type dropdown, select Curtain Wall - Storefront (Fig. 3.26).
4. Edit Type → Duplicate → Name = Storefront 2.

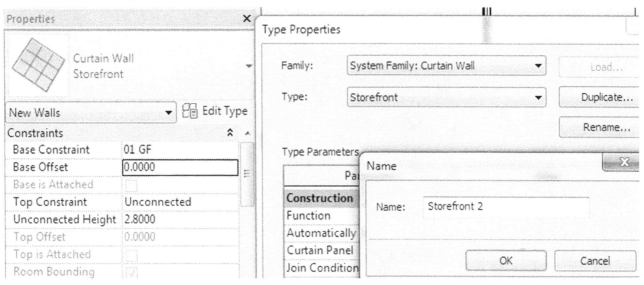

Fig. 3.26 – Edit type of Curtain Wall

5. In Type Parameters, make changes as shown in Fig. 3.27.

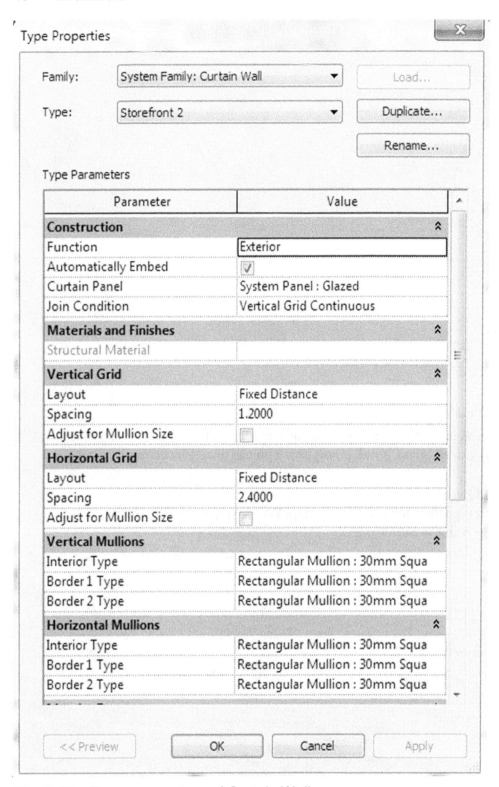

Fig. 3.27 – Type parameters of Curtain Wall

6. In Properties palette, make Base Constraint = 01 GF and Top Constraint = 02 FF.
7. Now draw the wall as shown in Fig 3.28.

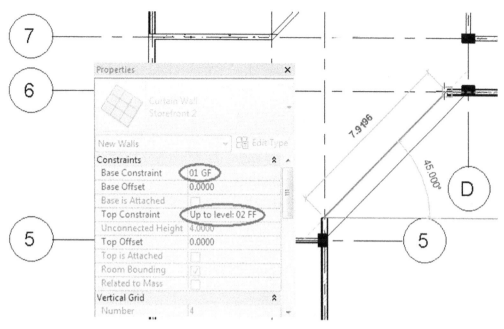

Fig. 3.28 – Draw Curtain Wall

8. Click  to Save Project As **Arch03a**

3.4 Floor

Like walls, a floor also consists of many layers for different purposes. We can edit the structure of floor to include layer of different materials.

3.4.1 Adjust the Structure of Floor

You will start with an existing floor and change its structure.

1. Open Project **Arch03a**
2. Save Project As **Arch03b**
3. Floor Plans → 01 GF
4. Architecture Tab → Build Panel → Floor tool.
5. Select Floor : Concrete-Domestic 425mm.
6. Click on Edit Type.
7. On Type Properties box, click on Duplicate.
8. Change Name = Concrete-Domestic 600mm → OK
9. On Type Properties box, Construction group, Structure parameter, click on Edit.
10. In the Edit Assembly dialogue box, insert Finish layer above Core Boundary as shown.
11. Select Functions and Materials of layers. Write thickness of each layer, select Structural Material and Variable for Structure layers as shown in Fig 3.29.
12. Press OK → OK.

Layers

	Function	Material	Thickness	Wraps	Structural Material	Var
1	Finish 1 [4]	Stone Floor	0.0100	☐	☐	☐
2	**Core Boundary**	**Layers Above Wrap**	**0.0000**			
3	Structure [1]	Concrete, Sand/Cement Screed	0.0500	☐	☐	☑
4	Structure [1]	Concrete, Cast In Situ	0.3400	☐	☑	☐
5	**Core Boundary**	**Layers Below Wrap**	**0.0000**			
6	Membrane Layer	Damp-proofing	0.0000			☐
7	Thermal/Air Layer	Rigid insulation	0.0500			☐
8		Site - Hardcore	0.1500	☐	☐	☐

Fig. 3.29 – Floor Structure

3.4.2 Draw Floor on Ground Floor Level

After selecting the floor type, you are still in floor sketch mode. You can start drawing boundary of the floor. Boundary of floor is a closed polygon with no gaps or overlaps. It is drawn in Magenta color. You will draw **only** one line on one side. Later on you will use trim/extend tool to join them.

1. On Modify | Create Floor Boundary contextual tab → Draw panel → select Pick Walls tool (Fig. 3.30).

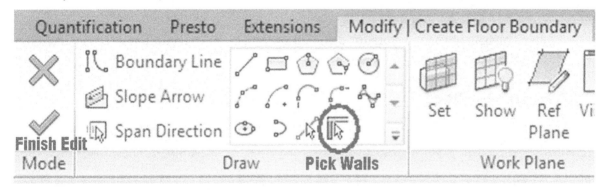

Fig. 3.30 – Pick Walls

2. Click all exterior walls. A Magenta line will be drawn on inner side. (If the Magenta line is drawn on outer side, click on blue double-arrow. Magenta line will come to inner side).
3. On Modify panel, select Trim/Extend tool.
4. Click at two lines (A and B) shown in fig. The two lines join.
5. Now select line tool in Draw panel.
6. Draw a line from C5 to D6.
7. Trim lines around C5. (Click on part of line which you want to **keep**).
8. Trim lines around D6.
9. Now the boundary is a closed polygon with no gaps or overlaps.

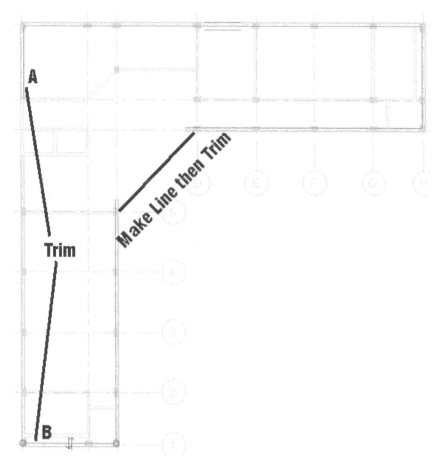

Fig. 3.31 – Draw Floor Boundary

10. In Mode panel, click on Finish Edit.
11. A dialog box appears

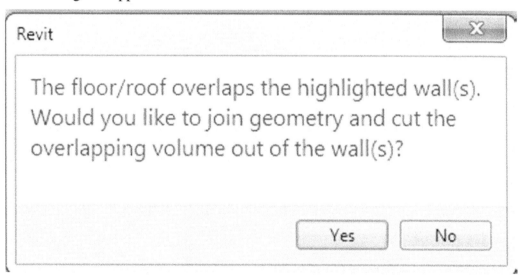

Fig. 3.32 – Floor Cutting Walls

12. Click **No**.
13. The floor is formed. You can see it in 3D view.
14. Select an exterior wall and press HH (Hide temporarily). View the floor and press HR (bring back the hidden wall).

3.4.3 Copy Floor to Other Levels

You will copy this floor to First Floor Level and modify the structure.

1. In 3D view, select floor.
2. On Modify | Floors contextual tab → Clipboard panel→ click Copy (Fig. 3.33).
3. Click Paste dropdown and select Aligned to Selected Levels.
4. Select 02 FF → OK

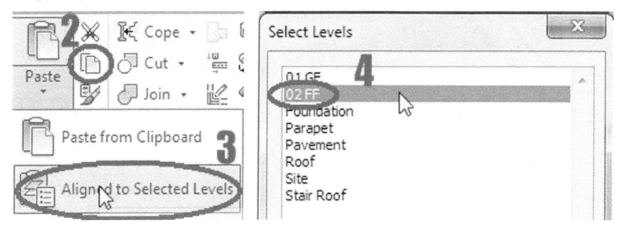

Fig. 3.33 – Copy Floor to other levels

5. The floor is copied to 02 FF level.
6. Select 02 FF level floor.
7. Edit Type → Duplicate → Rename → Concrete-Domestic 200mm (Fig. 3.34).

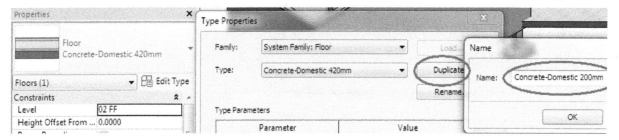

Fig. 3.34 – Edit Floor Structure

8. Edit Structure
9. Leave only layers shown in figure and delete others.
10. Change Thickness of Concrete layer (Fig. 3.35).

	Function	Material	Thickness	Wraps
1	Finish 1 [4]	Stone Floor	0.0100	
2	Core Bounda	Layers Above Wrap	0.0000	
3	Structure [	Concrete, Sand/Cement Screed	0.1900	
4	Core Bounda	Layers Below Wrap	0.0000	

Fig. 3.35 – Set Floor Structure

11. Press OK

12. On Modify | Floors contextual tab → Mode panel → click Finish ✓ .

13. A dialog box appears (Fig. 3.36).

Fig. 3.36 – Floor Cut Walls

14. Click **Yes**. (Floor will cut the walls) (Fig. 3.37).
15. A dialog box appears.

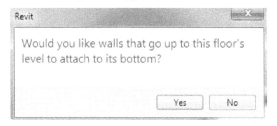

Fig. 3.37 – Walls attach to Floor

16. Click **No**. (Walls below will not attach to the bottom of slab).
17. Click 3D view on Quick Access Toolbar. Visual Style = Realistic (Fig. 3.38).

Fig. 3.38 – Set 3D Realistic style

18. In 3D view, Select 02 FF level floor. Type HH on keyboard to hide it temporarily. From Visual Styles, select Realistic.
19. You can see that floor has cut the overlapping volume out of exterior walls (Fig. 3.39).
20. Type HR to unhide the floor.

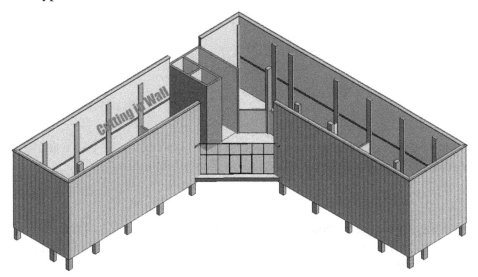

Fig. 3.39 – 3D Realistic view

3.4.4 Change Curtain Wall Properties

In the 3D view, you see that the curtain wall is passing through the 02 FF level floor. You will change the height of curtain wall so that it just touches the upper slab.

1. Note that the vertical grid has Justification to left (Start). You can make Justification to Center or End. Same for horizontal grid.
2. Select the curtain wall (Select the **whole wall** not just a panel or a mullion).
3. In Properties palette, make Top Offset = − 0.2000 (Fig. 3.40). Top of the wall will be below the floor.
4. Also justify vertical grid to End and press Apply.

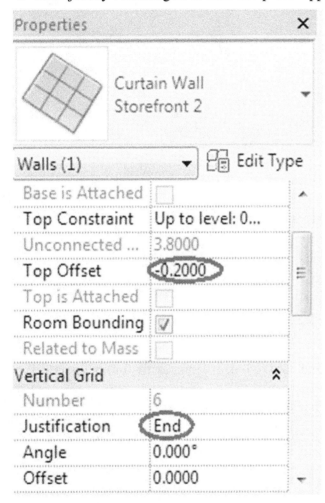

Fig. 3.40 – Curtain Wall Properties

3.5 Rooms

A room is a space bounded by room bounding elements such as walls, floor, ceiling etc. If you want to divide a large space into smaller parts, then you will draw a line called Room Separator.

3.5.1 Room Bounding

In general, when walls, floors or ceilings are added, their Room Bounding property is set to True. Before making rooms, you will make sure that walls are Room Bounding. (Also check for floors). You will also make the structural columns NOT Room Bounding.

1. Floor Plans → 01 GF.

2. Make a selection box around the whole building to select all elements.
3. Filter (Fig. 3.41).
4. Press Check None.
5. Check Walls only.

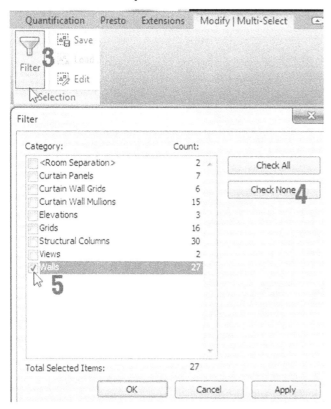

Fig. 3.41 – Filter the selection

6. Set Room Bounding Checked ☑ (True) (Fig. 3.42).

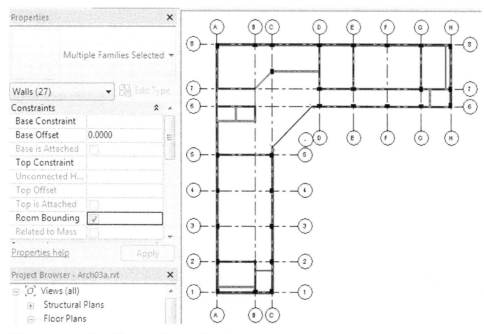

Fig. 3.42 – Set Room Bounding for walls

7. 3D view

8. Make a selection box around the whole building to select all elements.
9. Filter.
10. Check None.
11. Check Structural Columns only.
12. Set Room Bounding unchecked ☐ (False).

3.5.2 Room Area and Volume Setting

Each room has perimeter, area, volume and many other parameters. You will make rooms, so that areas and volumes are calculated from wall finish (and not from wall center).

1. Floor Plans → 01 GF
2. Architecture Tab → Room & Area Panel → Room & Area dropdown → Area and Volume Computation.
3. Make selection as shown in Fig 3.43.

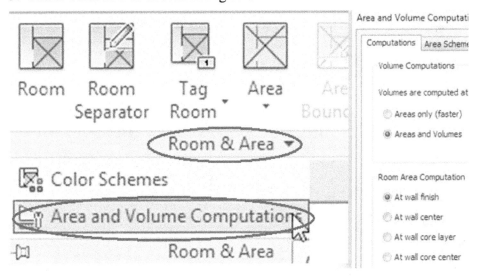

Fig. 3.43 – Room & Area Settings

3.5.3 Add Rooms

There are three types of walls on 01 GF level viz. exterior, interior and shear. Each of them should be room bounding.

1. Floor Plans → 01 GF
2. Architecture Tab → Room & Area Panel → Room tool.
3. Properties palette → Constraints group set the following:
   - Upper Limit = 02 FF
   - Limit Offset = 0.0
   - Base Offset = 0.0
4. Click in the North-West room near A8 intersection.
5. Room Tag appears in the room.
6. In the room tag, click on Room two times (slowly) and change it to Accounting (Fig. 3.44).
7. In the room tag, click on 1 two times (slowly) and change it to 101.

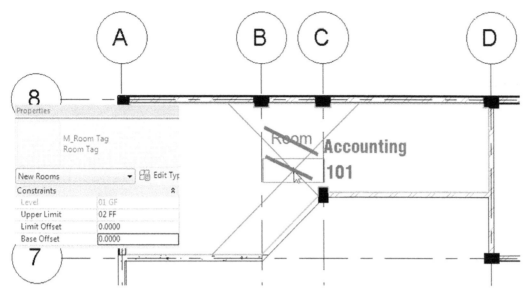

Fig. 3.44 – Change Room name and number

8. Now add rooms in other spaces as shown in Fig. 3.44.
9. Room numbers automatically increase.
10. You will change room names manually.
11. Architecture Tab → Room & Area Panel → Room Separator tool.
12. You will add two Room Separators to divide the big space in the middle into three parts viz. Corridor (107), Entrance (108) and Stairs (109).
13. Draw lines from grid 6 to 7 on grids B and D (Fig. 3.45).

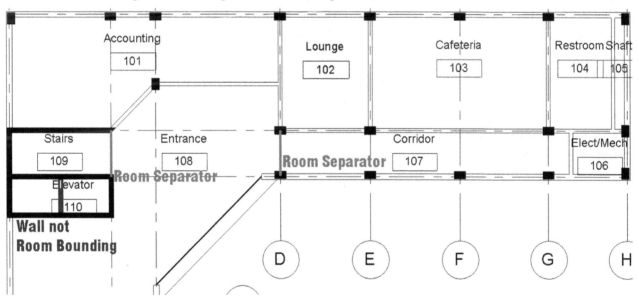

Fig. 3.45 – Set Room names and numbers on North side

14. The Elevator area is one room. The middle wall in Elevator room (110) is not Room Bounding.
15. Click on this wall and in Property palette, under Constraints group, uncheck Room Bounding.
16. Make other rooms as shown in Fig. 3.46.

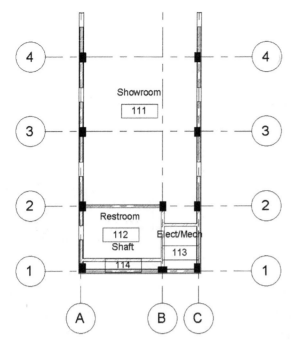

Fig. 3.46 – Set Room names and numbers on South side

3.5.4 Note on Adding Rooms

1. If room tags do not appear, then type VG → Model Categories tab → Visibility column → check Rooms → OK

2. When you are adding room and bring cursor inside a space, a big cross appears showing the extents of the room. If this big cross does not appear, it means that there is some problem in the boundaries. A side is open or a wall is not Room Bounding. To check this:

   - Press Esc.
   - On Modify | Place Room contextual tab → Room Panel → click on Highlight Boundaries (Fig. 3.47).
   - You will see all the room boundaries.
   - See carefully which side is open and close it.

Fig. 3.47 – Highlight Room Boundaries

3.6 Doors

Different families of doors are available in Revit library. Each family contains doors of similar construction and materials but different sizes.

When you add a door family, you can select a door type from properties palette.

If you want a door of size not available in the family, you can take any door, Edit Type, Duplicate and Rename it. Then you can adjust its parameters as you want.

3.6.1 Add Double Glass Doors in Concrete Walls

Doors are wall hosted components. They can be added in walls only. If you select a door, two sets of double arrows appear. They are used to flip the door.

1. Floor Plans → 01 GF
2. Architecture Tab
3. Build Panel
4. Door tool.
5. On Modify | Place Door contextual tab → Tag panel → select Tag on Placement (Blue) (Fig. 3.48).
6. On Modify | Place Door contextual tab → Mode panel → click on Load Family.

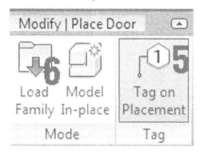

Fig. 3.48 – Load a Door family

7. From Doors folder, select M_Double-Glass 1.rfa.
8. In Properties palette → type selector → select type = M_Double-Glass 1 : 1830 x 2134mm.
9. Bring cursor on the wall for Accounting 101 between grids B and C.
10. The preview image the door appears. Move cursor to inner side of the wall and click. The door is added in the wall.
11. Similarly add two doors for Showroom 110 on grid 5.
12. Click on left door in the Showroom 110.
13. Temporary dimensions appear.
14. Focus on dimension from left side of the door to the left wall.
15. It should extend from left side of the door to the inner side of the wall. (If it is not from inner side of the wall, then click on the witness line control (small blue dot) at left end of the dimension, until it is on the inner side of the wall) (Fig. 3.49).
16. Click on the number and make it 1.20.
17. Do the same for the right door.

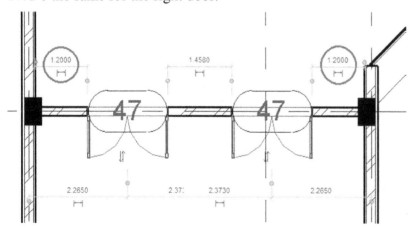

Fig. 3.49 – Glass Doors in Showroom

18. Select one door.
19. Edit Type → Type Mark = D01 → OK (Fig. 3.50).

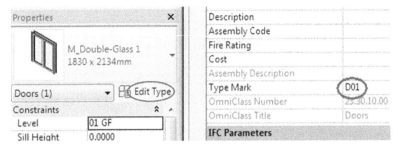

Fig. 3.50 – Change Door Type Mark

20. Tags of all three doors show D01.
21. Add one door for Cafeteria 103.

3.6.2 Add Single Doors in Concrete Walls

Now you will load and add single doors.

1. Door → Load Family → M_Single-Flush Vision.rfa.
2. In Properties palette , select type = M_Single-Flush Vision : 0915 x 2134mm.
3. Bring cursor on the wall of Lounge 102 (on grid 7 between grids D and E).
4. Move cursor to inner or outer side of the wall to flip the door up or down.
5. Press Spacebar to flip the door to left or right side.
6. Click to add the door.
7. Select the door. Edit Type → Type Mark = D02 → OK.
8. Door → In Properties palette → Type selector → select type = M_Single-Flush Vision : 0762 x 2134mm.
9. Bring cursor on the wall of Restroom 104 (on grid 7 between grids G and H). Click to add the door.
10. Select the door. Edit Type → Type Mark = D03 → OK.
11. Space for the door is very small. Click on the column at G7 and press Spacebar to rotate the column.
12. Now add a door of type = M_Single-Flush : 0915 x 2134mm for Elect/Mech 106. Make Type Mark = D04.
13. Similarly add doors in Restroom 112 and Elect/Mech 113 (Fig. 3.51).

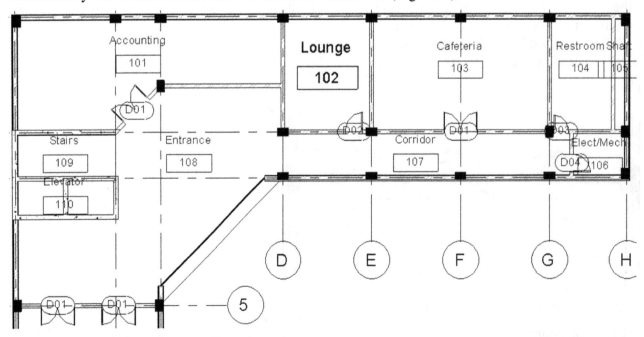

Fig. 3.51 – Doors on Ground Floor Level

3.6.3 Add Double Door in Curtain Wall

A door in curtain wall is a type of panel. To add a double panel door, you will delete the mullion in between two panels. You will replace that double panel with a Curtain Wall Storefront Double Door. So insert this door in the project from the Door library. Then you can replace it with a panel.

1. Insert Tab → Load from Library Panel → Load Family tool.
2. From Doors folder, select M_Curtain Wall-Store Front-Dbl.rfa → Open
3. View Tab → Create Panel → Elevation tool.
4. Add elevation in front of the curtain wall as shown in Fig. 3.52.

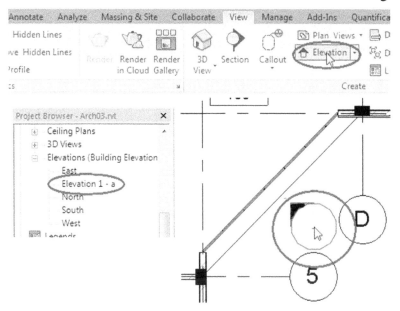

Fig. 3.52 – Add Elevation

5. The elevation also appears in Project Browser under Elevations group.
6. Double-click on Elevation 1 - a (or black head of the elevation near the wall).
7. Make Visual Style = Shaded.
8. Click on the fourth mullion from left. (You want to delete it but it is pinned)
9. Click on the pin-head to cancel pin (Fig. 3.53).

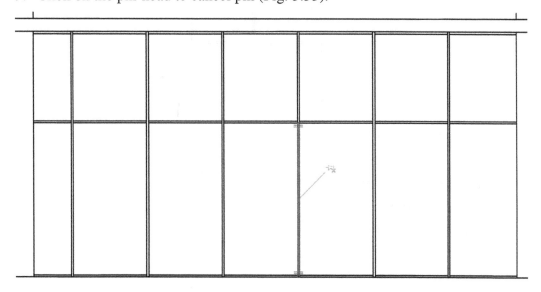

Fig. 3.53 – Remove a Mullion of Curtain Wall

10. Now press Delete to delete the mullion.
11. The mullion is deleted but the grid line is still there.
12. Click on the grid line.
13. Click on the pin-head to cancel pin (Fig. 3.54).
14. Modify | Curtain Wall Grids Contextual Tab → Curtain Grid Panel → Add/Remove Segments tool.
15. Click on the grid line to remove it. Press Esc.

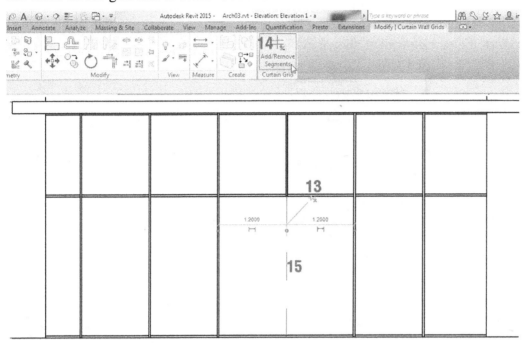

Fig. 3.54 – Remove Grid line of Curtain Wall

16. Bring cursor at the edge of the new double-panel. (**Do not click**).
17. Press Tab many times until the double-panel is highlighted. Click on it to select it (Fig. 3.55).

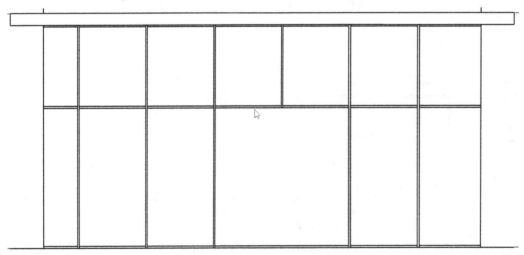

Fig. 3.55 – Select a Panel of Curtain Wall

18. From Properties panel, select type = Store Front Double Door (Fig. 3.56).

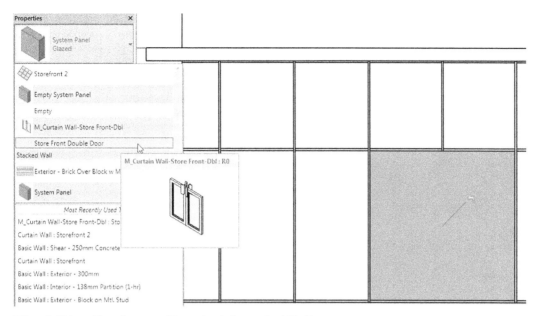

Fig. 3.56 – Replace a Panel of Curtain Wall

19. Panel Door is inserted into the curtain wall (Fig. 3.57).
20. See 3D view.

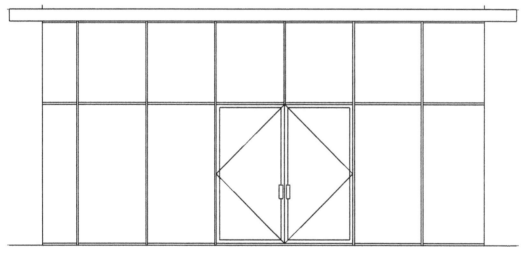

Fig. 3.57 – Panel Door of Curtain Wall

3.7 Windows

Different families of windows are available in Revit library. Each family contain windows of similar construction and materials but different sizes.

When you add a windows family, you can select a window type from properties palette.

If you want a window of size not available in the family, you can take any window, Edit Type, Duplicate and Rename it. Then you can adjust its parameters as you want.

3.7.1 Add Window in Concrete Walls

Like doors, windows are also wall hosted families. You can add a window to any type of wall in plan, section, elevation or 3D views.

When you select a window, a set of double arrows appear. It is used to flip the window inside out.

1. Floor Plans → 01 GF
2. Architecture Tab
3. Build Panel
4. Window tool.
5. On Modify | Place Window contextual tab → Tag panel → select Tag on Placement (Blue).
6. On Modify | Place Window contextual tab → Mode panel → click on Load Family (Fig. 3.58).

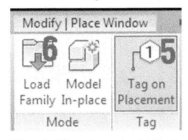

Fig. 3.58 – Load a Window family

7. From Windows folder, select M_Sliding with Trim.rfa.
8. In Properties palette , select type = M_Sliding with Trim : 0915 x 1220mm.
9. Bring cursor on the exterior wall (on grid 8) for Accounting 101 between grids B and C.
10. The preview image the Window appears.
11. Move cursor to outer side of the wall and click.
12. The Window (and tag) is added in the wall. (If you wan to flip the window inside out, then select the window and press Spacebar. Then select the tag. A four sided arrow appears. Drag it to new position).

3.7.2 Bring Window to Center Position

1. Click on the window to select it.
2. Edit Type → Type Mark = W01 → OK
3. The window tag changes to W01.
4. Annotate Tab → Dimension Panel → Aligned tool (Fig. 3.59).
5. Make an aligned dimension by clicking on grid A - then center of the window - then grid B - then somewhere above to place the dimension line.
6. Click on   EQ   above the dimension line.

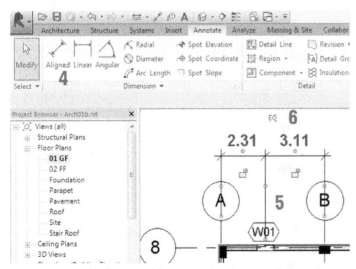

Fig. 3.59 – Bring Window to Center Position

7. The window moves to middle of the grids A and B by making EQual distance from both grids.
8. Click on dimension line and press Delete.
9. Press OK. (Do not press Unconstrain).
10. In the same way add other windows as shown in Fig. 3.60.

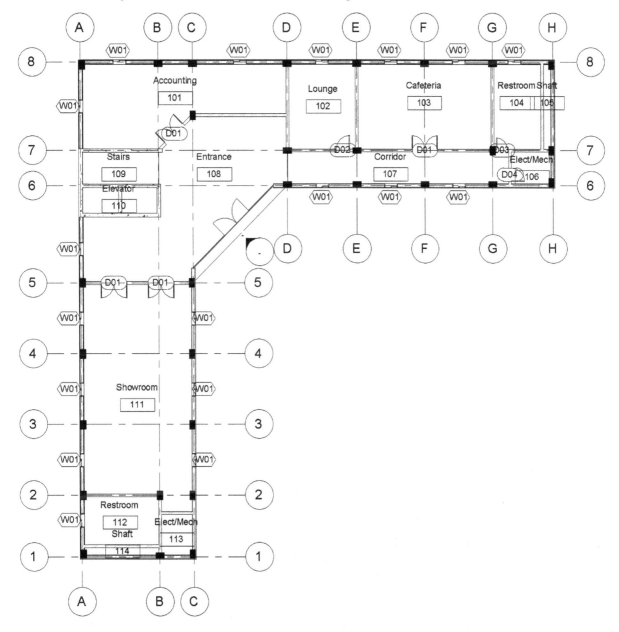

Fig. 3.60 – Placement of Windows on Ground Floor Level

3.7.3 Add Widow in Stair Area

You will add a window in the stair well.

1. Floor Plans → 01 GF.
2. On Architecture panel → Build panel → select Window tool.
3. Load Family → Windows → M_Casement 3x3 with Trim.rfa
4. In Properties palette → Type Selector → Select 0915 x 1525mm. Check that Tag on Placement is blue.
5. Edit Type → Duplicate → Name = 1200 x 1200mm → Height = 1.2, Width = 1.2 → OK (Fig. 3.61).

6. In Properties palette → Constraints group → Sill Height = 2.3

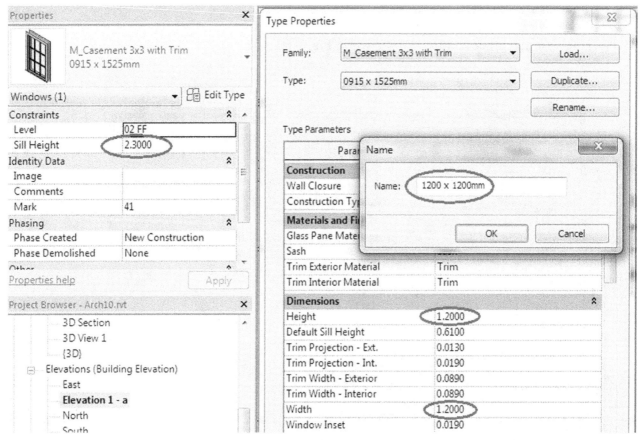

Fig. 3.61 – Edit Window Type

7. Place it in the exterior shear wall in the stair well with tag on outer side (Fig. 3.62).

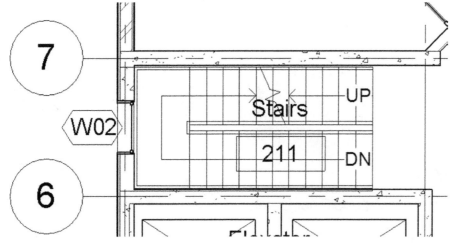

Fig. 3.62 – Window in stairwell

8. Make EQual distance from grids 6 and 7.
9. Edit Type → Type Mark = W02

10. Click [save icon] to Save Project As **Arch03b**

3.8 Internal Stairs

A stair consists of many components such as stair runs, landings, railing etc. You will add Stairs by Component. Each component of a stair is editable. First you will add stairs and then adjust its position.

1. Open Project **Arch03b.**
2. Save Project As **Arch03c.**
3. Floor Plans → 01 GF
4. Type VG→ Model Categories tab → Visibility column → unselect Rooms → OK
5. Rooms and Room Tags become invisible.
6. Zoom to room Stairs 109 (Space between grids 6 and 7 - A and B).
7. Architecture Tab → Circulation Panel → Stairs dropdown → Stair by Component (Fig. 3.63).

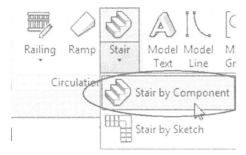

Fig. 3.63 – Stair by Component

8. From Properties palette → type dropdown → select Cast-In-Place : Monolithic Stair (Fig. 3.64).
9. Edit Type.
10. Duplicate → Name = Monolithic Stair 2.
11. Minimum Run Width = 1.000
12. OK
13. Set other properties as follows:

   - Base Level = 01 GF
   - Base Offset = 0.000
   - Top Level = 02 FF
   - Top Offset = 0.00
   - Desired Number of Risers = 24
   - Actual Tread Depth = 0.3000

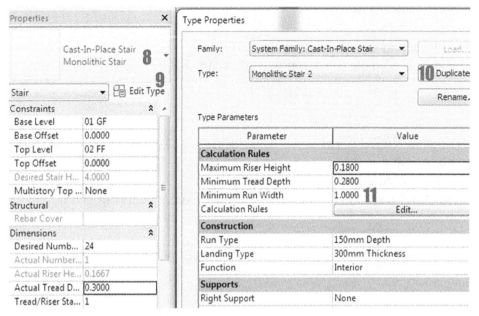

Fig. 3.64 – Stair properties

14. Click somewhere to start the stairs. (Point A in (Fig. 3.65).
15. Move cursor to left until you see 12 RISERS CREATED, 12 REMAINING. Click (Point B).
16. Move cursor vertically down by distance > 1m and click (Point C).
17. Move cursor to right until you see 12 RISERS CREATED, 0 REMAINING. Click (Point D).

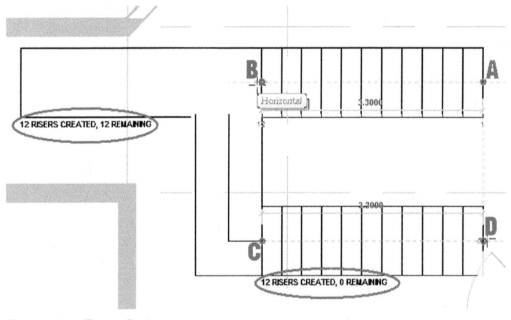

Fig. 3.65 – Draw Stairs

18. On Modify | Create Stair contextual tab → Modify panel → Align tool (Fig. 3.66).
19. Click line A on shear wall then line A' on stairs.
20. Click line B on shear wall then line B' on stairs.
21. Click line C on shear wall then line C' on stairs.

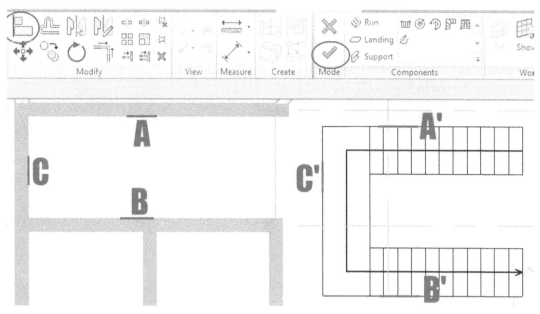

Fig. 3.66 – Align Stairs

22. On Modify | Create Stair contextual tab → Mode panel → Click Finish ✓ .
23. You will see the stairs as shown in Fig. 3.67.

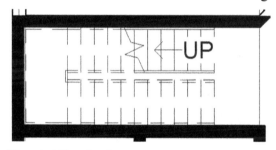

Fig. 3.67 – Stairs

24. Click on a riser to select stairs.
25. In Properties palette , make Multistory Top Level = Roof. The stairs will go upto Roof level.
26. On Annotate tab → Tag panel → click Tread Number tool.
27. Click on first run of stairs and then on second run of the stairs. Tread numbers will appear (Fig. 3.68).

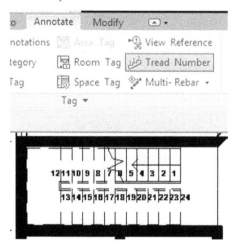

Fig. 3.68 – Tread Numbers

28. On View tab → Create panel → click Section tool. (or click on Section tool ⟨icon⟩ on Quick Access Toolbar),
29. Click left (point A) and right (point B) of the stairs to draw the Section Line.
30. Bring Extent line close as shown in Fig. 3.69

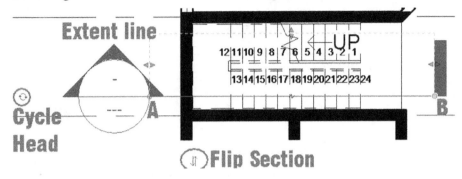

Fig. 3.69 – Draw Section

31. Double-click on the section-head.
32. You will see the stair section. You can add Tread Number in section also.

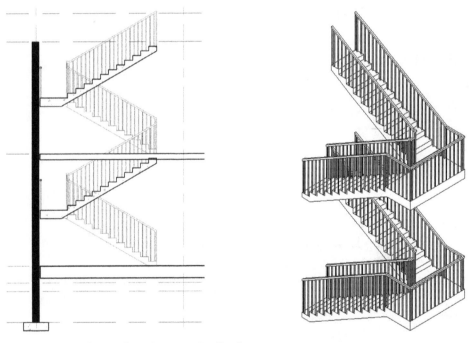

Fig. 3.70 – Stair Section and 3D view

33. See stairs in 3D view (Fig. 3.70). (Select walls or floor and press HH to hide them temporarily. Press HR to unhide).

3.9 Restrooms

You need to change the restroom floor finish, add bathroom stalls and other plumbing fixtures.

3.9.1 Change Floor Finish

In § 3.4.1 you created structure of the floor of 01 GF level. In the restroom, the floor structure will remain same but the finishing material will be different.

Floor Plans → 01 GF.

1. Zoom to Restroom 104.
2. On Modify tab → Geometry panel → click Split Face tool (Fig. 3.71).

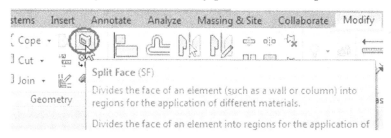

Fig. 3.71 – Split Face tool

3. Bring cursor on floor edge near grid H between grids 7 and 8 as shown in Fig. 3.72.
4. Floor edge is highlighted (blue line).
5. Click to select the floor.

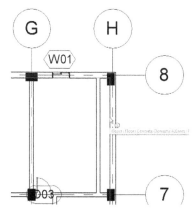

Fig. 3.72 – Select Floor

6. On Modify | Split Face > Create Boundary contextual tab → Draw panel → click Rectangle tool.
7. Draw rectangle (Magenta) as shown in Fig. 3.73.

8. Mode panel → click Finish ✓ .

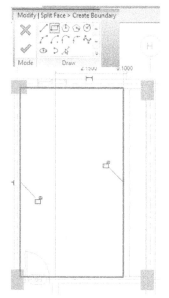

Fig. 3.73 – Split Face of Floor

9. The Restroom area is now split. You can paint a different material on it.
10. Visual Style = Realistic
11. On Modify tab → Geometry panel → Paint tool (Fig. 3.74).

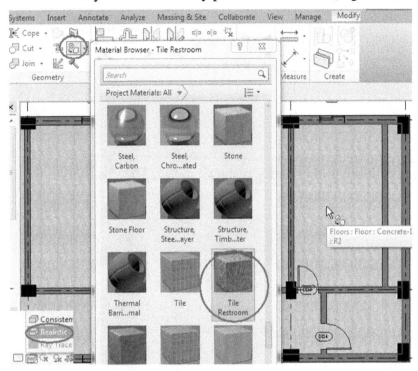

Fig. 3.74 – Paint the Split Face

12. Material Browser appears. Select Tile Restroom and click on the floor inside the restroom.
13. New material is painted.
14. Do the same for Restroom 112.

3.9.2 Add Toilet Partitions

Toilet Partition will added as a component.

1. Floor Plans → 01 GF.
2. Zoom to Restroom 104.
3. On Architecture tab → Build panel → click Component tool.
4. In Properties palette → Type Selector → select Toilet Stall1650 x 1000mm.
5. Edit Type → Duplicate
    - Rename = 1650 x 1500mm
    - Door Out = ☑
    - Width = 1500
    - Door Width = 1000

6. Toilet Stall is wall-hosted component therefore it can only be added on a wall. Bring cursor on the wall between Restroom 104 and Shaft 105. Image preview of toilet stall appears. Click on wall to add the toilet stall.
7. On Modify tab → Modify panel → click Align tool.
8. Click on line A then line A' to align the toilet stall with the wall as shown in Fig. 3.75.

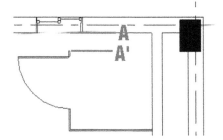

Fig. 3.75 – Paint the Split Face

9. Similarly add the component Toilet Stall 1650 x 1000mm and align them as shown in Fig. 3.76.
10. Also select the window in Restroom 104 and using Left-Right arrows on the keyboard, move it so that it is outside the toilet stall.

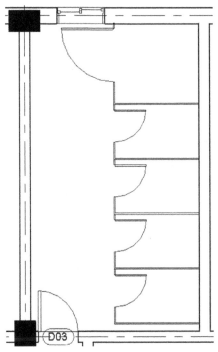

Fig. 3.76 – Toile Stalls

3.9.3 Add Water Closets

Water Closets are families added from the Revit Library.

1. Floor Plans → 01 GF.
2. Zoom to Restroom 104.
3. On System tab → Plumbing & Piping panel → click Plumbing Fixture tool.
4. Load Family → Plumbing → MEP → Fixtures → Water Closets → M_Water Closet - Flush Valve - Floor Mounted.rfa → Open.
5. From Type Selector, select Public - Flushing greater than 6.1 Lpf.

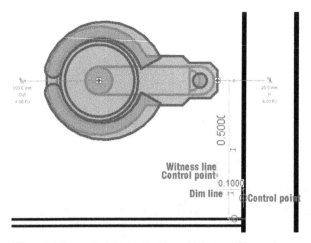

Fig. 3.77 – Add and align Water Closet

6. Bring cursor in the Toilet Stall : 1650 x 1500mm.
7. If the orientation of the a water-closet is not correct then press Spacebar to correct it. When orientation is correct, click to add the water-closet.
8. Select the water-closet. Temporary dimensions appear.
9. Controls for the witness line (the blue dots on the witness lines) in red circles should be as shown in the Fig. 3.77.
10. If a control is on another wall away from the water-closet, then drag the control to the nearby wall.
11. If the control is on the nearby wall but not on the inner side then click on the control until it is on the inner side.
12. When the controls are in correct position, then change the dimension text as shown in Fig. 3.77.
13. Copy water-closets in other stalls also as shown in Fig. 3.78.

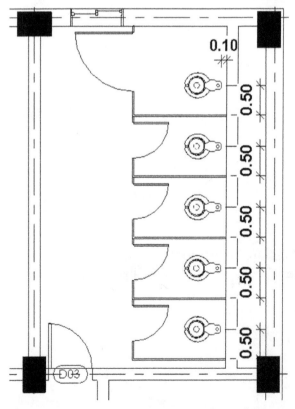

Fig. 3.78 – Copy Water Closets in other stalls

3.9.4 Add Sinks

Sinks are Plumbing fixtures added as Revit families.

1. Floor Plans → 01 GF.
2. Zoom to Restroom 104.
3. On System tab → Plumbing & Piping panel → click Plumbing Fixture tool.
4. From Type selector, select M_Lavatory - Wall Mounted - New: 510mm x 455mm - Public.
5. Bring cursor near the west side wall of the restroom. Click to add four sinks (Fig. 3.79).
6. Adjust distance of north side sink from inner face of the north side wall as 1.8m. (If the other end of the dimension is not on the north side wall, drag blue dot of the dimension to the north side wall. Click on the blue dot to position it on the inner face of the wall)
7. Adjust distance of south side sink from inner face of the south side wall as 1.5m. (If the other end of the dimension is not on the south side wall, drag blue dot of the dimension to the south side wall. Click on the blue dot to position it on the inner face of the wall)
8. On Annotate tab → Dimension panel → click Aligned tool.
9. Click in the center of each sink to add aligned dimension.

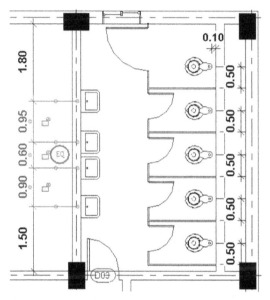

Fig. 3.79 – Adjust Sinks in Restroom 104

10. Select the aligned dimension and click on ⌴EQ⌴. All sinks will be at equal distance from each other.
11. Delete the dimension. Do not press Unconstrain.
12. Do the same in Restroom 112. Move the windows out of the stall (Fig. 3.80).

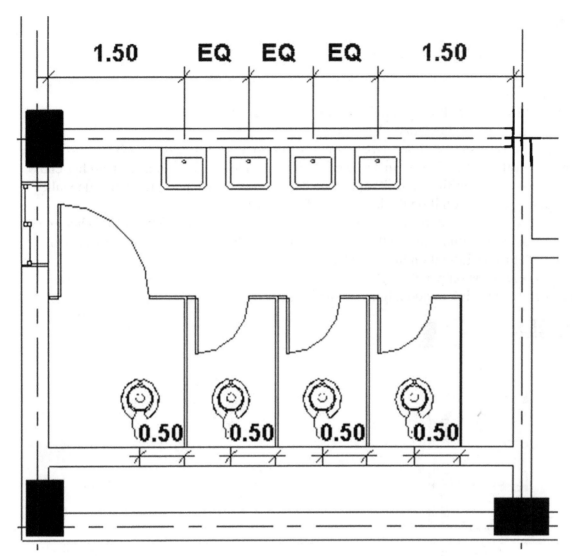

Fig. 3.80 – Adjust Sinks in Restroom 112

3.9.5 Add Floor Drain

Floor Drain is Plumbing fixtures added as Revit family.

1. Floor Plans → 01 GF.
2. Zoom to Restroom 104.
3. The floor drain will be below the floor level, therefore it will be invisible. To see, you must change the view range of the view. (If you do not change the view range, then the floor drain will be added but you will receive a message that None of the created elements are visible in the view).
4. Properties → Extents group → View Range → click Edit (Fig. 3.81).

   - Top : Associated Level (01 GF) : Offset = 2.3
   - Cut Plane : Associated Level (01 GF) : Offset = 1.2
   - Bottom : Associated Level (01 GF) : Offset = − 0.2
   - View Depth Level : Associated Level (01 GF) : Offset = − 0.2

5. Click OK

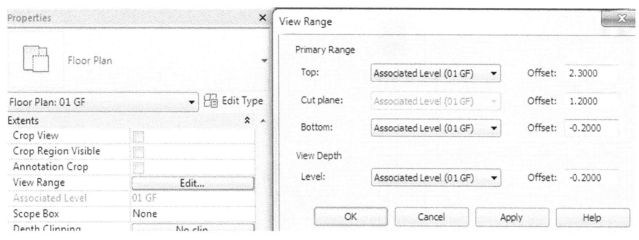

Fig. 3.81 – Change View Range

6. On System tab → Plumbing & Piping panel → click Plumbing Fixture tool.
7. Load Family → Plumbing → MEP → Fixtures → Drains → M_Floor Drain - Round.rfa → Open
8. Select 150 mm Strainer - 80 mm Drain.
9. In Properties palette, click Edit Type → set:
   - Strainer Height = 0.04
   - Body Height = 0.07
10. On Modify | Place Plumbing Fixture contextual tab → Placement panel → Click Place on Face (Fig. 3.82).

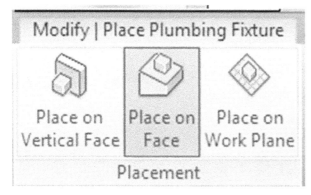

Fig. 3.82 – Placement : Place on Face tool

11. Click to add two Floor Drains in Restroom 104 as shown in Fig. 3.83. Adjust placement.
12. Select 150 mm Strainer - 100 mm Drain.
13. Change Strainer Height and Body Height as in step 9. Place in Shaft 105 as shown in Fig. 3.81.

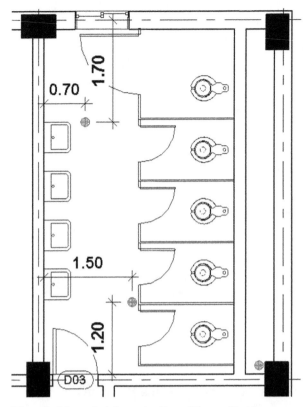

Fig. 3.83 – Add and align Floor Drains

3.9.6 Plumbing Fixtures on Upper Levels

Some elements can be copied to upper floors.

1. Floor Plans → 01 GF.
2. Select Toilet Stalls and Toilets. Copy - Paste to level 02 FF.
3. Floor Plans → 01 GF. Underlay = 01 GF
4. Add sinks and floor drains and align with those on 01 GF.

3.10 Ceiling

Ceilings are placed in Ceiling Plan view. In Project Browser, open the Ceiling Plans group. You will find Ceiling Plan views of many levels. (If Ceiling Plan view of a level is not present, then On View tab → Create panel → click Plan Views, Reflected Ceiling Plans tool. Select levels and press OK).

You can place ceiling in two ways.

- Automatic Ceiling. When you bring cursor inside an area enclosed by room-bounding elements and click, ceiling is placed.
- Sketch Ceiling. You use sketch tools from Draw panel and sketch ceiling as you want.

3.10.1 Place Ceiling in Rooms

In this project, you will place Automatic Ceiling.

1. Ceiling Plans → 01 GF.
2. On Architecture tab → Build panel → click Ceiling tool.
3. In Properties palette , select Compound Ceiling : 600 x 600mm Grid (Fig. 3.84).

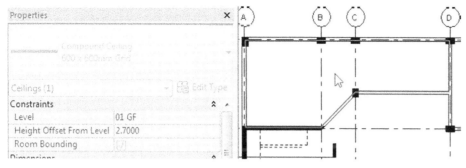

Fig. 3.84 – Add Ceiling in Accounting 101

4. Height Offset from Level = 2.700
5. Bring Cursor in Accounting 101. A red boundary will appear.
6. Click to place the ceiling.
7. In this way click in all rooms to place ceiling.
8. Do not place ceiling in 105 Shaft, 106 Elec/Mech, 110 Elevator, 113 Elec/Mech, 114 Shaft.

3.10.2 Edit Ceiling

As you see, a ceiling is placed in Corridor, Entrance and Stair area. You do not want to place ceiling in Stair area. You will edit the ceiling boundary.

1. Ceiling Plans → 01 GF.
2. Make a selection box that includes the ceiling in Entrance 108 (Fig. 3.85).

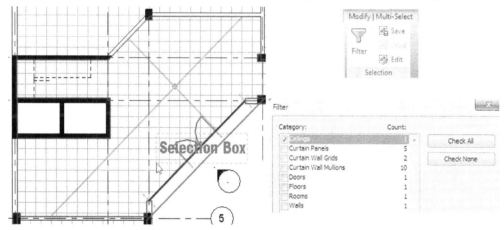

Fig. 3.85 – Select Ceiling in Entrance 108

3. On Modify | Multi-Select contextual tab → Selection panel → Click Filter.
4. In Filter dialog box, press Check None and select Ceilings only.
5. Ceiling in Corridor, Entrance and Stair area is selected.
6. On Modify | Ceilings contextual tab → Mode panel → Click Edit Boundary (Fig. 3.86).
7. Add a vertical line and a small horizontal line to separate stair area and delete 3 lines around stair area. (Use Trim to remove extra length).

Fig. 3.86 – Edit Boundary of Ceiling

8. Mode panel → click Finish ✓ .

3.10.3 Align Ceilings

Ceiling lines in neighboring rooms are not aligned. This can cause problems later on. You will use Align tool to align ceiling lines horizontally and vertically.

1. Ceiling Plans → 01 GF.
2. On Modify tab → Modify panel → Click Align tool.
3. Click on a ceiling line in the Entrance or Corridor area and then click on a ceiling line in a neighboring room to align.
4. Do this for vertical as well as horizontal ceiling lines.

3.10.4 Cover Ceiling Open End

In stair area there is no ceiling. Ceiling in Entrance 108 ends in stair area. In stair area, there is an open end of the ceiling. You need to cover this open end. You will place a wall there from ceiling to upper floor.

1. Floor Plans → 01 GF.
2. On Architecture tab → Build panel → Click Wall tool.
3. In Properties palette, select Type = Basic Wall : Interior - 79mm Partition (1-hr)
4. Edit Type → Duplicate → Name = Interior - 14mm Gypsum
5. In Type Properties dialog box, Structure → Edit
6. Make structure as shown in Fig. 3.87 → OK → OK

Layers

EXTERIOR SIDE

	Function	Material	Thickness	Wraps	Structural Material
1	Finish 1 [4]	Paint	0.0010	✓	
2	**Core Boundary**	**Layers Above**	**0.0000**		
3	Structure [1]	Gypsum Wall	0.0120		✓
4	**Core Boundary**	**Layers Below**	**0.0000**		
5	Finish 1 [4]	Paint	0.0010	✓	

Fig. 3.87 – Gypsum Wall structure

7. Set properties as below.
   - Base Constraint = 01 GF
   - Base Offset = 2.700
   - Top Constraint = Upto Level: 02 FF
   - Top Offset = −0.2
8. Draw wall from B6 to B7.
9. You will receive a message that the wall is not visible in this view. To see the wall, In Floor Plan properties, Extents group, View Range → Edit:
   - Top : Level Above (02 FF) : Offset = 0.0
   - Cut Plane : Associated Level (01 GF) : Offset = 2.8
   - Bottom : Associated Level (01 GF) : Offset = 0.0
   - View Depth Level : Associated Level (01 GF) : Offset = 0.0
10. Place a similar cover 5mm behind the curtain wall at entrance. Zoom to Entrance area.
11. On Architecture tab → Build panel → Click Wall tool.
12. In Properties palette, select Type = Interior - 14mm Gypsum
13. On Modify | Place Wall contextual tab → Draw panel → Click Pick Line. Offset = 0.005 (Fig. 3.88).

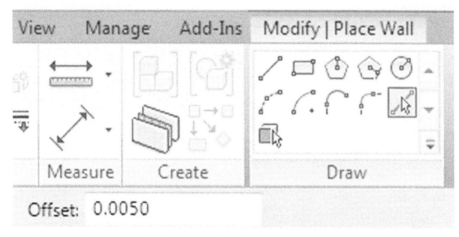

Fig. 3.88 – Pick Line with Offset

14. Bring cursor on inner side of the curtain wall and click. A wall will be added. Press Esc.
15. Select the new wall and drag both ends upto the ends of the curtain wall.
16. Change View Range as before.

3.11 Elevators

Like doors, some elevator components can also be hosted components. They can be added in walls only.

1. Floor Plans → 01 GF.
2. On Architecture tab → Build panel → Click Component tool.
3. In Properties palette , select M_Elevator Center 2032 x 1295mm.
4. Bring cursor near the wall. Image of elevator appears.
5. Move it to inside of the wall and click. An elevator is added.
6. Add the other elevator also (Fig. 3.89).

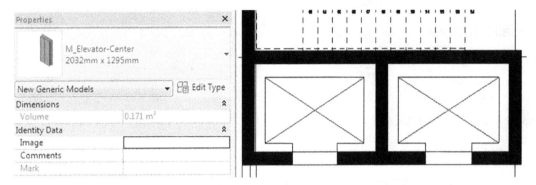

Fig. 3.89 – Add Elevators

7. Click 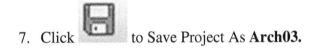 to Save Project As **Arch03.**

4 The Pavement Level

On the Pavement Level, you will add architectural elements such as External Stairs, Ramp and Pavement floor.

4.1 External Stairs

The external stairs are at the entrance of the building. They are 5 meter wide and consist of 4 steps between Pavement and 01 GF level.

1. Open Project **Arch03c.**
2. Save Project As **Arch04.**
3. Floor Plans → Pavement.
4. Zoom around the entrance of the building.
5. On Architecture tab → Model panel → Click Model Line tool.
6. Draw a model line starting from center of the Curtain Door (at 45°).
7. Draw two more model lines parallel to the central model line. Adjust distances as shown in Fig. 4.1.

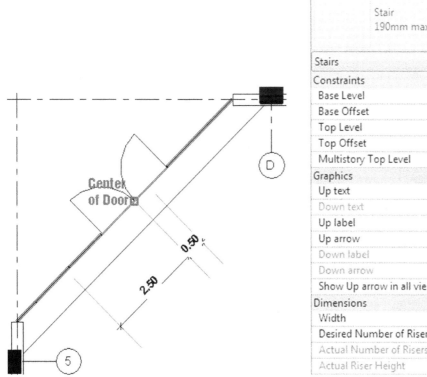

Fig. 4.1 – Model Lines for External Stairs

8. Architecture Tab → Circulation Panel → Stairs dropdown → Click on Stair by Sketch.
9. From Properties palette → type dropdown → select 190mm max riser 250mm going.
10. Set other properties as shown in Fig. 4.1.
11. Click on the end of north-east model line (Fig. 4.2).
12. Move cursor along the line. When you see "4 RISERS CREATED 0 REMAINING", click again.
13. Mode panel → click Finish Editing Mode.

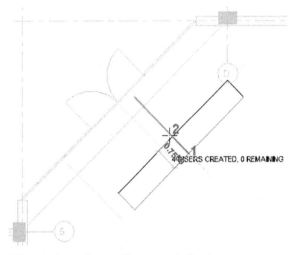

Fig. 4.2 – Draw External Stairs

14. On Modify tab → Modify panel → Click Align tool.
15. Click on edge of floor outside the entrance then click on upper edge of stairs.
16. The stairs align with the floor.
17. See 3D view (Fig. 4.3).

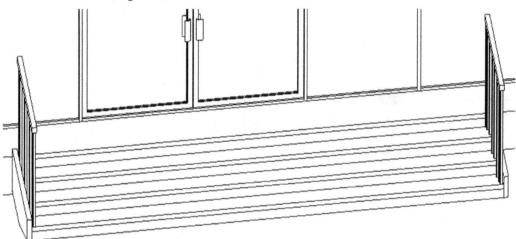

Fig. 4.3 – 3D view of External Stairs

18. Click on hand rail. Press Delete.
19. Select stairs. In Properties palette , click on Edit type (Fig. 4.4).
20. Set Left and Right Stringers = None.

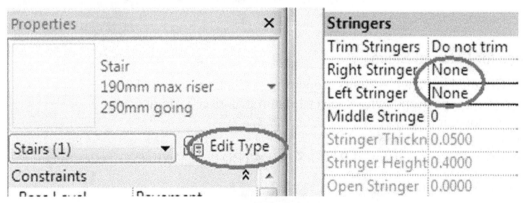

Fig. 4.4 – Remove stringers of External Stairs

21. The stairs look as shown in Fig. 4.5.

Fig. 4.5 – Final shape of External Stairs

4.2 Ramp

A ramp is used for wheeled objects such as wheel-chairs, strollers, carts to access a building easily.

4.2.1 Create a Ramp

The ramp is at the entrance of the building near the external stairs. It is 1 meter wide between Pavement and 01 GF level. Its slope is 1:2.

1. Floor Plans → Pavement.
2. Zoom around the entrance of the building.
3. On Architecture tab → Circulation panel → Click Ramp tool.
4. Set properties as shown in Fig. 4.6.

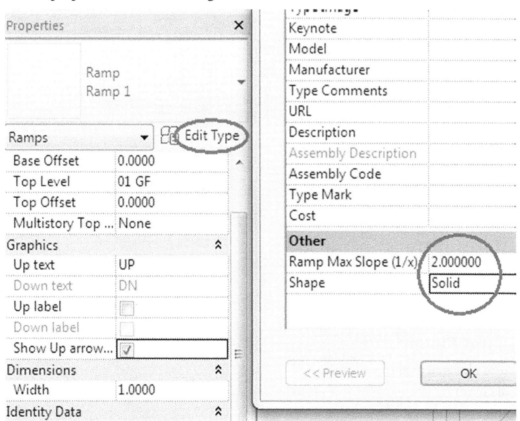

Fig. 4.6 – Ramp properties

5. Click on the end of south-west model line (Fig. 4.7).

6. Move cursor along the line. When you see "1.2 of inclined ramp created. 0 remaining", click again.

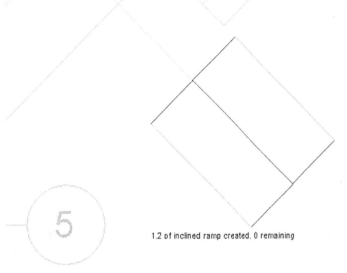

1.2 of inclined ramp created. 0 remaining

Fig. 4.7 – Draw Ramp

7. Mode panel → click Finish Editing Mode .
8. On Modify tab → Modify panel → Click Align tool.
9. Click on edge of floor outside the entrance the click on edge of the ramp.
10. The ramp align with the floor.
11. See 3D view.
12. Click on hand rail. Press Delete.
13. Floor Plans → Pavement.
14. Delete model lines.
15. 3D view looks as shown in Fig. 4.8.

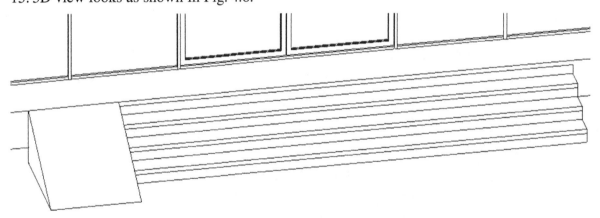

Fig. 4.8 – 3D view of Ramp

4.2.2 Edit the Ground Floor

The ground floor need to be changed near the entrance.

1. Floor Plans → Pavement.
2. Select the Ground Floor.
3. On Modify | Floors contextual tab → Mode panel → click Edit Boundary.
4. Change the boundary as shown in Fig. 4.9.

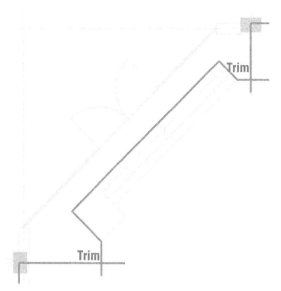

Fig. 4.9 – Edit Floor Boundary

5. Mode panel → click Finish Editing Mode .
6. A dialog box appears asking "....Would you like to join geometry....". Click on NO.

4.3 Pavement Floor

Pavement Floor is added all around the building.

4.3.1 Pavement Floor Structure

It is made of a layer of bricks over a layer of earth.

1. On Architecture tab → Build panel → Click Floor tool.
2. On Properties palette , select type = Generic 300mm (Fig. 4.10).
3. In Properties palette Edit Type → Duplicate → Name = Pavement Floor 300mm → OK.

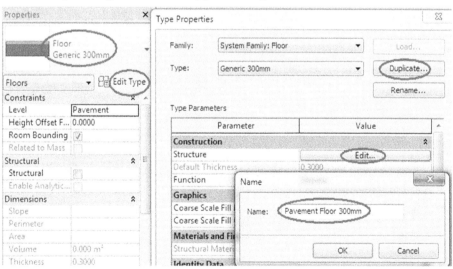

Fig. 4.10 – Edit Floor Type

4. On Type Properties → Construction group → Structure parameter → Edit.
5. On Edit Assembly dialogue box, click Insert to insert another layer.
6. Change materials from Material Editor.

7. Change thickness of layers as shown in Fig. 4.11.

	Function	Material	Thickness	Wraps	Structural Material	Var
1	Finish 1 [4]	Brick, Pavers	0.0750			✓
2	**Core Boundary**	**Layers Above W**	0.0000			
3	Structure [1]	Earth	0.2250		✓	
4	**Core Boundary**	**Layers Below W**	0.0000			

Fig. 4.11 – Edit Floor Structure

8. For material Brick, Pavers, change Cut Pattern to Brickwork (Fig. 4.12).

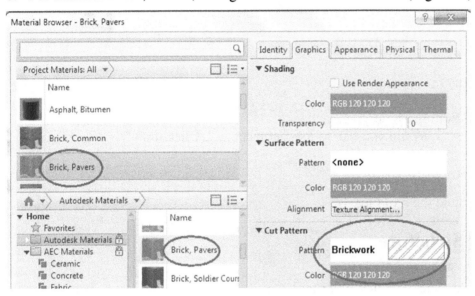

Fig. 4.12 – Edit Floor Material

9. For material Earth, change Cut Pattern to Earth.
10. Press OK.

4.3.2 Pavement Floor Placement

The pavement floor is all around the building. It is 2 meters from outer side of the exterior wall on all sides. At the entrance, it is 4 meters from the stairs.

1. Floor Plans → Pavement.
2. On Architecture tab → Build panel → Click Floor tool.
3. On Properties palette , select type = Pavement Floor 300mm.
4. On Modify | Create Floors Boundary contextual tab → Draw panel → click Pick Lines (Fig. 4.13).

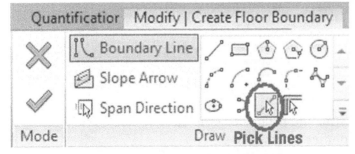

Fig. 4.13 – Pick Lines for Floor Boundary

5. Set Offset = 2.00
6. Bring cursor over the North exterior wall. When you see a blue dashed line, click.
7. Do the same on other sides of the building. *Note : Only ONE click on one side.*
8. On the entrance side, set Offset = 4.00 and click on start of external stair.
9. You will see as shown in Fig. 4.14.

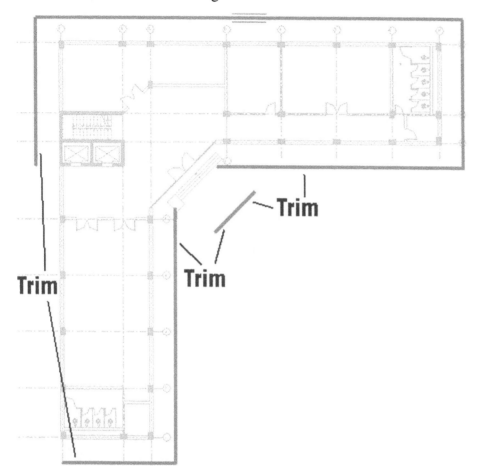

Fig. 4.14 – Floor Boundary Lines

10. On Modify tab → Modify panel → Click Trim tool   .
11. Click on lines where shown in Fig. 4.14.

12. Mode panel → click Finish Editing Mode   .

4.3.3 Pavement Floor Editing

The pavement floor placed in § 4.2.2 goes not only all around the building but also under the building. The part which is under the building has to be removed. To do this, you will edit the boundary of the floor and make a closed polygon inside the outer boundary.

1. Floor Plans → Pavement.
2. Select the pavement floor.
3. On Modify I Floors contextual tab → Mode panel → click Edit Boundary.
4. On Draw panel, select Pick Lines tool→ Offset = 0.0.
5. Click on outer line of the exterior wall, outer stairs, ramp etc (Fig. 4.15).
6. Trim lines where needed.

7. Mode panel → click Finish Editing Mode .

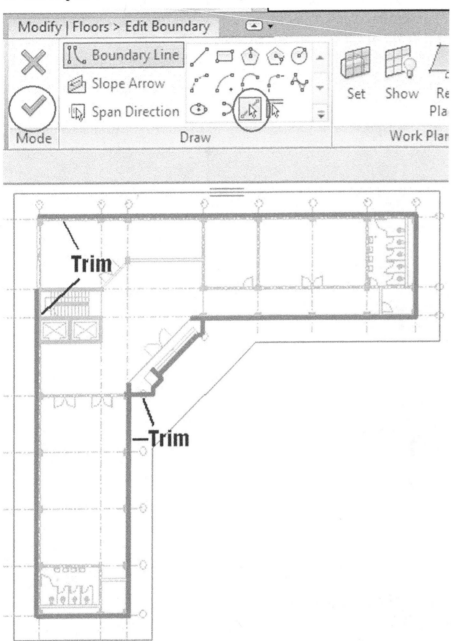

Fig. 4.15 – Edit Floor Boundary

8. Click to Save Project As **Arch04.**

5 The First Floor Level

On the First Floor Level, you will copy - paste elements from the Ground Floor Level and modify them where needed.

5.1 Widows

Windows layout on 02 FF level is almost same as on 01 GF level. Extra windows can be deleted and missing windows can added later on.

5.1.1 Copy Widows

You will copy windows on 01 GF level and paste them on 02 FF level.

1. Open Project Arch04.
2. Save Project As **Arch05.**
3. Floor Plans → 01 GF.
4. Make a selection box around the building to select all elements.
5. On Selection panel → click Filter tool.
6. Press Check None and then check Windows only (not Window Tags) → OK.
7. On Clipboard panel, press Copy.
8. On Clipboard panel → Paste dropdown → select Aligned to Selected Levels → 02 FF → OK.

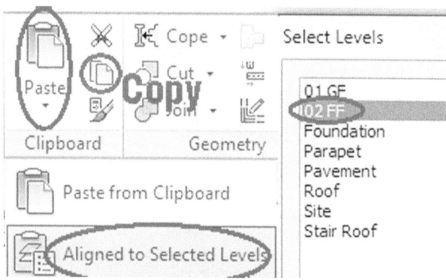

Fig. 5.1   – Copy - Paste Windows

9. All windows are copied to 02 FF level.

5.1.2 Tag Widows

Tags are not copied. So you will tag all windows on 02 FF level.

1. On Annotate tab → Tag panel → Click Tag All tool.
2. From Tag All Not Tagged dialog box, click on Category Window, M_Window Tag New. Press OK.

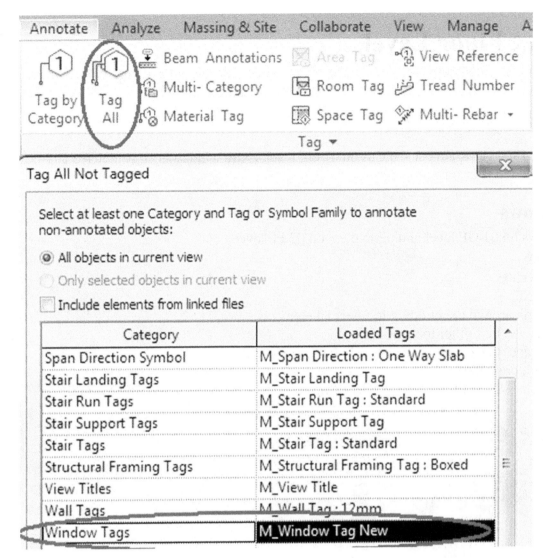

Fig. 5.2 – Add Window Tags

3. All windows are tagged.

5.1.3 Windows Flip

You added the windows by bringing the cursor to outer side of the exterior wall (§ 3.7.1 Step 10) so that the tag is placed on the outer side. The windows need to be flipped inside out.

1. 3D view.
2. Make a selection box to select all.
3. On Selection panel click Filter → Check None → Check Windows only.
4. Press Space Bar.

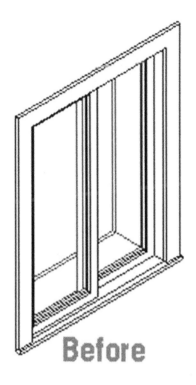
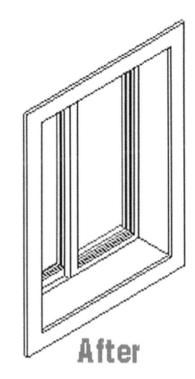

Fig. 5.3   – Flip Windows

5.2 Copy Interior Elements

1. Floor Plans → 01 GF.
2. Make a selection box to select all interior elements.

- Zoom to north-west part of the building.
- Select all interior parts as shown in Fig. 5.4.
- Zoom to south-west part of the building.
- Press Ctrl and select other elements.
- Ctrl-select **ADDS** to selection. Shift-select **SUBTRCTS** from selection
- Do not select shear walls, stairs and walls around shafts.

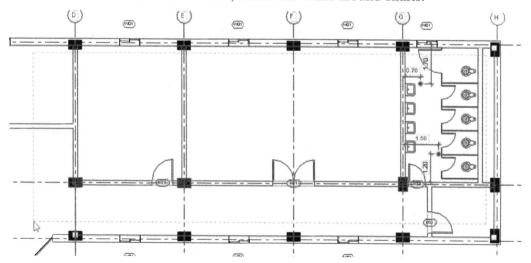

Fig. 5.4   – Select interior elements

3. On Selection panel → click Filter tool.

4. Select only the parts shown in Fig. 5.5 → OK.
5. On Clipboard panel, press Copy.
6. On Clipboard panel → Paste dropdown → select Aligned to Selected Levels → 02 FF → OK.
7. Floor Plans → 02 FF.
8. All selected elements are copied to 02 FF level.

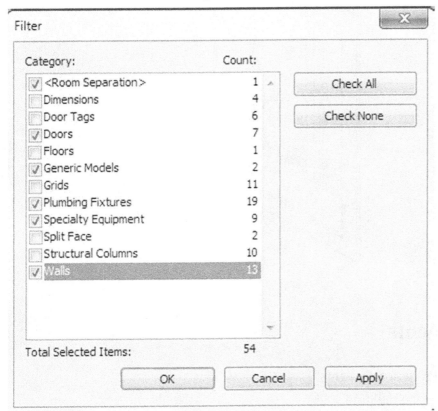

Fig. 5.5 – Filter Categories

5.3 Area Above Entrance

5.3.1 Split Walls

Exterior walls on grids C and 6 need to be split. One part will remain as it is. But other part will not go upto Parapet level. It will be upto 02 FF level. Also it will have no parapet cap.

1. Floor Plans → 02 FF.
2. Zoom to area between grids C-D and 5-6

3. On Modify tab → Modify panel → Click Split Element tool.
4. A knife cursor will appear. Click with it on exterior wall at D6 (Split exactly at grid D as shown in Fig. 5.6).
5. The wall is split in two parts.
6. Select the wall on west of grid D.
7. In Properties palette Edit Type → Duplicate → Name = Exterior - 300mm No Parapet → OK (Fig. 5.7).
8. On Type Properties → Construction group → Structure parameter → Edit.
9. On Edit Assembly dialogue box, select View = Section (Fig. 5.8).
10. Click on Sweeps.

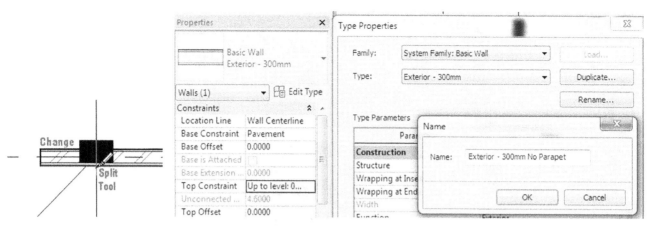

Fig. 5.6 – Split Wall   Fig. 5.7 – Edit Wall Type

11. Under Wall Sweeps, select the sweep 1.
12. Press Delete to delete it.
13. OK → OK → OK → OK

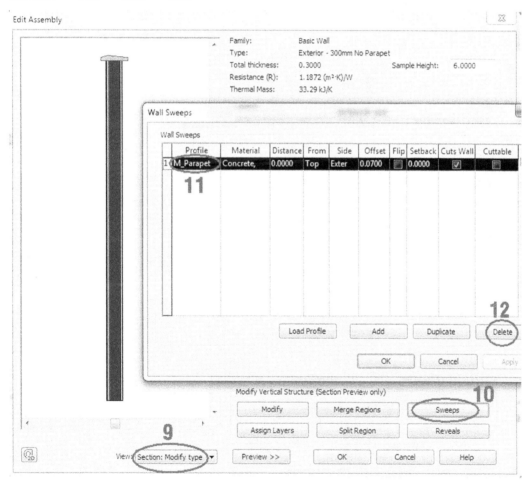

Fig. 5.8 – Remove Wall profile

14. In Properties palette, change Top Constraint = 02 FF (Fig. 5.9).
15. Now zoom near the column C5 and split the wall.
16. In Properties palette, change Type = Exterior - 300mm No Parapet and Top Constraint = 02 FF

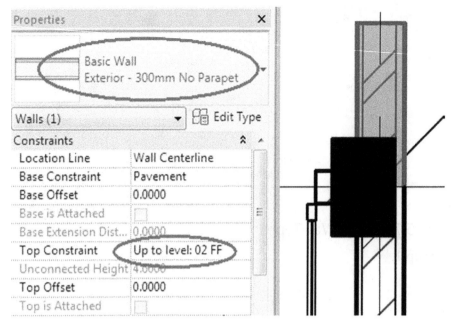

Fig. 5.9 – Change Wall type

17. See 3D view.

5.3.2 Change Exterior Wall

The area above entrance has no exterior wall. Now you will add an exterior wall.

1. Floor Plans → 02 FF.
2. Zoom to area between grids C-D and 5-6
3. On Architecture tab → Build panel → Click Wall tool.
4. In Properties palette, select Type = Exterior - 300mm and Top Constraint = Parapet.
5. Start from C5, go some distance to east, go to north-east at 45° until you see a blue dotted line extension from grid D. Finish at D6.
6. Adjust the distance of wall as shown in Fig. 5.10.

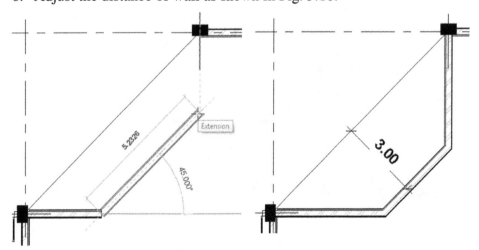

Fig. 5.10 – Add Wall

5.3.3 Change Floor

As you see in the Fig. 5.10, the 3 meter part is without floor. You will edit the boundary of the floor.

1. Floor Plans → 02 FF.

2. Select the floor. In mode panel, click Edit boundary.
3. Bring the floor boundary along the new wall (Fig. 5.11).

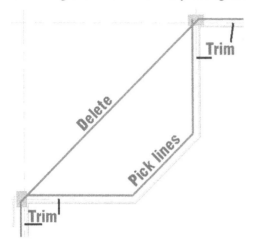

Fig. 5.11 – Edit Floor Boundary

4. Mode panel → click Finish Editing Mode ✓ .
5. For the dialog box asking Would you like wall ..., click No.
6. In 3D view, you can see that the floor is visible under the wall. You will lower the bottom of wall to cover it.
7. Select the three new walls. In Properties palette, change Base Offset = − 0.2

5.3.4 Add Curtain Windows

You can use curtain wall as a window. Actually you can embed a curtain wall inside a concrete wall. You will make a curtain window in three walls above the entrance. First you will make the wall joints as mitered.

1. Floor Plans → 02 FF. Zoom to walls above entrance.
2. On Modify tab → Geometry panel → click Wall Joints tool.
3. Click on the wall joint shown in Fig. 5.12.
4. On Option Bar, select Miter

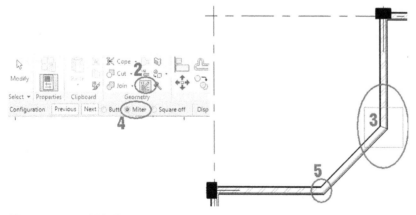

Fig. 5.12 – Wall Joints

5. Same for the other joint.
6. On Architecture tab → Build panel → click Wall tool.
7. On Properties palette, select type = Curtain Wall : Storefront
8. Edit Type → Duplicate → Name = Storefront Window

9. Set all Type Parameters as shown in Fig. 5.13.
10. On Properties palette, set
   - Base Constraint = 02 FF
   - Base Offset = 1.00
   - Top Constraint = Unconnected
   - Unconnected Height = 1.500

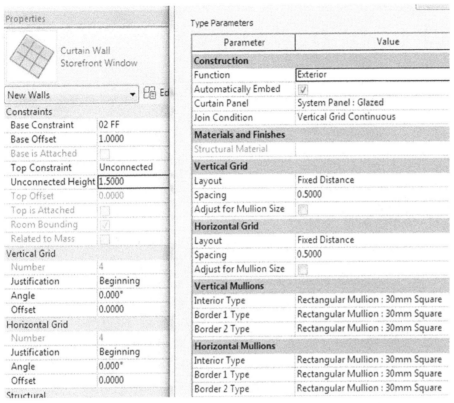

Fig. 5.13 – Edit Storefront Type

11. On Modify | Place Wall contextual tab → Draw panel → Click Pick Lines.
12. Click in the center of three walls above entrance (Fig. 5.14).

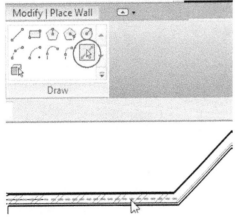

Fig. 5.14 – Pick Lines at Wall center

13. The 3D view will look as shown in Fig. 5.15.

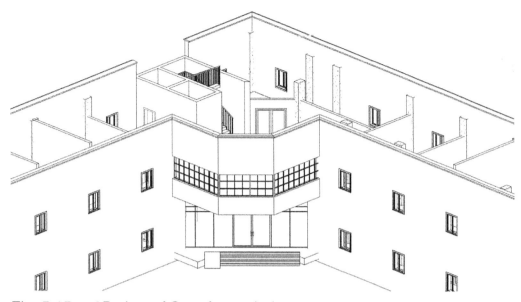

Fig. 5.15 – 3D view of Storefront window

5.4 Add Round Columns

The three walls above the entrance need structural support. You will add four columns. First you will add structural columns for support. For decoration, you will add architectural columns around them.

5.4.1 Add Structural Round Columns

1. Floor Plans → 02 FF. Zoom to walls above entrance.
2. On Architecture tab → Model panel → click Model Line tool.
3. In Draw panel, select Pick Lines (Fig. 5.16).
4. Set Offset = 0.35
5. Bring cursor over the inner side of the wall.
6. Click when blue dashed line appears.
7. Do the same for other three walls.

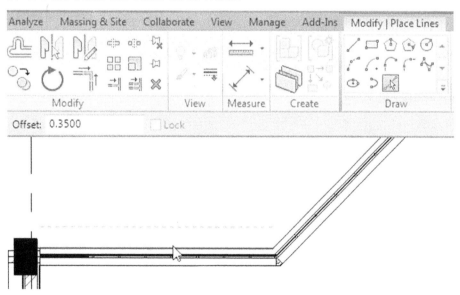

Fig. 5.16 – Add Model Lines

8. On Structure tab → Structure panel → click Column tool.

9. In Mode panel, click Load Family.
10. Structural Columns → Concrete → M_Concrete-Round-Column.rfa
11. In Properties palette, select type = 450mm
12. On Option bar select Height = Roof
13. Add four columns and move - align them as shown in Fig. 5.17.

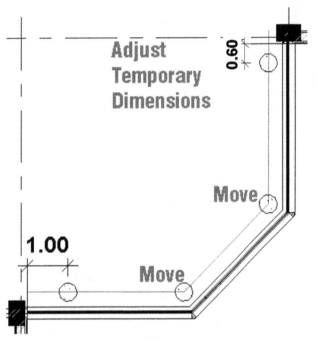

Fig. 5.17 – Add Structural Round Columns

14. Change appearance of round columns as explained in § 2.1.3.
15. Select all four round columns (Select first column. Ctrl-Select other three).
16. In Properties palette, set

   - Base Level = Foundation.
   - Base Offset = 0.00
   - Top Level = Roof
   - Top Offset = 0.00

5.4.2 Add Architectural Round Columns

Structural columns are load bearing. Architectural columns are like a cover around the structural columns for decoration purposes.

1. Floor Plans → 01 GF.
2. On Architecture tab → Build panel → Column dropdown → click Column: Architectural tool (Fig. 5.18).

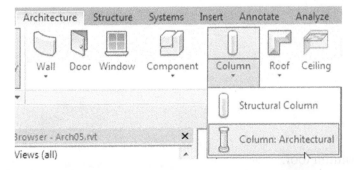

Fig. 5.18 – Architectural Column

3. Columna → M_Metal Clad Column.rfa.
4. Click at the center of four round structural columns.
5. See 3D view. Four architectural columns are placed around the four structural columns.
6. Select the four architectural columns. Set Top Offset = − 0.2. Now top of the columns is below the upper floor.
7. Select the front two architectural columns. Set Base Level = Pavement.

5.5 Wall - Floor Joint

The floor at 02 FF should be placed on structural material of the wall.

1. Floor Plans → 02 FF.
2. Make a selection box around the corner A8 → Filter → Check Floors only → OK.
3. Mode panel → Edit Boundary.
4. Align boundary lines with outer side of structural columns (Fig. 5.19).

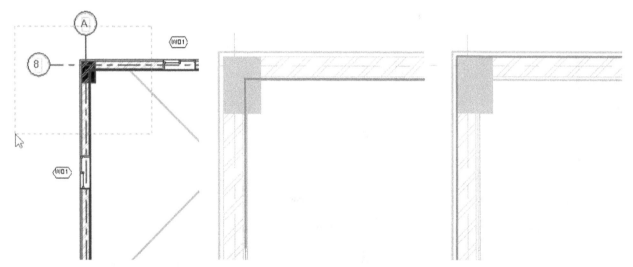

Fig. 5.19 – Align Floor Boundary with outer side of Structural Columns

5. Mode panel → Finish Edit.
6. Answer dialog boxes as shown in Fig. 5.20.

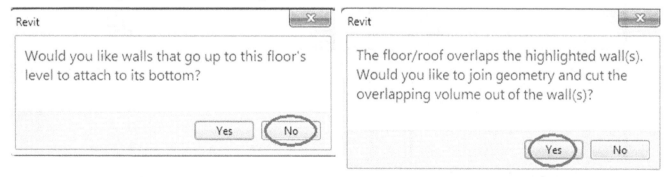

Fig. 5.20 – Edit Floor Dialog Boxes

7. On View tab → Create panel → click on Section tool. (or click on section tool in Quick Access Toolbar).

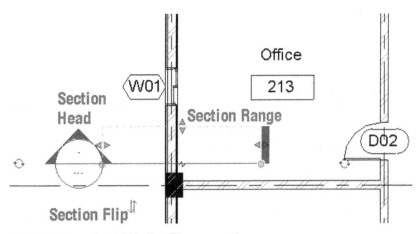

Fig. 5.21 – Add Wall - Floor section

8. Make a section on exterior wall. (If section head is not to the north side then click on the section-flip arrows). Bring the section-range line close so that no element other than the exterior wall is in the range (Fig. 5.21).
9. Double-click on the section-head to see the section.
10. You will see that the floor is now on the wall's structural material (Fig. 5.22).

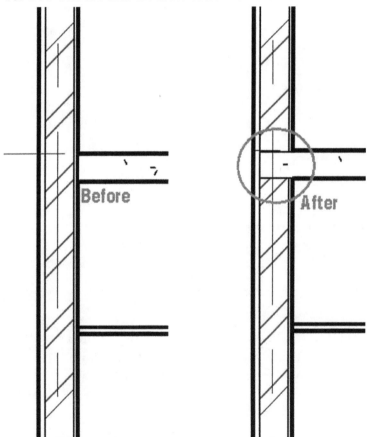

Fig. 5.22 – Wall - Floor section view

5.6 Remove Floor from Stair, Elevator and Shaft areas

You will edit the floor boundary to remove floor from Stair, Elevator and Shaft areas.

1. Floor Plans → 02 FF.
2. Make a selection box around the corner A8 → Filter → Check Floors only → OK.

3. Mode panel → Edit Boundary.
4. Edit boundary in the Stair and Elevator area near A6 as shown in Fig. 5.23.

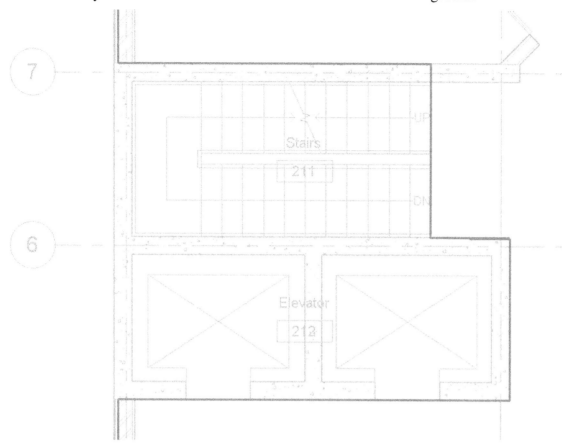

Fig. 5.23 – Floor Boundary in Stair and Elevator area near A6

5. Edit boundary in the Shaft area near A1 as shown in Fig. 5.24.

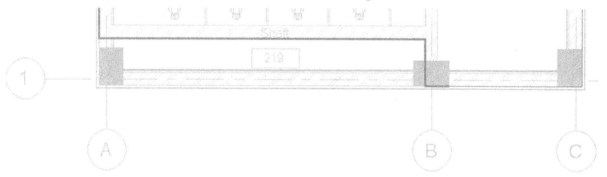

Fig. 5.24 – Floor Boundary in Shaft area near A1

6. Edit boundary in the Shaft area near H8 as shown in Fig. 5.25.

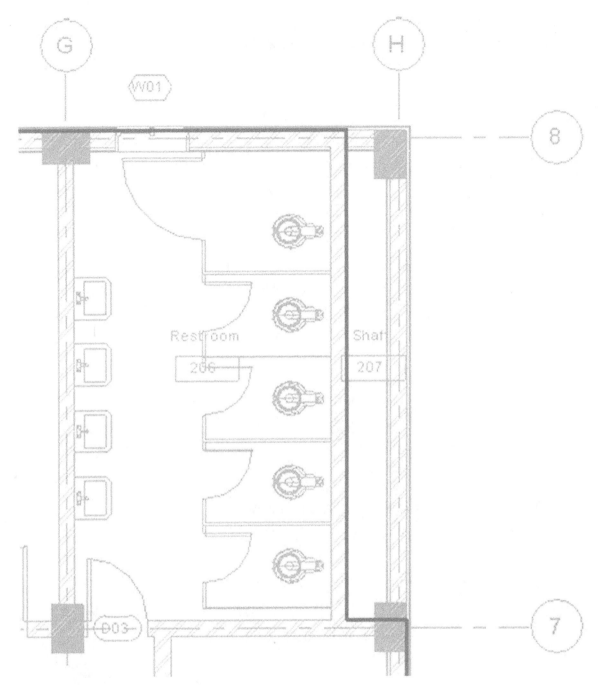

Fig. 5.25 – Floor Boundary in Shaft area near H8

7. Mode panel → Finish Edit.
8. Copy - Paste Floor from 02 FF level to 03 Roof level as explained in § 3.4.3.

5.7 Add Rooms

Just like on 01 GF, you will add rooms on 02 FF level also.

1. Floor Plans → 01 GF
2. Architecture Tab → Room & Area Panel → Room tool.
3. Properties palette → Constraints group set the following:

   • Upper Limit = Roof
   • Limit Offset = 0.0

- Base Offset = 0.0
4. Add rooms as you added in § 3.5.3.
5. The rooms will be as shown in Fig. 5.26.

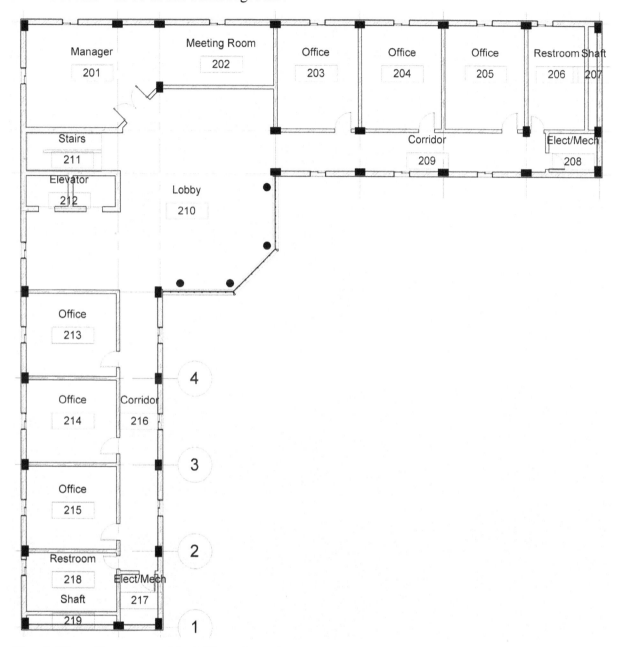

Fig. 5.26 – Rooms on First Floor Level

5.8 Ceiling

You will place ceiling on the ceiling plan of 02 FF level as you did for 01 GF level. Repeat the steps given in § 3.10 for 02 FF level.

1. Ceiling Plans → 02 FF.
2. On Architecture tab → Build panel → click Ceiling tool.
3. In Type Selector , select Compound Ceiling : 600 x 600mm Grid.
4. Height Offset from Level = 2.700

5. Place ceiling in all rooms except 207 Shaft, 208 Elec/Mech, 212 Elevator , 219 Shaft, 217 Elec/Mech.
6. Edit the ceiling in 210 Lobby as you did in § 3.10.2.
7. Align ceilings as you did in § 3.10.3.
8. Copy/Paste the gypsum wall you placed in § 3.10.4 from 01 GF level to 02 FF level.

9. Click  to Save Project As **Arch05.**

6 The Roof Level

On the Roof Level, you will copy - paste the floor from 02 FF level and modify its structure. Over the floor, you will add a roof. You will make slopes for rain water drainage. You need a room for stairs.

6.1 Floor structure for Roof Level

1. Open Project **Arch05.**
2. Save Project As **Arch06.**
3. Select the floor on Roof level → Edit Type → Duplicate → Name = Concrete-Domestic 150mm
4. Structure → Edit
5. Make changes as shown in Fig. 6.1.

	Function	Material	Thickness	Wraps	Structural Material	Variable
1	Core Boundary	Layers Above Wrap	0.0000			
2	Structure [1]	Concrete, Cast In Situ	0.1500	☐	✓	☐
3	Core Boundary	Layers Below Wrap	0.0000			

Fig. 6.1 – Floor Structure

6. 3D view looks as in Fig. 6.2.

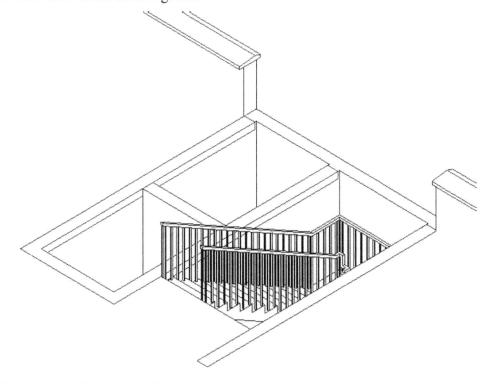

Fig. 6.2 – 3D view of Roof level

6.2 Some Safety Measures

On the roof, the openings are like deep holes. There are some other dangerous places to be taken care of. You will add elements to for safety purposes.

6.2.1 Add Railing

At the end of stairs, you will add a railing.

1. Floor Plans → Roof.
2. View Range Edit Cut Plane Offset = 1.2
3. On Architecture tab → Circulation panel → click Railing tool.
4. Draw a line at the end of the stairs as shown in Fig. 6.3.

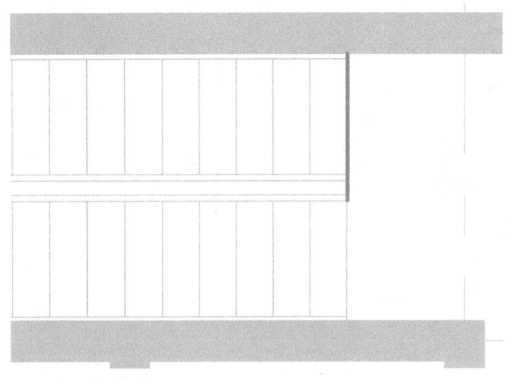

Fig. 6.3 – Add Railing

5. On Mode panel → click Finish ✓ .
6. Select the railing.
7. Press right or left-arrow to move the railing a little.

6.2.2 Walls around Stair and Elevator

There are shear walls around the stairs and elevators. But their height is up to Roof level. You will add another wall around the stairs and elevators.

1. Floor Plans → Roof.
2. Zoom around the stair and elevator area.
3. Properties palette → View Range → Edit.
    - Top = Associated Level, Offset = 2.3
    - Cut plane Offset = 0.5
    - Bottom = Associated Level, Offset = − 0.2
    - View Depth: Level = Associated Level, Offset = − 0.2
4. On Architecture tab → Build panel → click Wall tool.
5. In Type Selector , select Basic Wall : Exterior - 300mm No Parapet.
6. Edit Type → Duplicate → Name = Exterior - 225mm Roof Wall.
7. Structure → Edit → Make changes as shown in Fig. 6.4.

	Function	Material	Thickness	Wraps	Structural Material
1	Finish 1 [4]	Tile Wall	0.0120	☑	■
2	Membrane Layer	Damp-proofing	0.0000	☑	
3	**Core Boundary**	**Layers Above Wrap**	**0.0000**		
4	Structure [1]	Cement Block	0.2120	☐	☑
5	**Core Boundary**	**Layers Below Wrap**	**0.0000**		
6	Finish 2 [5]	Paint	0.0010	☑	☐

Fig. 6.4 – Roof Wall Structure

8. Add a wall as shown in Fig. 6.5 with:

- Type = Basic Wall: Exterior - 225mm Roof Wall.
- Base Constraint = Roof.
- Top Constraint = Up to level: Stair Roof.

9. Align outer side of this wall with outer side of shear wall.

10. Add a door (M_Single Flush Vision: 0915 x 2134) as shown in Fig. 6.5.

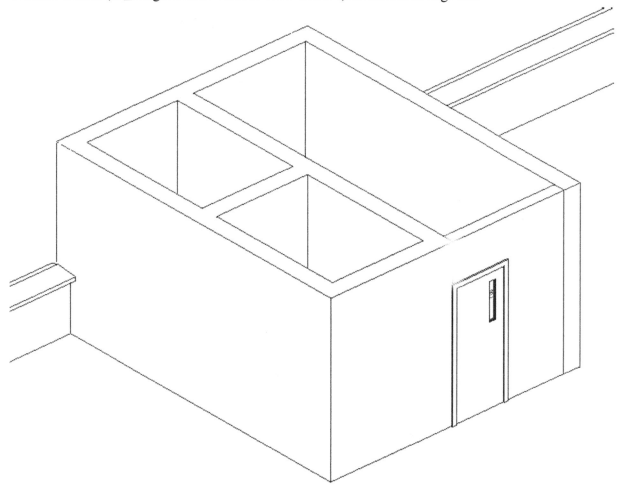

Fig. 6.5 – Walls around Stair and Elevator

6.3 Outer Side of Shear wall

The exterior wall has layers for damp-proofing, thermal-barrier and finishing on outer side. You will make similar layers for the shear wall on exterior side.

6.3.1 Add New Materials

You will add a new material for finishing of the outer side of the shear wall which will be the same as the finishing of the outer side of the exterior wall.

1. On Manage tab → Settings panel → click Materials to open the Material Browser.
2. Find the material Tile Wall, duplicate it and rename it as Tile Wall 2 (Fig. 6.6).
3. Select the material Tile Wall 2.
4. In Appearance tab, click on Duplicate this Asset.

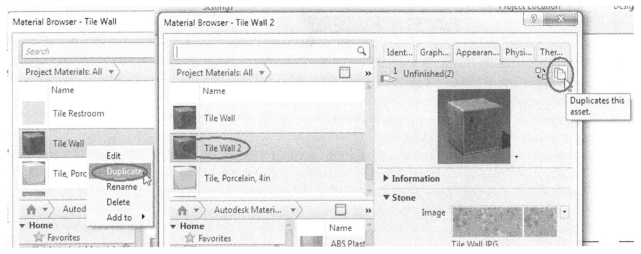

Fig. 6.6 – Material Tile Wall 2

5. Find the material Tile Wall, duplicate it and rename it as Tile Roof (Fig. 6.7).
6. Select the material Tile Roof.
7. In Appearance tab, change the image to Concrete.Cast-In-Place.Flat.Grey.2.jpg (in C:\Program Files (x86)\Common Files\Autodesk Shared\Materials\Textures\3\Mats folder).

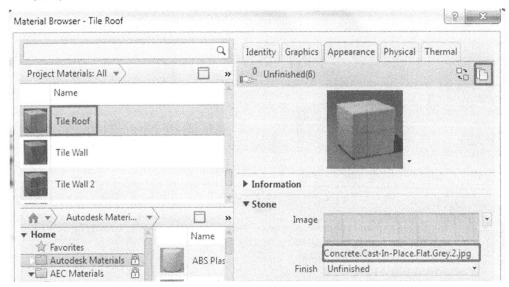

Fig. 6.7 – Material Tile Roof

8. In Appearance tab, click on Duplicate this Asset.

6.3.2 Change Shear Wall Structure

1. Floor Plans → 01 GF.
2. Visual Style = Hidden Line.
3. Detail Level = Fine.
4. Select the west side shear wall.
5. Structure → Edit → Change structure as shown in Fig. 6.8.

Layers

EXTERIOR SIDE

	Function	Material	Thickness	Wraps	St N
1	Finish 1 [4]	Tile Wall 2	0.0120	✓	
2	Thermal/Air Layer	Thermal Barriers - External Wa	0.0400	✓	
3	Membrane Layer	Damp-proofing	0.0000	✓	
4	**Core Boundary**	**Layers Above Wrap**	**0.0000**		
5	Structure [1]	Concrete, Cast In Situ	0.2480		✓
6	**Core Boundary**	**Layers Below Wrap**	**0.0000**		

Fig. 6.8 – Edit Structure of shear wall

6.3.4 Align Tile Pattern

You can see that the tile pattern of shear wall is not matching with that of the exterior wall. You will shift the tile pattern of the shear wall to align with that of the exterior wall.

1. Floor Plans → 01 GF.
2. On View tab → Windows panel → click Close Hidden (or on Quick Access Toolbar, click on 
).
3. Elevations → West → Visual Style = Realistic.
4. On View tab → Windows panel → click Tile (or press WT).
5. Select the west side shear wall in 01 GF.
6. In Properties palette, click Edit Type → Structure → Edit.
7. For layer 1, Material column, click on [...] to edit the material (Fig. 6.9).
8. In Material Editor, find and select Tile Wall 2.
9. Click on Appearance tab
10. Click on the Image.
11. On Texture Editor dialog box, change X or Y-offset for Position → OK → OK.

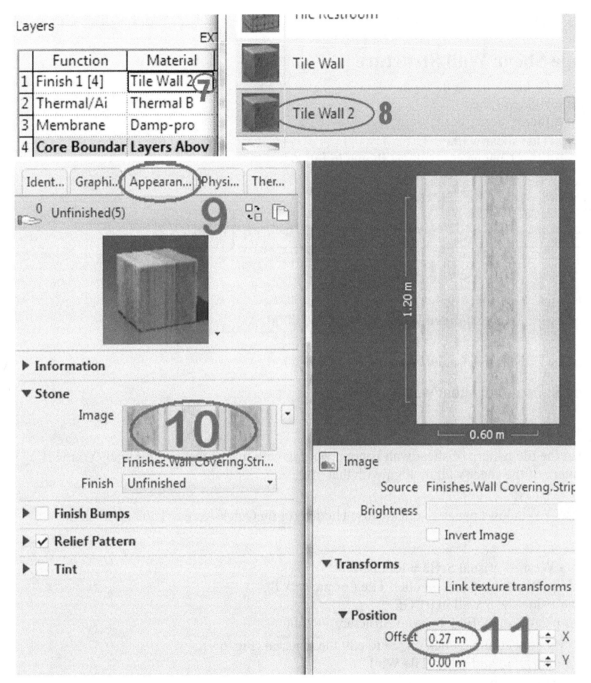

Fig. 6.9 – Align Tile Pattern

12. See the walls. The tile pattern of the shear wall has shifted.
13. Make adjustment until the wall patterns align with each other.

6.3.5 Joining Line of Patterns

You can see that although the tile patterns of shear wall is aligned with adjacent walls but the joining line is still visible. You need to remove (actually hide) this line.

1. Elevations → West.
2. On Modify tab → View panel → click Linework tool (Fig. 6.10).
3. In Line Style panel, Line Styles dropdown, select <Invisible Lines>.
4. Click on joining lines twice.
5. The joining lines will disappear.

6. Do the same in 3D view also.

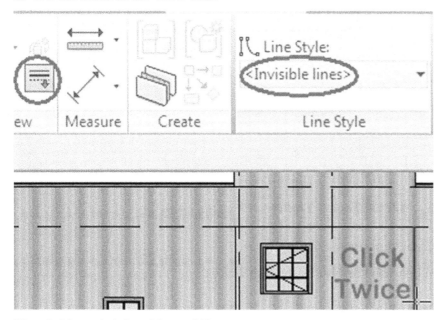

Fig. 6.10 – Joining Line of Patterns

6.4 Stair Roof

You will add a sloped roof above the stair and elevator area.

1. Floor Plans → Stair Roof.
2. Zoom around the stair and elevator area.
3. On Architecture tab → Build panel → Roof dropdown → Roof by Footprint.
4. In Properties palette, select type = Basic Roof: Generic -125mm
5. Edit Type → Duplicate → Name = Concrete - 100mm → OK (Fig. 6.11).

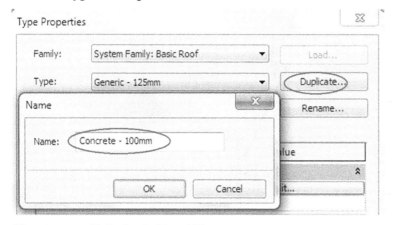

Fig. 6.11 – Edit Stair Roof Type

6. Structure → Edit → Change as shown in Fig. 6.12.

	Function	Material	Thickness	Wraps	Va
1	Core Boundary	Layers Above Wrap	0.0000		
2	Structure [1]	Concrete, Cast-in-Place gray	0.1000	☐	☐
3	Core Boundary	Layers Below Wrap	0.0000		

Fig. 6.12 – Edit Stair Roof Structure

7. In Draw panel, select Pick Walls.
8. On Option Bar, select Overhang, set Offset = 0.6 (Fig. 6.13).

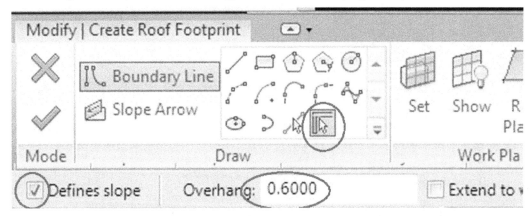

Fig. 6.13 – Stair Roof settings for Overhang with Slope

9. Bring cursor on north shear wall. When you see blue dashed line, click.
10. Same on south shear wall.
11. On Option Bar, deselect Defines slope (Fig. 6.14).

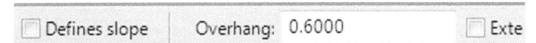

Fig. 6.14 – Stair Roof settings for Overhang without Slope

12. Click on east and west shear walls (Fig. 6.15).

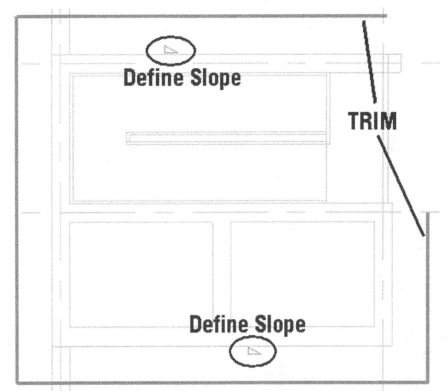

Fig. 6.15 – Stair Roof Footprint

13. Trim north and east lines.

14. On Mode panel → click Finish   .
15. See 3D view.
16. There is a gap under the sloped roof.
17. Select the brick wall.
18. On Modify Wall panel, click on Attach Top/Base (Fig. 6.16).
19. On Option Bar, select Top

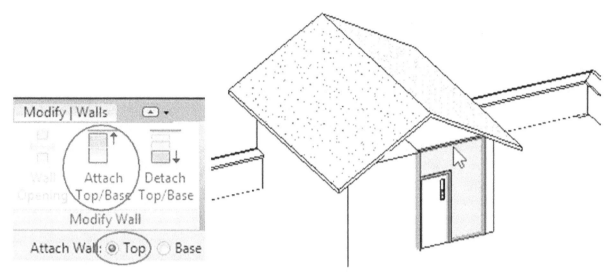

Fig. 6.16 – 3D view of stair Roof

20. Click on sloped roof.
21. The wall attaches to the sloped roof.
22. Similarly attach other walls to the roof.
23. Copy - Paste window in the west side shear wall (from 02 FF level to Roof level. Sill Height = 2.00).

6.5 Roof

You will add a roof over the concrete floor.

1. Floor Plans → Roof.
2. On Architecture tab → Build panel → Roof dropdown → Roof by Footprint.
3. In Properties palette, select type = Basic Roof: Warm Roof - Concrete
4. Edit Type → Duplicate → Name = Warm Roof - Insulated → OK
5. Structure → Edit → Change as shown in Fig. 6.17.

	Function	Material	Thickness	Wraps	Variable
1	Finish 1 [4]	Tile Roof	0.0100		
2	**Core Boundary**	**Layers Above Wrap**	**0.0000**		
3	Structure [1]	Concrete, Sand/Cement Screed	0.0500		✓
4	Thermal/Air	Rigid insulation	0.0500		
5	Membrane L	Damp-proofing	0.0000		
6	Substrate [2]	Asphalt, Bitumen	0.0200		
7	**Core Boundary**	**Layers Below Wrap**	**0.0000**		

Fig. 6.17 – Edit Structure of Roof

6. In Draw panel, select Pick Walls.
7. On Option Bar, un-select Overhang, set Offset = 0.0

8. Bring cursor on inner side of north exterior wall.
9. When wall becomes blue, press Tab. A series of walls become blue. Now **Click**.
10. Delete, Trim lines to adjust the footprint as shown in Fig. 6.18.

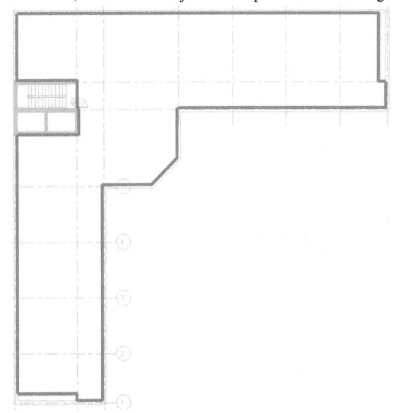

Fig. 6.18 – Roof Footprint

11. On Mode panel → click Finish ✔ .
12. Lower part of the stair door is in the roof. You will raise it up by the thickness of the roof.
13. Select stair door. In Properties palette, change Sill Height = 0.13.

14. Click 💾 to Save Project As **Arch06.**

7   The Site Level

On the site level, you will make a toposurface around the building. On it, you will make roads, trees, parking etc. An easy way is that you go to site plan view and export it as Autodesk Autocad® drawing. Make roads, parking etc. with lines, arcs, polylines and link the drawing back in Autodesk Revit®.

7.1 Export the Model

The site view of the BIM Model will be exported as DWG file. You need to export the floors only because all the site elements are outside the floors and inner details are not needed to make the site plan.

1. Open Project **Arch06.**
2. Save Project As **Arch07.**
3. Floor Plans → Site.
4. Make a big selection box to select all.
5. On Selection panel, click on Filter.
6. Unselect Floors. Press OK.
7. Press HH to hide temporarily all elements other than floors.
8. → Export → CAD Formats → DWG (Fig. 7.1).

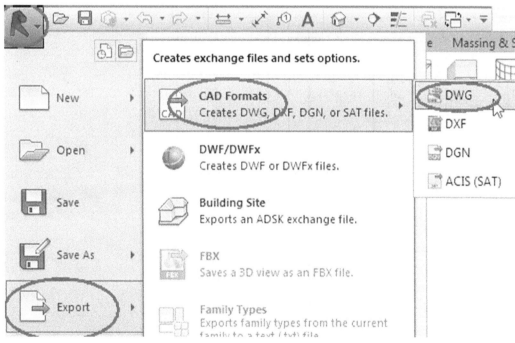

Fig. 7.1 – Export CAD

9. In the "Export with Temporary Hide/Isolate" dialog box, click on "Leave the Temporary Hide/Isolate mode on and export".
10. Save the DWG file. Press HR to unhide the temporarily hidden elements.
11. Open this file and make all elements as **polylines**. Units = **Meters**. Save.

7.2 Import CAD File

The CAD file will be imported as a layout in the BIM Model. Polylines in CAD file be used to make site elements in the Model.

1. Floor Plans → Site.
2. On Insert tab → Link panel → click Link CAD tool.
3. Navigate to SitePlan.dwg in the Download Folder (page v).
4. Select values as shown in Fig. 7.2.

Fig. 7.2 – Import CAD

5. Align north side of pavement floor in CAD file with north side of pavement floor in BIM Model (Modify tab → Modify panel → Align tool → Click on BIM Model → Click on CAD file).
6. Align west side of pavement floor in CAD file with west side of pavement floor in BIM Model.
7. Select the four elevation symbols one by one and move them out of the drawing area.
8. The site plan will look like Fig. 7.3.

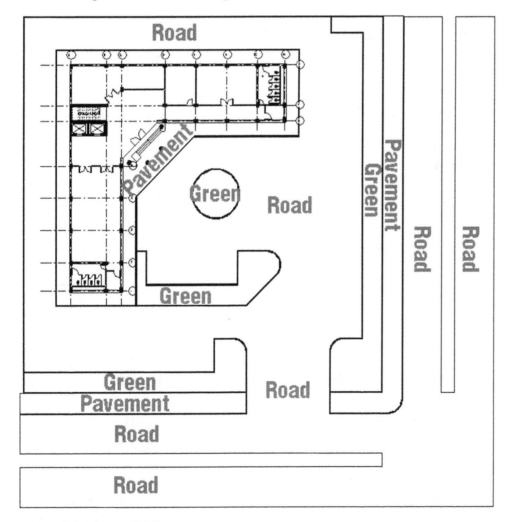

Fig. 7.3 – Align CAD

7.3 Boundary Wall

1. Floor Plans → Site.
2. On Architecture tab → Build panel → click Wall tool.
3. In Properties Palette , click on Element dropdown.
4. Select Basic Wall : Generic - 140mm Masonry.
5. Set properties as shown in Fig. 7.4.

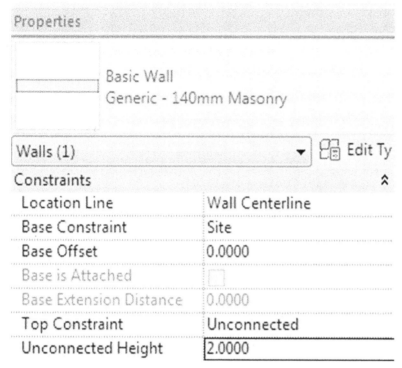

Fig. 7.4 – Boundary Wall properties

6. Draw panel → Pick Lines.
7. Pick lines shown in Fig. 7.5.

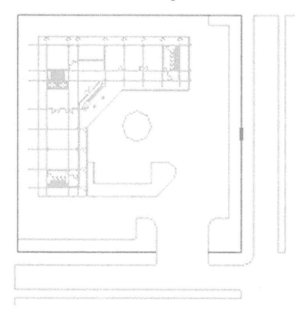

Fig. 7.5 – Draw Boundary Wall

7.4 Pavement Curb

7.4.1 Pavement Curb Structure

Pavement curb is made of concrete. In the BIM model, it will be made as a concrete wall with a wall sweep on top.

1. Floor Plans → Site.
2. On Architecture tab → Build panel → click Wall tool.
3. In Properties Palette , click on Element dropdown.
4. Select Basic Wall : Generic - 200mm.
5. Click on Edit Type.
6. In Type Properties box, click on Duplicate.
7. Change Name = Pavement - Curb → OK
8. In Type Properties box, Construction group, Structure parameter, click on Edit.
9. In the Edit Assembly dialogue box, Make changes as shown in Fig. 7.6.

	Function	Material	Thickness	Wraps	Stru Ma
1	Core Boundary	Layers Above Wrap	0.0000		
2	Structure [1]	Concrete, Precast	0.1500		✓
3	Core Boundary	Layers Below Wrap	0.0000		

Fig. 7.6 – Pavement Curb Structure

10. Click on Preview to see the graphical display of structure. (See § 3.2.2).
11. For View, select Section.
12. Click on Sweeps
13. Click Load Profile. Add M_Pavement Sweep.rfa.
14. Make following settings.

- Profile : M_ Pavement Sweep : 125mm wide
- Material : Concrete, Precast
- From : Top
- Side : Exterior
- Offset : 0.00
- Cuts Walls : ☑

15. OK → OK.

7.4.2 Add Pavement Curb

Pavement curb is placed along the pavement floor.

1. Floor Plans → Site.
2. On Architecture tab → Build panel → click Wall tool.
3. In Properties Palette, click on Element dropdown.
4. Select Basic Wall : Pavement - Curb.
5. Set properties as shown in Fig. 7.7.

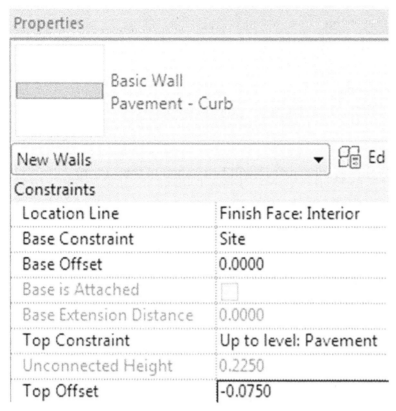

Fig. 7.7 – Pavement Curb properties

6. Draw panel → Pick Lines
7. Click on the line as shown in Fig. 7.8.

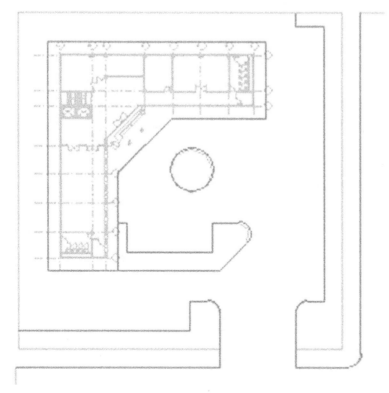

Fig. 7.8 – Draw Pavement Curb

7.5 Site Regions

Site has different parts.

- Outer part is a toposurface covered with sand.
- Road and parking is covered with asphalt.
- Inside the boundary wall of the building, there are some green areas covered with grass.

7.5.1 Add Toposurface

There is a big outer square in the linked CAD file. A toposurface will be created in this square.

1. Floor Plans → Site.
2. Properties palette → Extents group → View Range → Edit → View Depth → Offset = −0.1
3. On Massing & Site tab → Model Site panel → click Toposurface tool.
4. On Options bar, set Elevation = −0.9 (Fig. 7.9.)

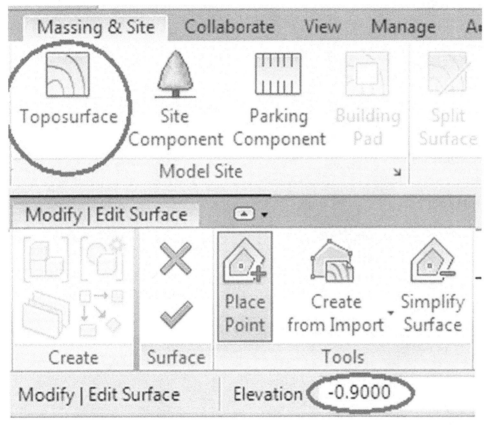

Fig. 7.9 – Toposurface settings

5. Click on four corners of the outer big square in the CAD file.
6. Surface panel → Finish Surface.
7. Select the surface.
8. Properties palette → Material → Sand (Fig. 7.10).

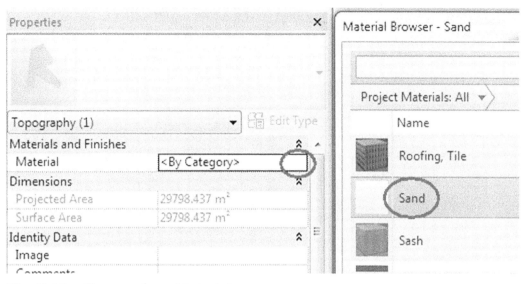

Fig. 7.10 – Toposurface Material

7.5.2 Roads

Roads area is subregion of the toposurface. You will make a closed boundary and then apply asphalt material.

1. On Massing & Site tab → Model Site panel → click Subregion tool.
2. Draw panel → Pick Lines.
3. Pick lines as shown in Fig. 7.11. Trim where needed.

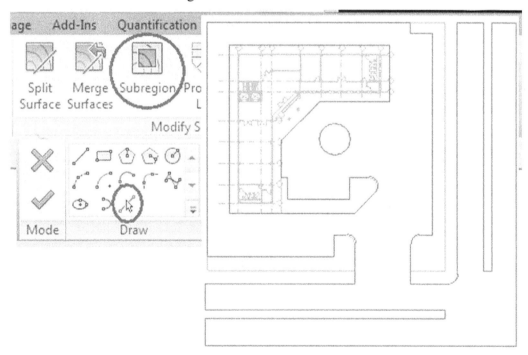

Fig. 7.11 – Pick Lines for Roads

4. Mode panel → Finish.
5. Select the subregion.
6. Properties palette → Material → Asphalt, Road (Material Browser → Site - Hardcore → Right-click → Duplicate → Rename = Asphalt, Road → Appearance tab → Image = C:\Program Files

(x86)\Common Files\Autodesk Shared\Materials\Textures\3\Mats\ Sitework.Paving - Surfacing.Asphalt.bump.jpg) (Fig. 7.12).

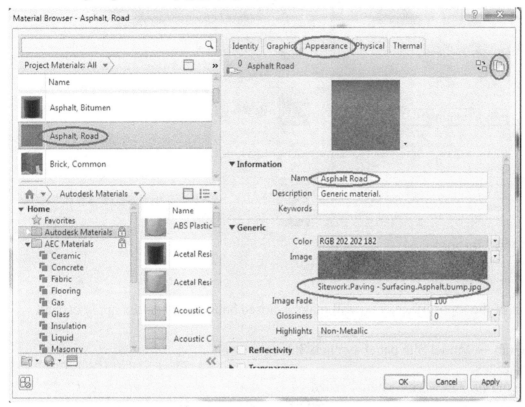

Fig. 7.12 – Road Material

7.5.3 Green Areas

Green area are floors made of material earth with a finishing material grass. You will select pavement floor, duplicate it and change its structure.

7. Floor Plans → Pavement.
8. On Architecture tab → Build panel → click Floor tool.
9. In Properties Palette, click on Element dropdown.
10. Select Floor : Pavement 300mm.
11. Edit Type → Duplicate → Name = Grass Area 300mm.
12. Structure → Edit
13. For Layer 1 (Finish 1 [4]), click 🔲 in Material column.
14. Make a new material Grass (Material Browser → Sand → Right-click → Duplicate → Rename = Grass → Appearance tab → Image = C:\Program Files (x86)\Common Files\Autodesk Shared\Materials\Textures\3\Mats\SiteWork.Planting.Grass.Bermuda2.jpg) (Fig. 7.13).
15. In Properties palette → Constraints group → Level = **Pavement**
16. Draw panel → Pick Lines (Fig. 7.14 left).
17. Pick lines as shown in Fig. Trim where needed.
18. **Note : There are four green areas. Make them one-by-one (not altogether).**
19. Mode panel → Finish.

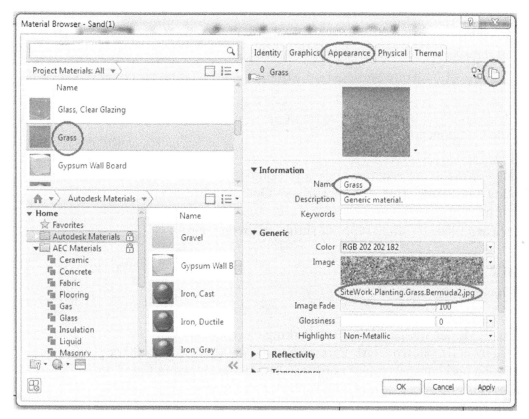

Fig. 7.13 – Grass Material

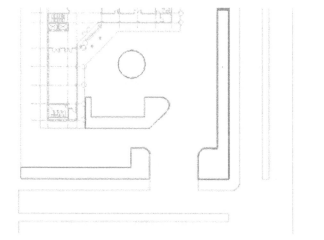

Fig. 7.14 – Draw Green Area

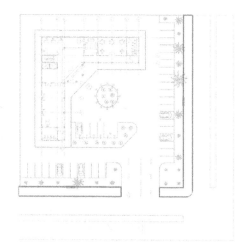

Pavement along Road

7.5.4 Pavement along Road

You will make pavement floor along the roads.

1. Floor Plans → Site.
2. On Architecture tab → Build panel → click Floor tool.
3. In Properties Palette, click on Element dropdown.
4. Select Floor : Pavement 300mm.
5. In Properties palette → Constraints group → Level = Pavement
6. Draw panel → Pick Lines.
7. Pick lines as shown in Fig. 7.14 (right). Trim where needed. Close with line where open.
8. Mode panel → Finish.

7.6 Site Components

You will add planting, parking spaces, vehicles and people on site. (Many other site components are also available in the library).

7.6.1 Planting

Plants, trees, shrubs are Site Components.

1. Floor Plans → Site.
2. On Massing & Site tab → Model Site panel → click Site Component tool.
3. Load Family → Planting → M_RPC Tree - Tropical.rfa → Open.
4. Place different types of trees in green areas.
5. Load M_RPC Shrub.rfa and place different types of shrubs in green areas.

7.6.2 Parking Space

Parking spaces are Site Components.

1. Floor Plans → Site.
2. On Massing & Site tab → Model Site panel → click Parking Component tool.
3. Properties palette → Element dropdown → M_Parking Space : 4800 x 2400mm 90 deg.
4. Press Tab to rotate. Place a parking space (near north-east corner) as shown in Fig. 7.15.
5. Click on parking space. Click on Flip L-R tool.
6. Align the parking space. (click A - A' - B - B')

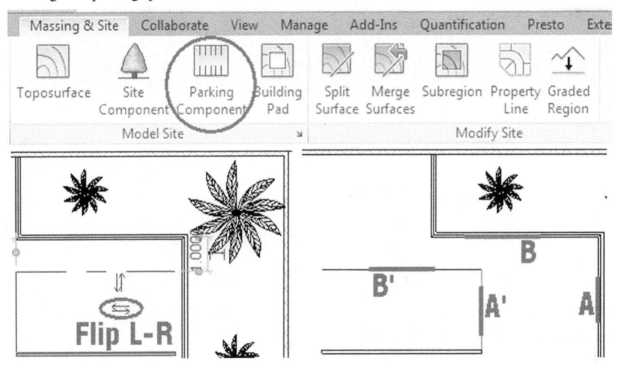

Fig. 7.15 – Parking Space

7. Click on parking space.
8. On Modify tab → Modify panel → click Array tool (Fig. 7.16).
9. Check settings on the Option bar.
10. Select corner of the parking space and drag to south side.
11. Write 2.4 and press Enter.
12. Number 2 appears in the count box. Change it to 18.

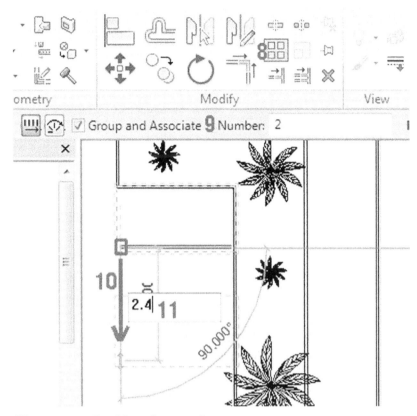

Fig. 7.16 – Parking Space Array

13. Similarly add a parking space near the entrance of the building.
14. Click on the parking space and flip it left-right and up-down.
15. Align as shown in Fig. 7.17.

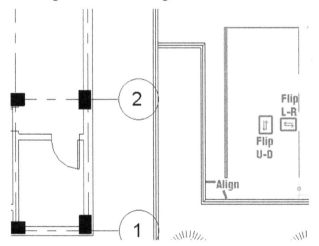

Fig. 7.17 – Parking Space

16. Array 4 times.
17. Similarly add parking spaces near the south boundary wall.

7.6.3 Vehicles

Vehicles are Site Components.

1. Floor Plans → Site.
2. On Massing & Site tab → Model Site panel → click Site Component tool.

3. Load Family → Entourage → M_RPC Beetle.rfa → Open.
4. Place Vehicles in different parking spaces.

7.6.4 People

People are Site Components.

1. Floor Plans → Site.
2. On Massing & Site tab → Model Site panel → click Site Component tool.
3. Load Family → Entourage → M_RPC Male.rfa → Open.
4. Place Alex at some place.
5. Load Family → Entourage → M_RPC Female.rfa → Open.
6. Place Tina at some place.

7.6.5 More Site Components

Parking Symbols are Site Components. Street lights Components.

1. Floor Plans → Site.
2. On Massing & Site tab → Model Site panel → click Site Component tool.
3. Load Family → Site → Parking → M_Parking Symbol - ADA.rfa → Open.
4. Similarly add M_Direction Arrows - Straight.rfa, M_Direction Arrows - Straight & Turn.rfa, M_Pavement Stripe.rfa.
5. On Architecture tab → Build panel → click Component tool.
6. Mode panel → Load Family → Lighting → MEP → External → M_Street Light - Standard.rfa
7. Add street lights on the site (Fig. 7.18).

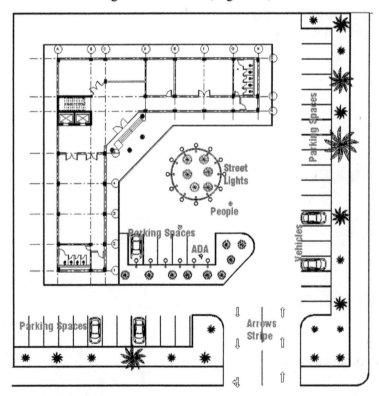

Fig. 7.18 – Street Lights

8. Click ![save] to Save Project As **Arch07.**

8 Architectural Design Documentation

You have finished creating an architectural Building Information Modeling (BIM) model. It is time to extract different kinds of information from this model. In this chapter you will extract information about different building elements in the form of Schedules.

8.1 Door Schedule

You have different kinds of doors on different floor levels. You will add a schedule in your project in which you will add different fields of information about doors.

8.1.1 A simple Door Schedule

1. Open Project Arch07.
2. Save Project As **Arch08.**
3. On View tab → Create panel → Schedules dropdown → click Schedules/Quantities tool.
4. In New Schedule dialog box → Category listbox → click Doors (Fig. 8.1).

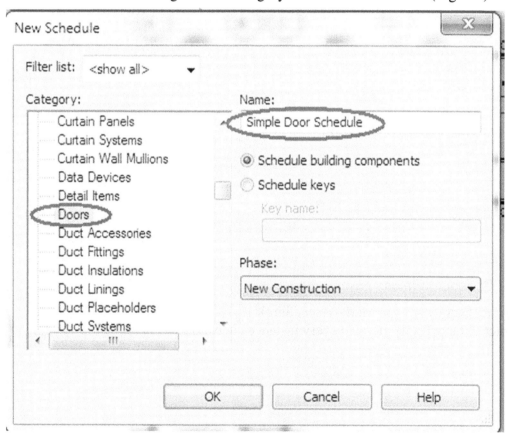

Fig. 8.1 – Create Simple Door Schedule

5. Name = Simple Door Schedule → OK.
6. On Fields tab, from Available Fields listbox, select the following fields and add them (double-click or press Add →) to Schedule Fields listbox.

   - Family and Type.
   - Height
   - Type Mark

- Width

7. Select a field and using Move Up and Move Down buttons, arrange the fields as shown in Fig. 8.2.

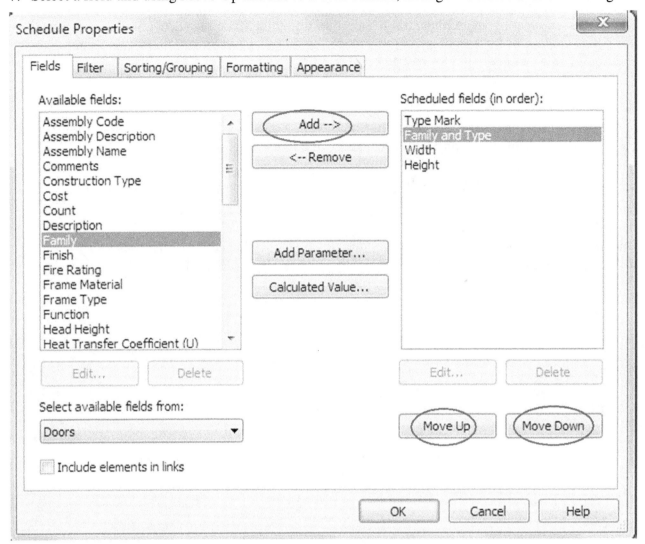

Fig. 8.2 – Simple Door Schedule Fields

8. On Sorting/Grouping tab, Sort by = Type Mark (Ascending).
9. Unselect Header, Footer, Grand Totals, Itemize every instance checkboxes (Fig. 8.3).

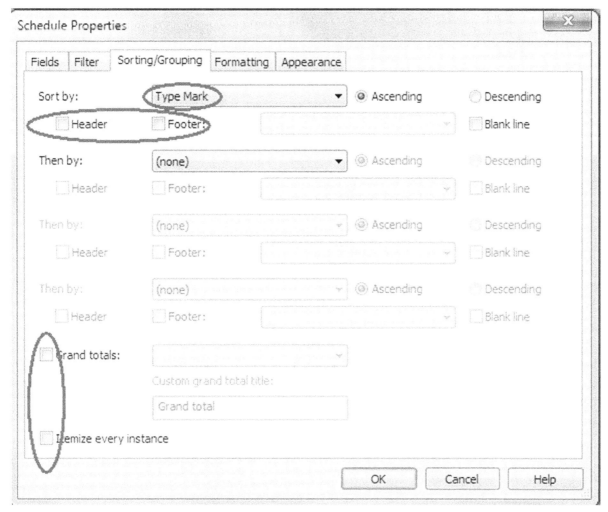

Fig. 8.3 – Simple Door Schedule Sorting

10. You will get a schedule as shown in Fig. 8.4.

<Simple Door Schedule>			
A	B	C	D
Type Mark	Family and Type	Width	Height
D01	M_Double-Glass 1: 1830 x 2134mm	1.83	2.13
D02	M_Single-Flush Vision: 0915 x 2134mm	0.92	2.13
D03	M_Single-Flush Vision: 0762 x 2134mm	0.76	2.13
D04	M_Single-Flush: 0915 x 2134mm	0.92	2.13
D05	M_Curtain Wall-Store Front-Dbl: Store Front Double Door	2.37	2.36

Fig. 8.4 – Simple Door Schedule

8.1.2 A More Detailed Door Schedule

You have created your first schedule showing information extracted from your BIM model. Now you can add more details to it.

1. In Project Browser, expand Schedules/Quantities node. You will find Simple Door Schedule you just created.
2. Simple Door Schedule → Right-click → Duplicate View → Duplicate → click (Fig. 8.5).

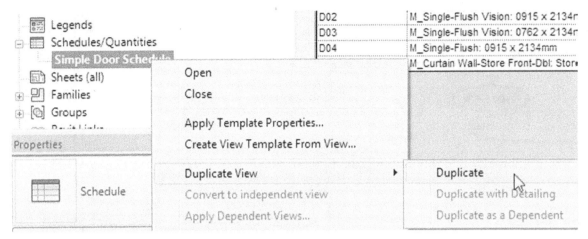

Fig. 8.5 – Duplicate Door Schedule

3. In Project Browser → Schedules/Quantities node, you will see Simple Door Schedule Copy 1.
4. Right-click on it and click on Rename.
5. Enter Name = Detailed Door Schedule.
6. In Properties palette → Other group → Fields parameter → press Edit.
7. You will see the Schedule Properties dialog box, **Fields** tab.
8. Add Cost and Level to Scheduled Fields (double-click at Cost and Level in Available Fields).
9. Press Add Parameter (Fig. 8.6).
10. On Parameter Properties dialog box, set

- Parameter Type = Project Parameter
- Name = Hardware
- Discipline = Common
- Type = Text
- Group parameter under = Other
- Select Type

11. Arrange fields as shown in Fig. 8.6.

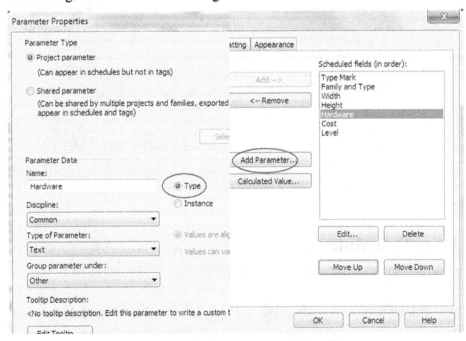

Fig. 8.6 – Add Parameter in Door Schedule

12. Click **Sorting/Grouping** tab (Fig. 8.7).

- Sort by = Level. Select Header and select Footer.
- Then by = Type Mark. Unselect Header and unselect Footer.
- Select Grand totals
- Select Itemize every instance.

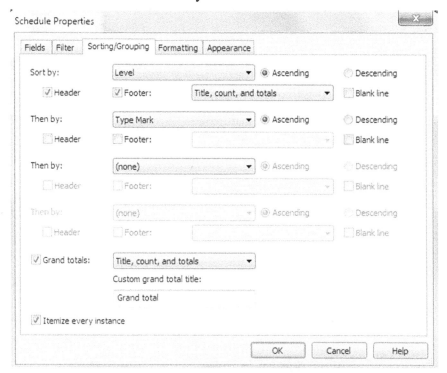

Fig. 8.7 – Sorting and Grouping Door Schedule

13. Click **Formatting** (Fig. 8.8).

- Type Mark → Heading = Door Number
- Family and Type → Heading = Door Type
- Cost → Alignment = Right, Select Calculate totals
- Level → Select Hidden field

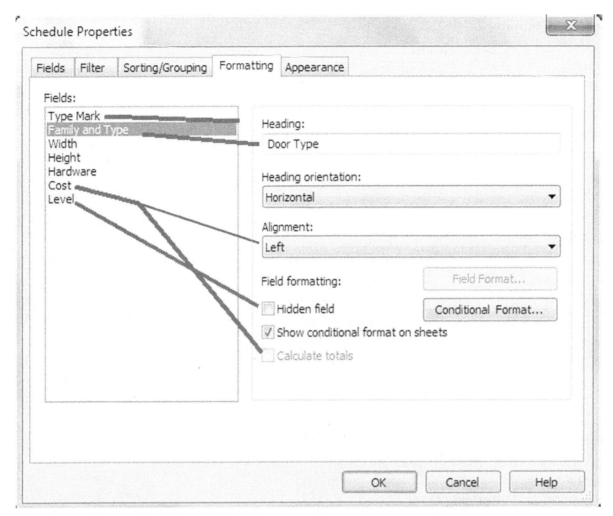

Fig. 8.8 – Formatting Door Schedule

14. OK

15. In the schedule, write Hardware and Cost for only one door of its type and press Enter. A dialog box will appear asking "This change will be applied to all Elements of type .....". Press OK.

- D01 → Hardware = Aluminum and Glass, Cost = 1200.
- D02 → Hardware = Wood and Glass, Cost = 700.
- D03 → Hardware = Wood and Glass, Cost = 600.
- D04 → Hardware = Wood, Cost = 650.
- D05 → Hardware = Glass, Cost = 800.

16. The final form of the schedule will be as shown in Fig. 8.9.

<Detailed Door Schedule>

A	B	C	D	E	F
Door Number	Door Type	Width	Height	Hardware	Cost
01 GF					
D01	M_Double-Glass 1: 1830 x 2134mm	1.83	2.13	Aluminum and Glass	1200.00
D01	M_Double-Glass 1: 1830 x 2134mm	1.83	2.13	Aluminum and Glass	1200.00
D01	M_Double-Glass 1: 1830 x 2134mm	1.83	2.13	Aluminum and Glass	1200.00
D01	M_Double-Glass 1: 1830 x 2134mm	1.83	2.13	Aluminum and Glass	1200.00
D02	M_Single-Flush Vision: 0915 x 2134mm	0.92	2.13	Wood and Glass	700.00
D03	M_Single-Flush Vision: 0762 x 2134mm	0.76	2.13	Wood and Glass	600.00
D03	M_Single-Flush Vision: 0762 x 2134mm	0.76	2.13	Wood and Glass	600.00
D04	M_Single-Flush: 0915 x 2134mm	0.92	2.13	Wood	650.00
D04	M_Single-Flush: 0915 x 2134mm	0.92	2.13	Wood	650.00
D05	M_Curtain Wall-Store Front-Dbl: Store Front Double Door	2.37	2.36	Glass	800.00
01 GF: 10					8800.00
02 FF					
D01	M_Double-Glass 1: 1830 x 2134mm	1.83	2.13	Aluminum and Glass	1200.00
D02	M_Single-Flush Vision: 0915 x 2134mm	0.92	2.13	Wood and Glass	700.00
D02	M_Single-Flush Vision: 0915 x 2134mm	0.92	2.13	Wood and Glass	700.00
D02	M_Single-Flush Vision: 0915 x 2134mm	0.92	2.13	Wood and Glass	700.00
D02	M_Single-Flush Vision: 0915 x 2134mm	0.92	2.13	Wood and Glass	700.00
D02	M_Single-Flush Vision: 0915 x 2134mm	0.92	2.13	Wood and Glass	700.00
D02	M_Single-Flush Vision: 0915 x 2134mm	0.92	2.13	Wood and Glass	700.00
D03	M_Single-Flush Vision: 0762 x 2134mm	0.76	2.13	Wood and Glass	600.00
D03	M_Single-Flush Vision: 0762 x 2134mm	0.76	2.13	Wood and Glass	600.00
D04	M_Single-Flush: 0915 x 2134mm	0.92	2.13	Wood	650.00
D04	M_Single-Flush: 0915 x 2134mm	0.92	2.13	Wood	650.00
02 FF: 11					7900.00
Roof					
D02	M_Single-Flush Vision: 0915 x 2134mm	0.92	2.13	Wood and Glass	700.00
Roof: 1					700.00
Grand total: 22					17400.00

Fig. 8.9 – Detailed Door Schedule

17. You can export this schedule as a Tab delimited text file. You can open this file in Microsoft Excel®.
18. Similarly you can make a Windows Schedule.

8.1.3 Add Room Information in Door Schedule

You can add room information in a door schedule. There are two types pf room information:-

- **To Room**: Room into which the door opens.
- **From Room**: Room from which you open the door.

You can add information about To and From room. You can use this information to tag a door.

1. In the Project Browser, select Detailed Door Schedule.
2. On the Properties palette → Fields parameter → Edit.
3. Fields tab → Select available fields drop-down → select To Room (Fig. 8.10).

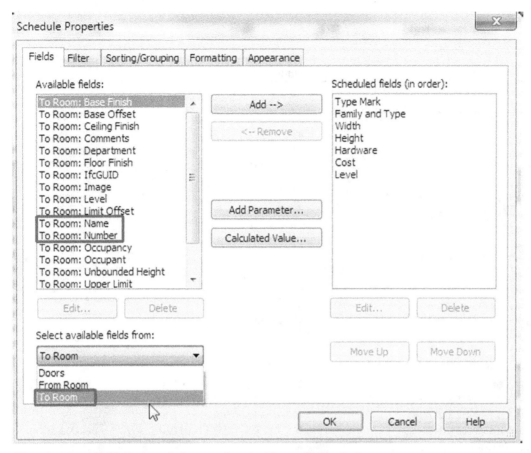

Fig. 8.10 – Add Room Information in Door Schedule

4. From Available fields, add To Room: Number and To Room: Name into Scheduled fields.
5. Fields tab → Select available fields drop-down → select From Room.
6. From Available fields, add From Room: Number and From Room: Name into Scheduled fields.
7. OK.

8.2 Room Schedule

You will make a Room Schedule.

1. On View tab → Create panel → Schedules dropdown → click Schedules/Quantities tool.
2. In New Schedule dialog box → Category listbox → click Rooms.
3. Name = Room Schedule → OK.
4. On Fields tab, from Available Fields listbox, select the following fields and add them (double-click or press Add --->) to Schedule Fields listbox.

- Number
- Name
- Perimeter
- Area
- Volume

5. Select a field and using Move Up and Move Down buttons, arrange the fields as shown above.
6. Click **Sorting/Grouping** tab.

- Sort by = Level. Select Header and select Footer.
- Then by = Number. Unselect Header and unselect Footer.

7. OK. Room Schedule looks as shown in Fig. 8.11.

\<Room Schedule\>

A	B	C	D	E
Number	Name	Perimeter	Area	Volume
01 GF				
101	Accounting	39.41	62 m²	167.75 m³
102	Lounge	20.70	26 m²	71.14 m³
103	Cafeteria	30.60	54 m²	145.42 m³
104	Restroom	18.00	19 m²	50.32 m³
105	Shaft	12.50	3 m²	11.16 m³
106	Elect/Mech	9.80	6 m²	22.15 m³
107	Corridor	36.81	33 m²	88.66 m³
108	Entrance	46.72	92 m²	249.34 m³
109	Stairs	14.69	11 m²	43.63 m³
110	Elevator	13.59	9 m²	34.63 m³
111	Showroom	47.81	108 m²	292.55 m³
112	Restroom	16.79	17 m²	45.01 m³
113	Elect/Mech	9.80	6 m²	22.15 m³
114	Shaft	11.29	2 m²	9.99 m³
01 GF: 14				
02 FF				
201	Manager	25.71	40 m²	109.28 m³
202	Meeting Room	19.70	22 m²	58.48 m³
203	Office	20.70	26 m²	71.14 m³
204	Office	20.70	26 m²	71.20 m³
205	Office	20.70	26 m²	71.20 m³
206	Restroom	18.00	19 m²	50.32 m³
207	Shaft	12.50	3 m²	11.17 m³
208	Elect/Mech	9.80	6 m²	22.45 m³
209	Corridor	36.80	33 m²	88.67 m³
210	Lobby	49.72	115 m²	311.44 m³
211	Stairs	14.69	11 m²	43.75 m³
212	Elevator	13.59	9 m²	34.63 m³
213	Office	19.49	24 m²	63.74 m³
214	Office	19.49	24 m²	63.74 m³
215	Office	19.49	24 m²	63.68 m³
216	Corridor	36.61	33 m²	88.90 m³
217	Elect/Mech	9.80	6 m²	22.44 m³
218	Restroom	16.79	17 m²	45.01 m³
219	Shaft	11.29	2 m²	9.99 m³
02 FF: 19				

Fig. 8.11 – Room Schedule

8.3 Add Calculated Field

You can add a new field in the schedule based on a formula involving existing fields. For example you know that the floor cost rate is 275 per square meter. You can add a Floor Cost field with formula:-

Floor Cost = 275 x Area

1. In the Project Browser, select Room Schedule.
2. On the Properties palette → Fields parameter → Edit.
3. Fields tab → Click on Calculated Value. Set (Fig. 8.12):
    - Name = Floor Cost.
    - Type = Currency.
4. In Formula field, write 275*
5. Click on ...

6. From Fields, select Area.

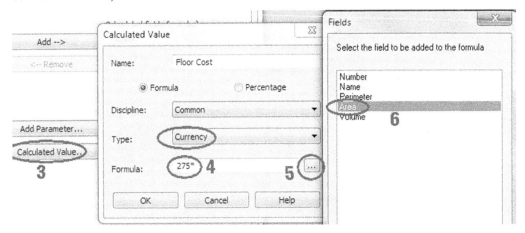

Fig. 8.12 – Add Calculated Field in Room Schedule

7. Change Formula = 275*(Area/1m/1m).
8. OK
9. On Formatting tab, select currency unit symbol as shown in Fig. 8.13.

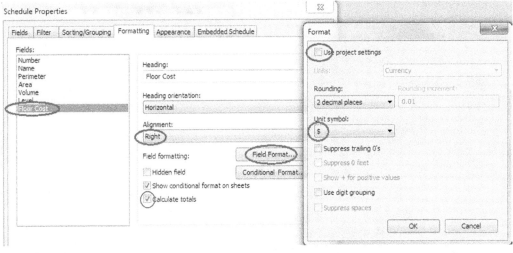

Fig. 8.13 – Formatting Calculated Field in Room Schedule

10. OK → OK.
11. You will see Floor Cost for each room.

12. Click  to Save Project As **Arch08.**

9 Presentation of Architectural Design

Your architectural Building Information Modeling (BIM) model is complete. You will print different views and schedules for presentation. Most of the views (floor plans, elevations etc.) are already present in the model. But you may need to make some more views.

9.1 The Title Block

There are many ways to make a title block. You may have done some work in AutoCad® and a title block may be ready as DWG file. You can import the same file in Revit® and modify it.

Now you will make A1 title block.

1. Open the file "title_block_a1.dwg" in the Download Folder (page v). Change Name, ID# etc. → Rotate the North by 120 degrees → Save As "Title Block A1 B.dwg".
2. Start Revit → Families → New.
3. Family templates folder → Titleblocks → A1 metric.rft (You will see a rectangle of A1 size).
4. On Insert tab → Import panel → click Import CAD tool.
5. Navigate to the file you saved in step 1.
6. Make adjustments as shown in Fig. 9.1.

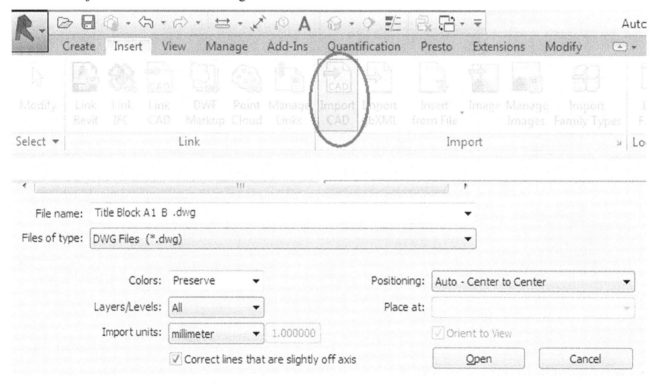

Fig. 9.1 – Import CAD Title block

7. Press Open.
8. You will see the imported cad title block.
9. Zoom to the lower right part of the title block.
10. On Create tab → Text panel → click Label tool (Fig. 9.2).
11. Click in the empty box under SCALE.

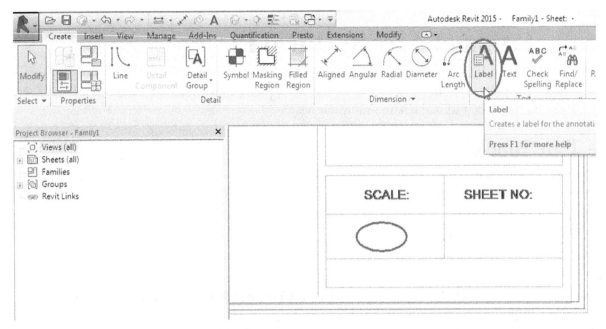

Fig. 9.2 – Add Label on Title block

12. In the Edit Label dialog box, add Scale to Label Parameters and change its Sample Value to 1:100 as shown in Fig. 9.3.

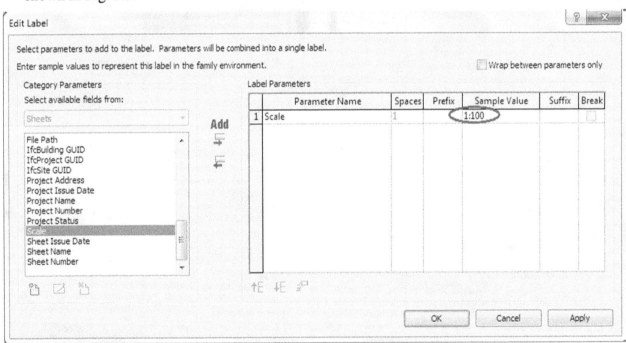

Fig. 9.3 – Edit Label

13. Press OK then Esc.
14. Select the Scale label.
15. In Properties palette, change Vertical Align = Middle, Horizontal Align = Center.
16. Click Edit Type → Duplicate → Name = 5mm → Text Size = 5mm.
17. Under the box SHEET NO., add a label with parameter Sheet Number and Sample Value = Arch 101. Adjust its properties as in step 15-16.
18. In the box DRAWING NAME, add a label with parameter Sheet Name and Sample Value = PLAN. Adjust its properties as in step 15-16 (Fig. 9.4).

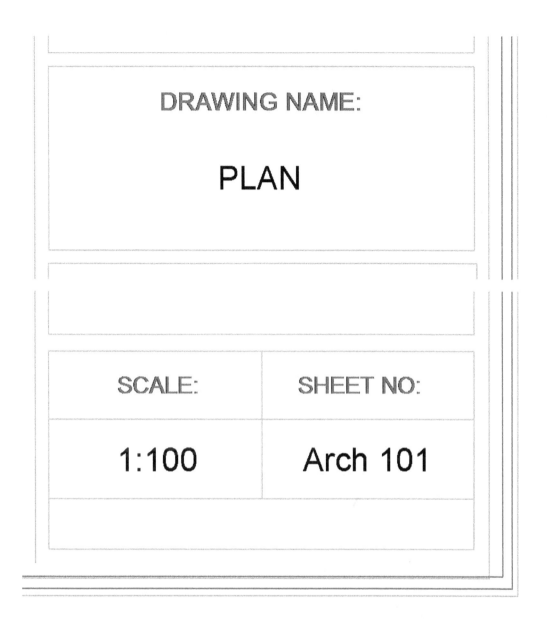

Fig. 9.4 – Edited Labels

19. Save As → Family → Arch A1.rfa
20. Similarly you can make A0 title block.

9.2 Sheets for the Ground Floor

Now the title block is ready. You can open a new sheet, add title block and add ground floor view to it.

9.2.1 A Simple Sheet for the Ground Floor

You will make a simple sheet from the ground floor view.

1. Open Project **Arch08.**
2. Save Project As **Arch9.**
3. Floor Plans → 01 GF
4. You see that many unwanted elements are visible in the view. You will hide them.
5. On View tab → Graphics panel → click Filters tool (Fig. 9.5).

6. Click on New
7. Name = Pavement → OK.
8. In Categories list, select Floors
9. Filter Rules → Filter by → Type Name → equals → Pavement 300mm

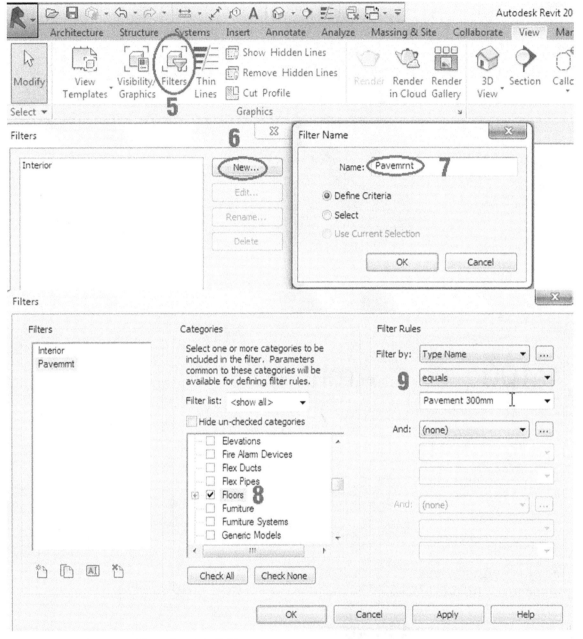

Fig. 9.5 – Create Filter for Visibility

10. Similarly make anew filter → Name = Grass Area → Category = Floors → Filter Rules → Filter by → Type Name → equals → Grass Area 300mm
11. Similarly make anew filter → Name = Outer → Category = Walls → Filter Rules → Filter by → Type Name → equals → Generic - 140mm Masonry
12. Floor Plans → 01 GF → Right-click → Duplicate View → Duplicate (Fig. 9.6).

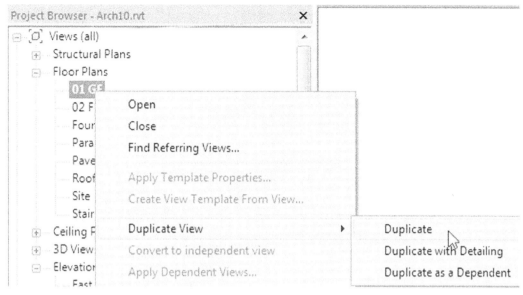

Fig. 9.6 – Duplicate a view

13. You will get another view 01 GF Copy 1.
14. Floor Plans → 01 GF Copy 1→ Right-click → Rename = 01 GF Simple
15. VG

- On Model Categories tab, unselect Entourage, Parking, Planting, Roads, Site, Topography
- On Annotation Categories tab, unselect Elevations
- On Filters tab, add Grass Area, Pavement, Outer and unselect their visibility (Fig. 9.7) → OK.

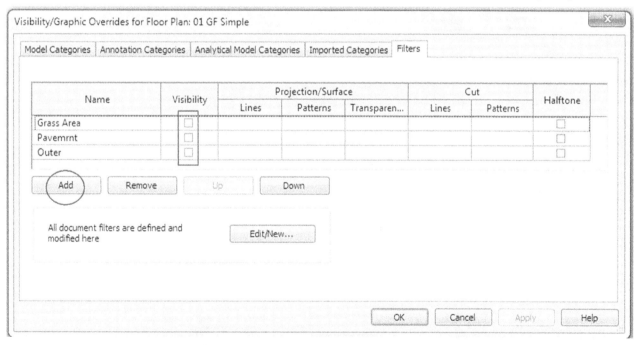

Fig. 9.7 – Using Filters for Visibility

16. Project Browser → Sheets → Right-click → New Sheet (Fig. 9.8).
17. Click on Load.
18. Navigate to Arch A1.rfa (You saved in § 9.1 step 19).

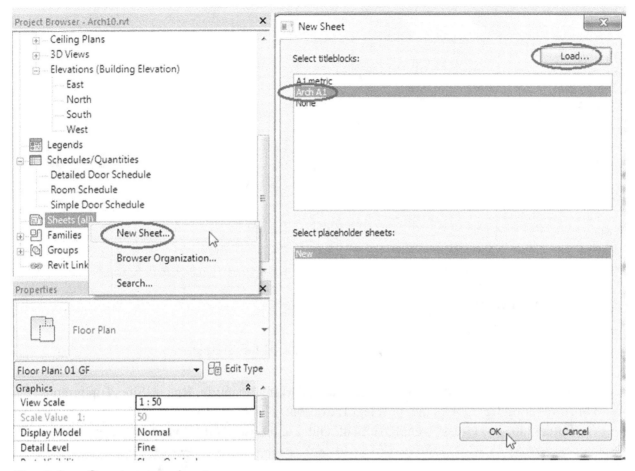

Fig. 9.8 – Create new sheet

19. OK.
20. Titleblock is added.
21. From Floor Plans, drag 01 GF Simple to the middle of the sheet area (Fig. 9.9).
22. In the Viewport Properties palette, change View Scale = 1:100.
23. Select the Titleblock. In the Properties palette, change Sheet Name = Ground Floor Plan, Sheet Number = Arch 101.
24. You can see the changes on the sheet.
25. You don't see the Room tags ! No problem.
26. Double-click 01 GF Simple.
27. On Annotate tab → Tag panel → click Tag All tool.
28. Click Room Tags → OK.
29. In Project Browser, expand Sheets (all) → Double-click Arch 101 Ground Floor Plan → Room Tags are shown.

9.2.2 Scale Symbol on Sheet

1. On View tab → Symbol panel → click Symbol tool.
2. From Type selector, select M_Sheet Scale : 1:100.
3. Click on the sheet.
4. The scale symbol is added as shown in Fig. 9.9.

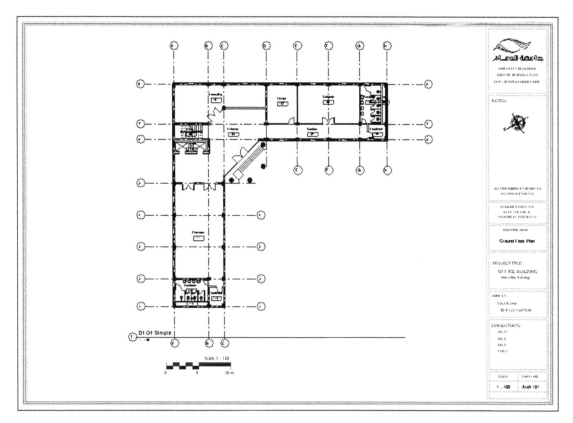

Fig. 9.9 – Simple Sheet for the Ground Floor

9.2.3 Working Drawing Sheet for the Ground Floor

Working drawing displays all the required dimensions. You will duplicate 01 GF Simple and add dimensions to it. Units of dimensions will be millimeters.

For a wall, you will make 3 dimension lines:

- a dimension line showing overall length (using Individual References).
- a dimension line showing dimensions between grids (Entire Wall).
- a dimension line close to the wall showing dimensions of openings (Entire Wall).

1. Floor Plans → 01 GF Simple → Right-click → Duplicate View → Duplicate → Rename = 01 GF Working.
2. Select a grid → Drag the small circle at the end of the grid (where it meets the bubble) little away from the building to make some space for the dimensions.
3. On Annotate tab → Dimension panel → click Aligned tool.
4. Select Type = Diagonal - 2.5mm Arial.
5. Edit Type → Duplicate → Rename = Diagonal Dim 1.
6. Change Units Format as shown in Fig. 9.10.

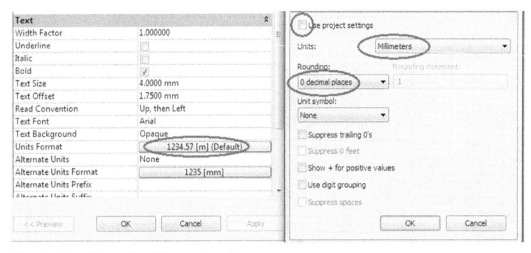

Fig. 9.10 – Units for Dimension Lines

7. OK → OK.
8. Make a dimension showing overall length.
9. On Annotate tab → Dimension panel → click Aligned tool (Fig. 9.11).
10. On the Option bar, Pick: Individual References

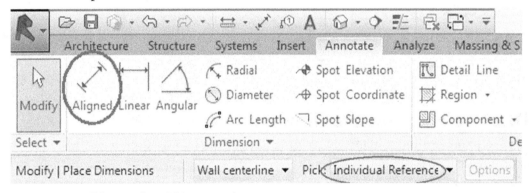

Fig. 9.11 – Dimension Lines setting

11. On the north side, click on grid A then H → Move the cursor little away from the wall and click to place the dimension line.
12. Make a dimension showing dimensions of openings.
13. On Annotate tab → Dimension panel → click Aligned tool.
14. On the Option bar, Pick: Entire Wall. Click on Options (Fig. 9.12).

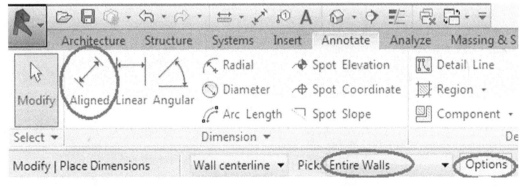

Fig. 9.12 – Entire Wall Dimension

15. In Auto Dimensions Options dialog box, select Openings - Widths as shown in left side of Fig. 9.13.

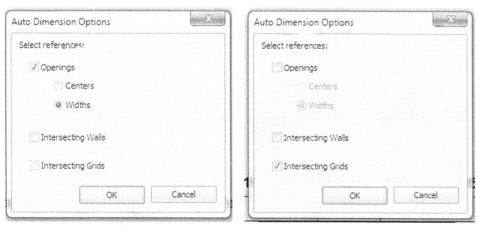

Fig. 9.13 – Auto Dimension options

16. Select the north side wall→ Move the cursor little away from the wall and click to place the dimension line.
17. If you feel that a witness line is on a wrong point, then:
    - click on the dimension line to select it.
    - drag the middle blue circle on the wrong witness line to correct position.
18. Make a dimension showing dimensions between the grids.
19. On Annotate tab → Dimension panel → click Aligned tool.
20. On the Option bar, Pick: Entire Wall. Click on Options.
21. In Auto Dimensions Options dialog box, select Intersecting Grids as shown in right side of Fig. 9.13.
22. Select the north side wall→ Move the cursor little away from the wall and click to place the dimension line.
23. The north side wall will look as shown in Fig. 9.14.

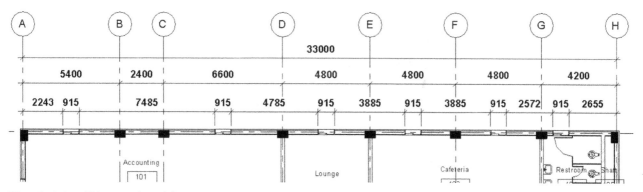

Fig. 9.14 – Dimension Lines

24. In the same way add dimensions in the entire view.
25. Project Browser → Sheets → Right-click → New Sheet.
26. From titleblocks, select Arch A1.rfa → OK → Titleblock is added.
27. From Floor Plans, drag 01 GF Working to the middle of the sheet area.
28. In the Viewport Properties palette, change View Scale = 1:100.
29. Select the Titleblock. In the Properties palette, change Sheet Name = Ground Floor Plan - Working Drawing, Sheet Number = Arch 102 (Fig. 9.15).

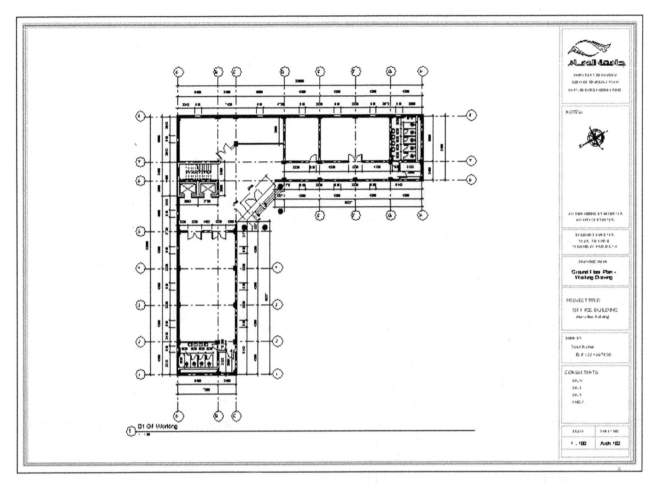

Fig. 9.15 – Working Drawing Sheet for the Ground Floor

9.2.4 Furniture Layout for the Ground Floor

You will add furniture e.g. tables, chairs etc. on the ground floor plan. You will duplicate 01 GF Simple and add furniture on it.

1. Floor Plans → 01 GF Simple → Right-click → Duplicate View → Duplicate → Rename = 01 GF Furniture.
2. Zoom to Accounting 101.
3. On Architecture tab → Build panel → click Component tool.
4. Load Family → Furniture → Tables → M_Desk.rfa
5. Place some desks in the room
6. Component → Load Family → Furniture → Seating → M_Chair-Executive.rfa
7. Place some chairs with the desks.
8. In the same way, load furniture from the library and place in different rooms.
9. Project Browser → Sheets → Right-click → New Sheet.
10. From titleblocks, select Arch A1.rfa → OK → Titleblock is added.
11. From Floor Plans, drag 01 GF Furniture to the middle of the sheet area.
12. In the Viewport Properties palette, change View Scale = 1:100.
13. Select the Titleblock. In the Properties palette, change Sheet Name = Ground Floor Plan - Furniture Layout, Sheet Number = Arch 103 (Fig. 9.16).

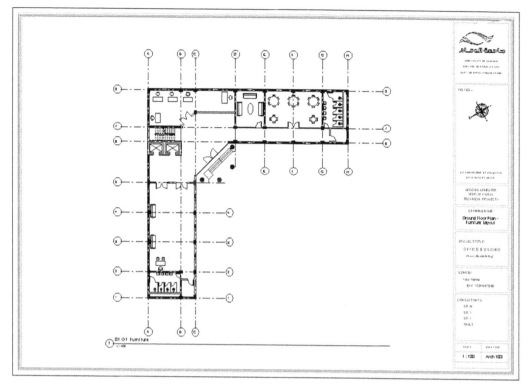

Fig. 9.16 – Furniture Layout for the Ground Floor

14. If you open sheets Arch 101 or Arch 102, you see that furniture is also visible. To hide the furniture from Arch 101, Floor Plans → 01 GF Simple → VG → unselect Furniture. Same for Arch 102.
15. Similarly you can make sheets for other floors.

9.3 Placing Multiple Views on a Sheet

In § 10.3 you placed one view on a sheet. You can place more than one view on a sheet. Each view can have its own scale.

9.3.1 Placing North and West Elevations

You will place North and West elevations on a sheet.

1. Project Browser → Elevations (Building Elevation) → North.
2. You see that toposurfaces and many other elements are visible in the view. You need to hide them.
3. VG
   - On Model Categories tab, unselect Entourage, Parking, Planting, Roads, Site.
   - On Filters tab, add Outer and unselect its visibility → OK.
4. Large toposurface is still visible. You want to keep it visible near the building but not far away. So you will crop the view.
5. On the View Control bar (Fig. 1.5), press Show Crop Region and Crop View.
6. A rectangle appears around the view. Click on this rectangle. Move the blue handles on left and right side to crop.
7. When crop handles are adjusted, then press Hide Crop Region.
8. You may also change the Visual Style to Realistic.
9. Do the same for West elevation.
10. Project Browser → Sheets → Right-click → New Sheet.
11. From titleblocks, select Arch A1.rfa → OK → Titleblock is added.

12. From Elevations, drag North to the upper part of the sheet area.
13. From Elevations, drag West to the lower part of the sheet area.
14. In the Viewport Properties palette, change View Scale = 1:100.
15. Select the Titleblock. In the Properties palette, change Sheet Name = Elevations - North & West, Sheet Number = Arch 104.

9.3.2 Placing Sections

You will place 2 sections on a sheet.

1. Project Browser → Floor Plans → 01 GF Simple.
2. On View tab → Create panel → click Section tool (or click on Section tool on the Quick Access Toolbar).
3. Click on left of grid A between grids 6 and 7.
4. Click on right of grid H between grids 6 and 7.
5. A section line is drawn.
6. Select the section line → Section panel → click Split Segment.
7. Cursor becomes a knife. Split the section line between grids C and D.
8. Select the section line → Properties palette → Change View Name = A-A' (Fig. 9.17).

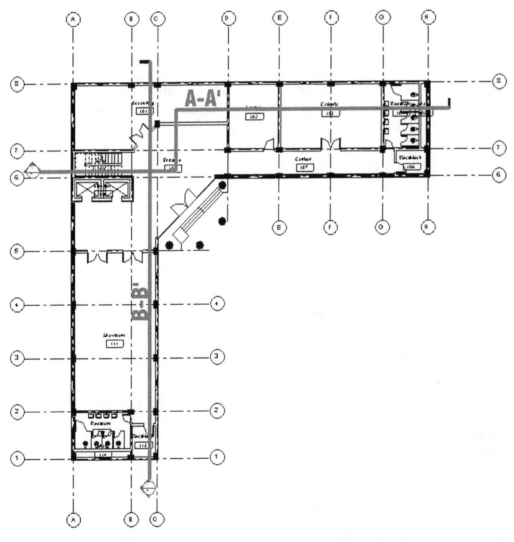

Fig. 9.17 – Draw Sections

9. Double-click on the section head. You will see the section A-A' view.
10. On Annotate tab → Tag panel → click Tag All tool.
11. Select Door Tags → OK → Door tags are added to the view.
12. Similarly add window tags.
13. Add different vertical dimensions e.g. floor to ceiling, ceiling to upper slab, height of interior walls.
14. Similarly make a section B-B' starting from below grid 1 to above grid 8 between grids B and C. Double-click on the section head. You will see the section B-B' view.
15. Project Browser → Sheets → Right-click → New Sheet.
16. From titleblocks, select Arch A1.rfa → OK → Titleblock is added.
17. From Sections, drag A-A' to the upper part of the sheet area.
18. From Sections, drag B-B' to the lower part of the sheet area.
19. In the Viewport Properties palette, change View Scale = 1:100.
20. Select the Titleblock. In the Properties palette, change Sheet Name = Sections, Sheet Number = Arch 105.
21. If you want to hide a section line visible in that view, then VG → Annotation Categories tab → unselect Sections.

9.4 Placing Schedules on Sheets

Similar to the views, you can place schedules on the sheets also.

9.4.1 Room Schedule for Ground Floor

You made a Room Schedule in § 8.2. This schedule is for the whole building. You want to place the ground floor part of this schedule in the sheet Arch 101.

1. Project Browser → Schedules/Quantities → Room Schedule → Right-click → Duplicate View → Duplicate.
2. You will see Room Schedule Copy 1 → Right-click → Rename = Room Schedule 01 GF.
3. Double-click Room Schedule 01 GF to see the schedule → In Properties palette → Filter → Edit → Filter by : Level : equals : 01 GF (Fig. 9.18).

Fig. 9.18 – Filter Room Schedule

4. Double-click sheet Arch 101
5. Drag Room Schedule 01 GF on the sheet (Fig. 9.19).

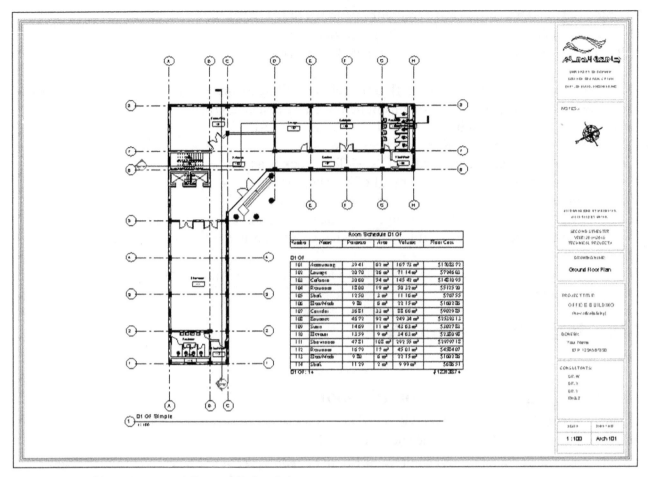

Fig. 9.19 – Plan view and Room Schedule

9.4.2 Multiple Schedules on a Sheet

You can place more than one schedules on one sheet.

1. Project Browser → Sheets → Right-click → New Sheet.
2. From titleblocks, select Arch A1.rfa → OK → Titleblock is added.
3. From Schedules/Quantities, drag Room Schedule to the upper part of the sheet area.
4. From Schedules/Quantities, drag Detailed Door Schedule to the lower part of the sheet area.
5. Select the Titleblock. In the Properties palette, change Sheet Name = Room and Door Schedule, Sheet Number = Arch 107.

9.5 Placing 3D Perspective Views on Sheets

You will use the Camera tool to make exterior or interior 3D perspective views. These views can be placed on the sheets as wireframe, hidden line or rendered image.

9.5.1 Exterior Perspective View

You will place a camera outside the building on the road.

1. Floor Plans → 01 GF.
2. On View tab → Create panel → 3D View dropdown → click Camera tool.
3. Click on a south-east point to specify the camera position.
4. Click on a north-west point to specify the target point (Fig. 9.20).

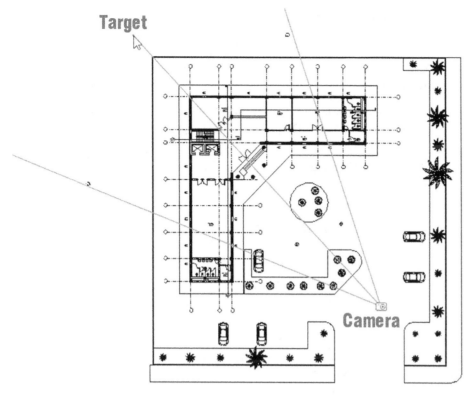

Fig. 9.20 – Place Camera

5. A view named 3D View 1 appears on the screen (Fig. 9.21).
6. You can also see blue control grips on the crop region. Drag the control grips to resize the view.

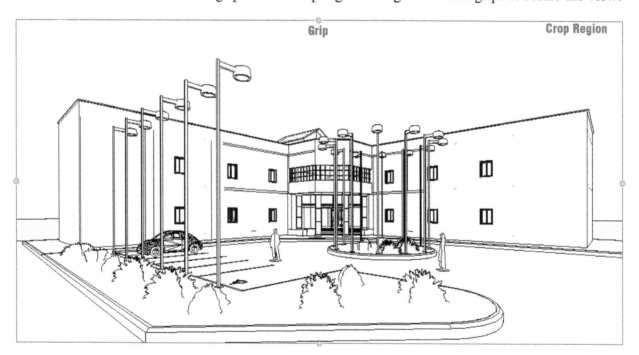

Fig. 9.21 – Camera view

7. You can change the visual style (View Control bar → Visual Styles)
8. You can change the view properties in Properties palette.

9.5.2 Rendering Exterior Perspective View

To render the view, you need to make some adjustments in the Rendering dialog box.

1. On View tab → Graphics panel → click Render tool. Rendering dialog box appears.
2. Make the settings of different parameters (Fig. 9.22):
   - Select **Quality** from Settings dropdown. Draft is poor quality but fast. Best is slow.
   - Select **Resolution** as Screen or Printer. More DPI means better picture but bigger file.
   - Select **Lighting** from Scheme dropdown. Select Sun for day-time rendering and Artificial for night-time rendering. You can also select Sun Setting (position of sun, day of year, time of day etc.)
   - Select **Background** from Style dropdown. You can also select and image as background.
3. For **day-time** rendering, select Quality = Medium, Resolution = Screen, Lighting Scheme = Exterior: Sun only, Background Style = Few Clouds
4. Click on Render on top of the dialog box. You will see a rendered image.
5. Click on Adjust Exposure... and make the image Brighter.
6. Click on Export... to save the picture as .jpg or .png image.
7. Click on Save to Project... , Name = Exterior Day → OK.
8. For **night-time** rendering set Lighting Scheme = Exterior: Artificial only.
9. Adjust Exposure and Save to Project... , Name = Exterior Night → OK
10. Project Browser → Sheets → Right-click → New Sheet.
11. From titleblocks, select Arch A1.rfa → OK → Titleblock is added.
12. From Renderings, drag Exterior Day to the upper part of the sheet area.
13. From Renderings, drag Exterior Night to the lower part of the sheet area.
14. Select the Titleblock. In the Properties palette, change Sheet Name = Exterior Rendering.
15. Double-click an image and adjust its width or height (Fig. 9.23).

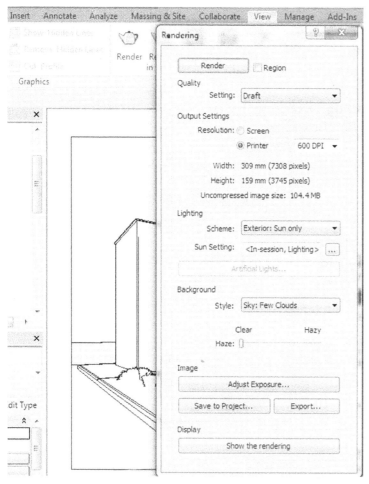

Fig. 9.22 – Rendering settings

Fig. 9.23 – Rendered views

9.6 3D Section View

You can see 3D section of the model.

1. 3D Views → {3D} → right-click → Duplicate View → Duplicate → {3D} Copy 1 → right-click → Rename → 3D Section.
2. Press VG → Annotation Categories → ☑ Section Boxes (Fig. 9.24).
3. In Properties palette → Extents group → Section Box ☑

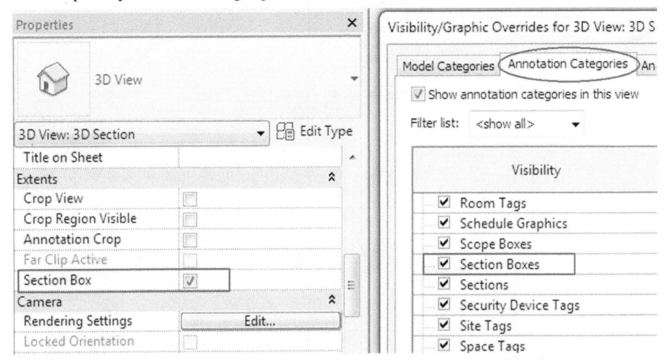

Fig. 9.24 – Section Box settings

4. A section box is visible with 6 control points on left, right, up, down, front, back (Fig. 9.25).

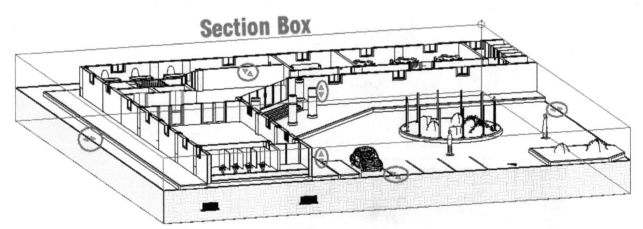

Fig. 9.25 – 3D Section view

5. Move these control points to see a 3D section.
6. After adjusting the controls, press VG→ Annotation Categories → unselect Section Boxes

9.7 Multiple Views with Different Scales

You can add multiple views on the same sheet with different scales.

1. Floor Plans → 01 GF Furniture
2. On View tab → Create panel → click Callout tool.
3. Make a rectangle around Cafeteria 103.
4. A new view 01 GF Furniture - Callout 1 is created in Floor Plans.
5. Floor Plans → Double-click 01 GF Furniture - Callout 1.
6. Adjust the crop region and press Hide Crop Region on the View Control toolbar.
7. In Properties palette → Graphics group → View Scale = 1:50.
8. Sections → Double-click B-B'
9. On View tab → Create panel → click Callout tool.
10. Make a rectangle around top of wall on grid 8.
11. A new view B-B' - Callout 1 is created in Sections.
12. Sections → Double-click B-B' - Callout 1.
13. Adjust the crop region and press Hide Crop Region on the View Control toolbar.
14. In Properties palette → Graphics group → View Scale = 1:20.
15. Project Browser → Sheets → Right-click → New Sheet.
16. From titleblocks, select Arch A1.rfa → OK → Titleblock is added.
17. From Floor Plans, drag 01 GF Furniture - Callout 1 to the upper left part of the sheet area.
18. From Sections, drag B-B' - Callout 1 to the upper right part of the sheet area.
19. From 3D Views, drag 3D Section to the lower part of the sheet area.
20. Select the Titleblock. In the Properties palette, change Sheet Name = Multiple Views.
21. All views are added with different scales (Fig. 9.26).

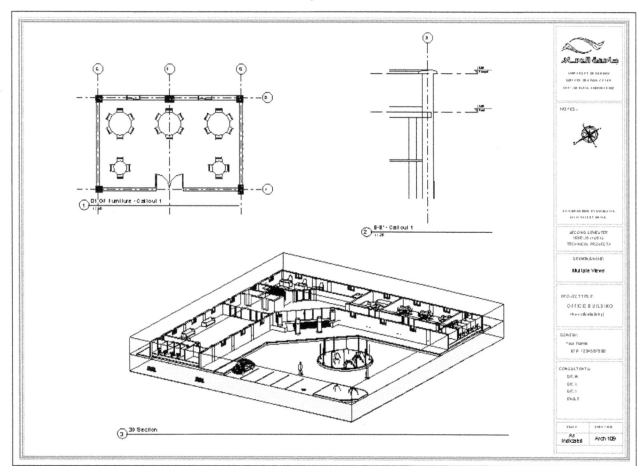

Fig. 9.26 – Sheet with views at multiple scales

9.8 Printing the Sheets

Your sheets are complete in Revit. Now you want to print them on paper. You can try one of the following ways.

1. If a printer is directly connected to you computer, then click on Revit button ![icon] and select Print.
2. Install a PDF printer and print views as PDF files. Later on print these PDF files on a printer.
3. ![icon] → Export → CAD Formats → DWG. Open the exported file in AutoCAD and save as PDF file. Later on print this PDF file on a printer.

4. Click ![save icon] to Save Project As **Arch09.**

10 Material Tags

You have made walls and floors with many layers of different materials. You can show details of layers by adding material tags on the layers. The tag will show the material used in a layer.

10.1 Material Tags in Section

1. Open Project **Arch09.**
2. Save Project As **Arch10.**
3. Floor Plans → 01 GF.
4. On Quick Access Toolbar (or on View tab → Create panel) click Section tool.
5. Add a section line to the north of the grid 4 including grids A and B.
6. Adjust extents of the section view as shown in Fig. 10.1.

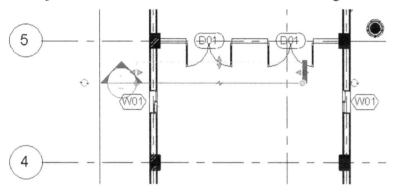

Fig. 10.1 – Draw Section

7. Double-click on the head of the section.
8. On the View Control bar, set:

   - Scale = 1:25
   - Detail Level: Fine
   - Visual Style: Hidden Line

9. Project Browser → Sections → Section 1 → right-click → Rename = Materials Section.
10. Zoom to Roof level.
11. On Annotate tab → Tag panel → click Material Tag tool.
12. Bring cursor on the top layer of the roof.
13. Material tag will appear.
14. Click 1 - 2 - 3 as shown in Fig. 10.2.

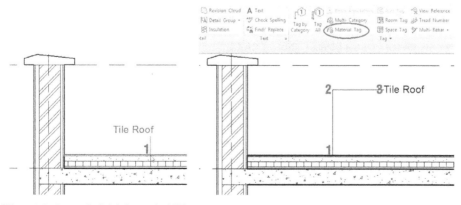

Fig. 10.2 – Add Material Tag

15. Do the same for other layers of the roof by placing tags according to the order of layers.

10.2 Material Tags in Callout

1. Floor Plans → 01 GF.
2. On View tab → Create panel → Callout dropdown → click Rectangle.
3. Draw a callout around west exterior wall including part of stairs and elevators (Right of Fig. 10.3).
4. A view named 01 GF - Callout 1 appears under Floor Plans node of Project Browser. Rename it as 01 GF - Materials Callout.
5. Double-click on 01 GF - Materials Callout.
6. On the View Control bar, set:

   - Scale = 1:20
   - Detail Level: Fine
   - Visual Style: Hidden Line

7. Add material tags as explained in § 10.1.

10.3 Material Tags on a Sheet

1. Project Browser → Sheets → Right-click → New Sheet → Select titleblock Arch A1 → OK.
2. Select the Titleblock. In Properties palette, make:

   - Sheet Number = Arch 110.
   - Sheet Name = Materials.

3. Drag the views Materials Section and 01 GF - Material Callout on the sheet.
4. The sheet looks as shown in Fig. 10.3.

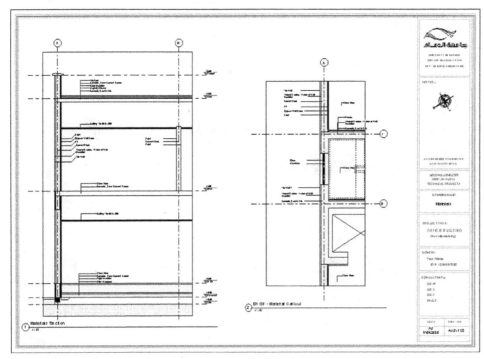

Fig. 10.3 – Sheet with Material Tags

5. Click [save icon] to Save Project As **Arch10.**

Part 2 . Structure

11 New Structural Project

You have completed the architectural design of your Revit project. Now you will start the structural design based on the architectural model. You have already made grids, columns, shear walls, stairs etc. in your architectural model. You don't need to make them again. You will just collaborate with the architectural model and copy these elements in your structural model.

11.1 Starting a New Structural Project

You will start your work with a project StrProject.rvt. You will download this file from the Download Folder (page v).

1. Open Revit → Projects → Open.
2. Select **str_project.rvt** → Open
3. Save Project As **Str01.**

11.2 Copy/Paste Element Types

You created some new element types in your architectural model. The equivalent types are not present in the structural model. One way is that you create them again. Or you can copy those elements from architectural model and paste them in the structural model. (After pasting, you will delete these elements. What you really want is to load the element types, not the elements themselves).

1. 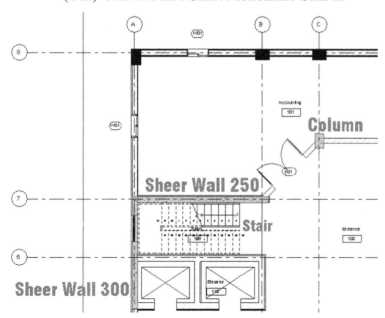 → Open → Project → Arch05.rvt. (You saved this project at the end of chapter 5. You can take any project you saved at the end of chapter 5 or later. If you didn't save it, then download it from Download Folder (page v)).
2. Floor Plans → 01 GF.
3. Select (Fig. 11.1)

    - Basic Wall: Shear - 250mm Concrete
    - (Ctrl) Basic Wall: Shear - 300mm Concrete
    - (Ctrl) M_Concrete-Rectangular-Column: 400 x 600mm.
    - (Ctrl) Cast-in-Place Stair: Monolithic Stair 2.

Fig. 11.1 – Select Structural Elements for copying

4. On Modify | Multi-select contextual tab → Clipboard panel → Click Copy to Clipboard.
5. On Quick Access Toolbar → Switch Windows dropdown → Select Str01.rvt - Structural Plans: Level 1 (Fig. 11.2).

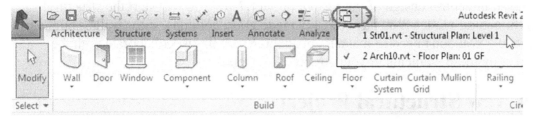

Fig. 11.2 – Switch Windows

6. On Modify tab → Clipboard panel → Paste dropdown → Aligned to Current View
7. Select the newly pasted walls and column → Press Delete (Leave the stairs).
8. On Quick Access Toolbar → Switch Windows dropdown → Select Arch09.rvt.
9. Close all views of Arch09.rvt.

11.3 Link with Architectural Project

You will link your structural project with the architectural project you finished before. Then you will be able to copy elements from the architectural project.

1. Floor Plans → Level 1.
2. On Insert tab → Link panel → click Link Revit tool.
3. Browse to Arch05.rvt. (You saved this project at the end of chapter 5. You can take any project you saved at the end of chapter 5 or later. If you didn't save it, then download it from the Download Folder (page v)). (Fig. 11.3).

Fig. 11.3 – Link with Architectural Project

4. Click on Open. The architectural project is inserted.
5. Align copied stairs with the stairs in the architectural model.

11.4 Copy/Monitor Elements

First you will match the elements in both structural and linked model by setting the copy options. Then you will copy elements from linked model to the structural model in appropriate view i.e. grids in elevation view, columns in 3D view, walls in plan view etc.

11.4.1 Copy Options

Before you copy the elements from linked model into the structural model, you will set copy options for different element types.

1. On Collaborate tab → Coordinate panel → Copy/Monitor dropdown → click Select Link.
2. Click on the linked model you just inserted.
3. On Copy/Monitor contextual tab → Tools panel → Click Options.
4. On Levels tab, choose as shown in Fig. 11.4.

Fig. 11.4 – Copy/Monitor Options: Levels Tab

5. On Grids tab, choose as shown in Fig. 11.5.

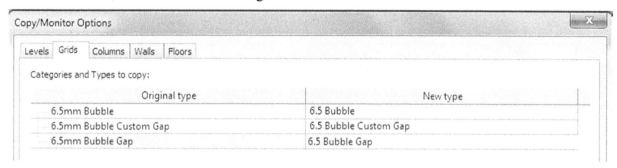

Fig. 11.5 – Copy/Monitor Options: Grids Tab

6. On Columns tab, choose as shown in Fig. 11.6.

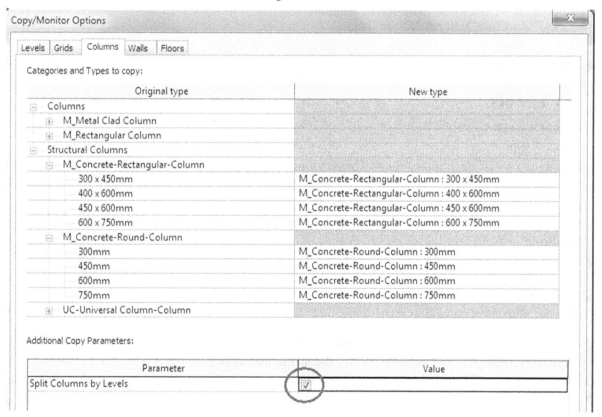

Fig. 11.6 – Copy/Monitor Options: Columns Tab

7. On Walls tab, choose as shown in Fig. 11.7.

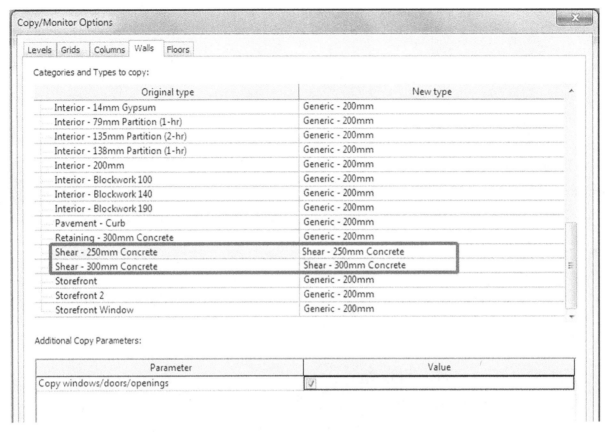

Fig. 11.7 – Copy/Monitor Options: Walls Tab

8. On Copy/Monitor contextual tab → Copy/Monitor panel → click Finish ✔ .

11.4.2 Copy Levels

You will copy levels in an elevation view.

1. Elevations → South.
2. On Collaborate tab → Coordinate panel → Copy/Monitor dropdown → click Select Link.
3. Click on the linked mode.
4. On Copy/Monitor contextual tab → Tools panel
5. Click Copy (Fig. 11.8).
6. Select ☑Multiple.
7. Make a selection box which includes all the levels.
8. Click Filter.
9. Press Check None → Select Levels → OK.
10. Click Finish (small button on option bar).

11. On Copy/Monitor contextual tab → Tools panel → click Finish ✔ .
12. All the levels from linked model are copied into the structural model.
13. But there are two levels viz. Level 1 and Level 2, which are present in the structural model when you created the project. These levels are not needed anymore. Delete these two levels (Select a level → right-click → Delete).
14. On View tab → Create panel → Plan Views dropdown → click Structural Plan (Fig. 11.9).

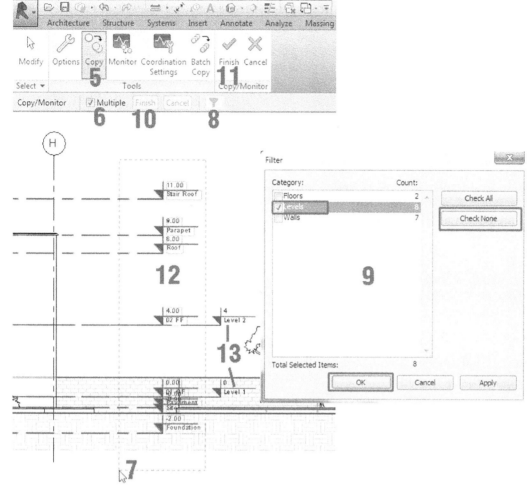

Fig. 11.8 – Copy Levels

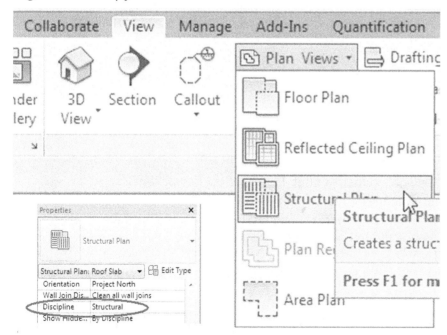

Fig. 11.9 – Create Structural Plan Views

15. List of levels appear → Select all the levels → OK.

16. All the levels appear in the Project Browser under Structural Plans node.
17. You don't need Structural Plans for Pavement and Parapet. Right-click on each in the Project Browser and delete.
18. For all other Structural Plans, click each in the Project Browser one by one and in the Properties palette, change its **Discipline = Structural** (Fig. 11.9).

11.4.3 Copy Grids

You will copy grids in a structural plan view.

1. Structural Plans → 01 GF.
2. On Collaborate tab → Coordinate panel → Copy/Monitor dropdown → click Select Link.
3. Click on the linked mode.
4. On Copy/Monitor contextual tab → Tools panel
5. Click Copy.
6. Select ☑Multiple.
7. Make a selection box which includes all the grids.
8. Click Filter.
9. Press Check None → Select Grids → OK.
10. Click Finish (small button on option bar).

11. On Copy/Monitor contextual tab → Tools panel → click Finish ✓ .
12. All the grids are copied into the structural model.
13. To check this, select the linked model and press HH to hide the linked model temporarily. You will see all the grids. Press HR to unhide the linked model.

11.4.4 Copy Columns

You will copy Columns in a 3D view.

1. 3D View → {3D}.
2. On Collaborate tab → Coordinate panel → Copy/Monitor dropdown → click Select Link.
3. Click on the linked mode.
4. On Copy/Monitor contextual tab → Tools panel
5. Click Copy.
6. Select ☑Multiple.
7. Make a selection box which includes all the columns.
8. Click Filter.
9. Press Check None → Select Structural Columns → OK.
10. Click Finish (small button on option bar).

11. On Copy/Monitor contextual tab → Tools panel → click Finish ✓ .
12. All the columns are copied into the structural model.
13. To check this, select the linked model and press HH to hide the linked model temporarily. You will see all the columns. Press HR to unhide the linked model.
14. The columns are split by levels. They should only be split at 01 GF and 02 FF levels only. For this, you can delete columns at Site and Pavement levels. Then change the height of columns at Foundation level up to 01 GF.
15. Elevations → South → Select the linked model → Press HH to hide the linked model temporarily.
16. Make a selection box to select all elements between Site and 01 GF.
17. Filter → Check None → Select Structural Columns → Delete.
18. Make a selection box to select all elements between Foundation and Site.
19. Filter → Check None → Select Structural Columns.

20. In Properties palette, change Top Level = 01 GF.
21. 3D Views → {3D} → Select all → Filter → Check None → Select Structural Columns.
22. In Properties palette → under Materials and Finishes group → Structural Material = Cast-in-Place gray Col.

11.4.5 Copy Shear Walls

You will copy Shear Walls in a structural plan view.

1. Structural Plans → 01 GF.
2. On Collaborate tab → Coordinate panel → Copy/Monitor dropdown → click Select Link.
3. Click on the linked mode.
4. On Copy/Monitor contextual tab → Tools panel
5. Click Copy.
6. Select ☑Multiple.
7. Select the shear walls.
8. Click Finish (small button on option bar).
9. On Copy/Monitor contextual tab → Tools panel → click Finish ✓ .
10. The shear walls are copied into the structural model.
11. To check this, select the linked model and press HH to hide the linked model temporarily. You will see the shear walls.
12. To change the fill color of wall in a structural plan view, press VG and set cut pattern as shown in Fig. 11.10.

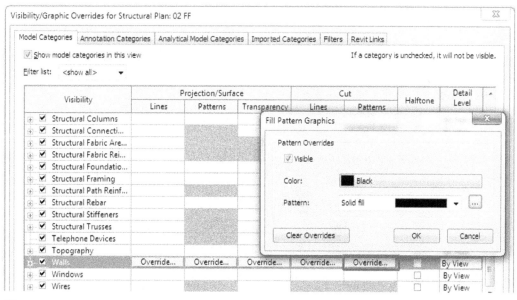

Fig. 11.10 – Walls' Cut Pattern

11.4.6 Copy Dimension Styles

You will copy Dimension Style in a structural plan view.

1. Structural Plans → 01 GF.
2. On Manage tab → Settings panel → click Transfer Project Standards tool (Fig. 11.11).
3. Check None → Select Dimension Styles → OK.
4. On Duplicate Types dialog box, press New Only.

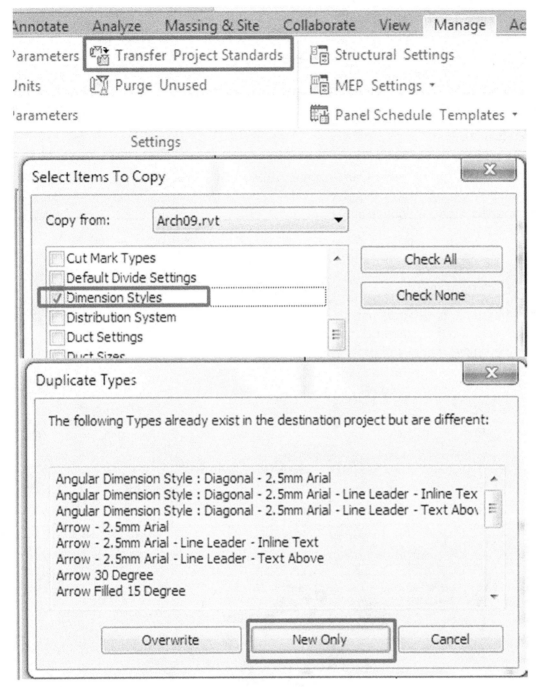

Fig. 11.11 – Copy Dimension Styles

5. Click [save icon] to Save Project As **Str01.**

12 The Foundation Level

You have copied all required elements from the architectural model. Now you will add new structural elements in the structural project. You will start from the Foundation level.

12.1 Foundations

You will place rectangular footings under the columns and bearing footings under the shear walls.

12.1.1 View Range

Foundations are below the level. At Foundation Level, Columns are visible. But if you make Foundations, they are not visible by default because they are below the level. You should make changes in the View Range.

1. Open Project **Str01.** (You can get this file from Download Folder (page v)).
2. Save Project As **Str02.**
3. Structural Plans → Foundation
4. In Properties Palette , under Extents group, View Range → Edit

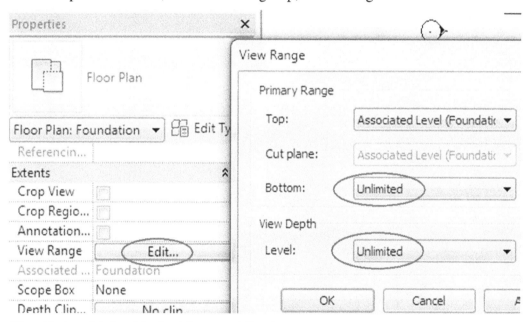

Fig. 12.1 – Link with Architectural Project

5. Make Bottom and View Depth Level = Unlimited.

12.1.2 Isolated Foundations

You will place Isolated Foundation under each column.

1. Structural Plans → Foundation
2. Structure Tab → Structure Panel → Foundation → Isolated
3. In Properties palette, select Type = M_Footing-Rectangular_New: 1800 x 1200 x 450
4. Edit Type → Type Mark = F1
5. Click At Columns

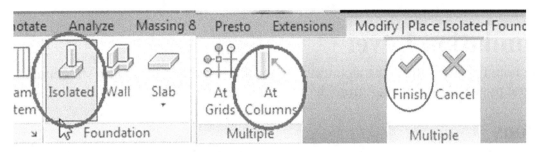

Fig. 12.2 – Isolated Foundations At Columns

6. Make a selection box around the columns and click Finish.
7. Isolated foundations are added under all columns. See 3D View.

12.1.3 Wall Foundations

You will place Wall Foundations under the Structural Walls.

1. Structural Plans → Foundation
2. Structure Tab → Structure Panel → Foundation → Wall
3. In Properties palette, select Type = Wall Foundation: Bearing Footing - 900 x 300.
4. Edit Type → Type Mark = F2.
5. Click on Select Multiple.
6. Make a selection box around shear walls from Top-left to Bottom-right.
7. Click Finish.

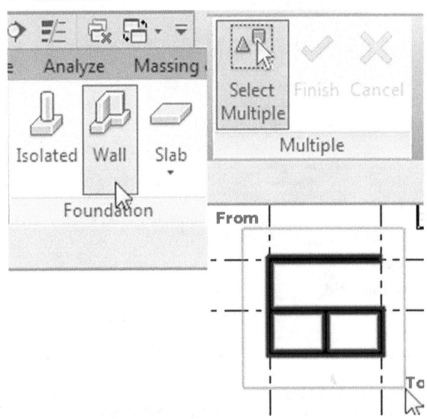

Fig. 12.3 – Wall Foundations

8. Wall Foundations are placed under the Shear Walls.
9. 3D View appears as shown in Fig. 12.4.

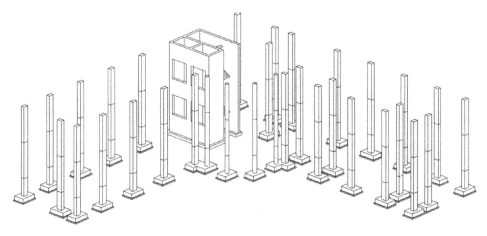

Fig. 12.4 – Isolated and Wall Foundations in 3D view

12.2 Dimensions

You will add dimensions in the foundation plan.

1. Structural Plans → Foundation
2. On Annotate tab → Dimension panel → click Aligned tool.
3. In Properties palette, select Type = Linear Dimension Style: Diagonal Dim 1.
4. Add dimensions (of type = Diagonal Dim 1) between grids and overall dimension on each side.

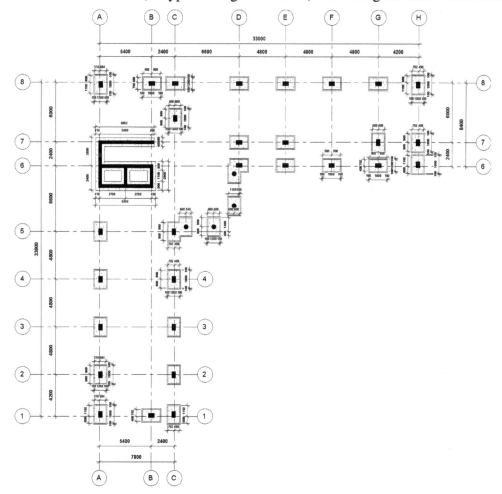

Fig. 12.5 – Dimensions for Isolated and Wall Foundations

5. Select a dimension of type = Diagonal Dim 1 → Edit Type → Duplicate → Name = Diagonal Dim 2 → In Text group → Text Size = 2mm.
6. Add dimensions (of type = Diagonal Dim 2) around foundations.

12.3 Foundation Tags

You will add tags to the foundations.

1. Structural Plans → Foundation
2. On Annotate tab → Tag panel → click Tag by Category tool.
3. Click on each foundation.
4. Select tag and move the four-sided arrow to adjust its position.

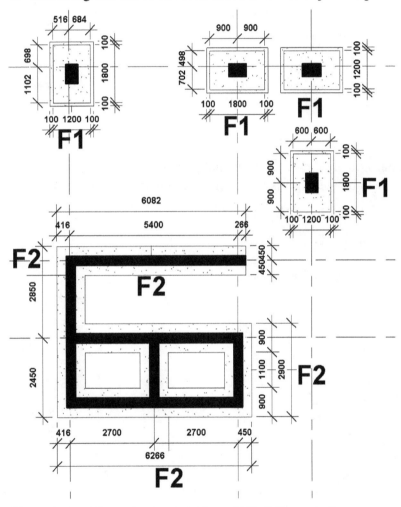

Fig. 12.6 – Tags for Isolated and Wall Foundations

5. Click 💾 to Save Project As **Str02.**

13 The Ground Floor Level

You will add ground beams, slabs and slab edges on the Ground Floor level. But first of all you will add outer dimensions. Or you can copy them from the Foundation plan.

1. Structural Plans → Foundation.
2. Select the outer dimensions of type = Diagonal Dim 1.
3. On Modify | Dimensions contextual tab → Clipboard panel → Click Copy.
4. Click Paste → Aligned to selected Views → 01 GF → OK.
5. Structural Plans → 01 GF.
6. You will see that outer dimensions are copied.

13.1 Columns

You have copied columns from the architectural model in § 11.4.4. You need to make some changes in the column layout.

1. Open Project **Str02.**
2. Save Project As **Str03.**
3. Structural Plans → 01 GF.
4. On Structure tab → Structure panel → click Column tool.
5. Load Family → Structural Columns → Concrete → M_Concrete-Square-Column.rfa.
6. In Properties palette, select M_Concrete-Square-Column: 450 x 450mm.
7. On Modify | Place Structural Column contextual tab → Depth = Foundation (Fig. 13.1).

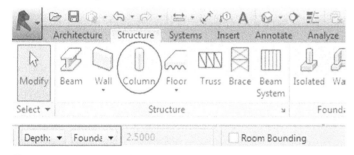

Fig. 13.1 – Add Columns

8. Place two columns at C6 and C7.
9. Structural Plans → Foundation (Fig. 13.2).
10. Place an Isolated footing 1000 x 1000 x 450 (Type Mark = F3) under columns at C6 and C7.

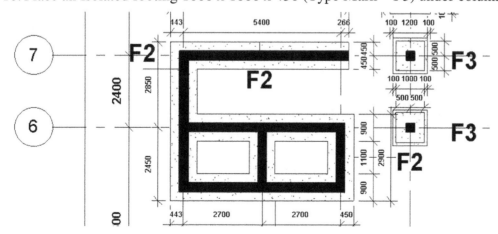

Fig. 13.2 – Add Foundations

13.2 Ground Beams

Ground beams are concrete beams placed on 01 GF level. You will create different types of beams.

1. Structural Plans → 01 GF → Right-click → Duplicate View → Duplicate with Detailing (Fig. 13.3).
2. 01 GF Copy 1 is created → Right-click → Rename = 01 GF Framing.

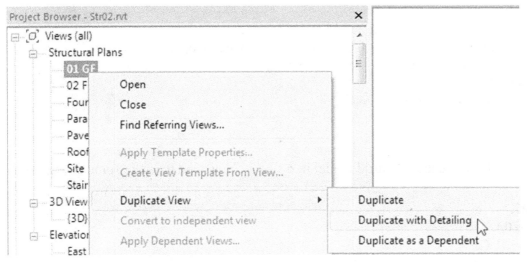

Fig. 13.3 – Duplicate View

3. Structural Plans → 01 GF Framing.
4. On Structure tab → Structure panel → click Beam tool.
5. In Properties palette, select Type = M_Concrete-Rectangular Beam: 300 x 600mm.
6. Properties palette → Edit Type → Duplicate → Name = 200 x 600mm GB1 → OK (Fig. 13.4).
7. b = 0.2, h = 0.6, Type Mark = GB1 → OK.

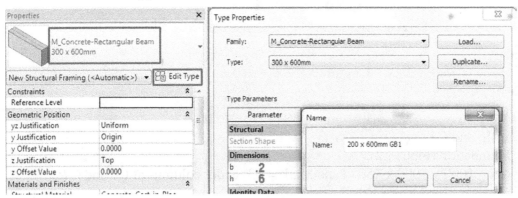

Fig. 13.4 – Edit Beam type

8. Check that Tag on Placement is selected.
9. Add beams from center of a column to center of other column wherever the distance between columns is **4800**mm.
10. Note that the tag GB1 appears above each beam.
11. The ground beams on the outer sides of the building are aligned with outer sides of the columns.
12. On Modify tab → Modify panel → click Align tool.
13. Click on outer side of the column then on outer side of the beam (Fig. 13.5).

Fig. 13.5 – Align Beam with Column

14. In this way, align all outer beams with columns. Leave the inner beams form center to center of columns (Fig. 13.6).

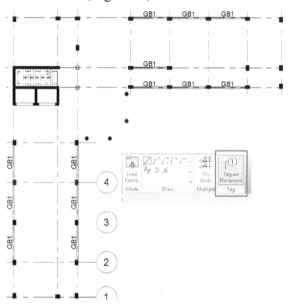

Fig. 13.6 – Ground Beams GB1

15. On Structure tab → Structure panel → click Beam tool.
16. In Properties palette, select Type = M_Concrete-Rectangular Beam: 200 x 600mm GB1.
17. Properties palette → Edit Type → Duplicate → Name = 200 x 600mm GB2 → OK
18. Type Mark = GB2 → OK.
19. Check that Tag on Placement is selected.
20. Add beams from center of a column to center of other column where ever the distance between columns is **2400**mm.
21. Similarly make (Fig. 13.7)

- GB3 = 6000mm
- GB4 = 4200mm
- GB5 = 5400mm
- GB6 = 7800mm
- GB7 = 6600mm
- GB8 = 4600mm
- GB9 = 1348mm
- GB10 = 2850mm
- GB11 = 2970mm
- GB12 = 3600mm

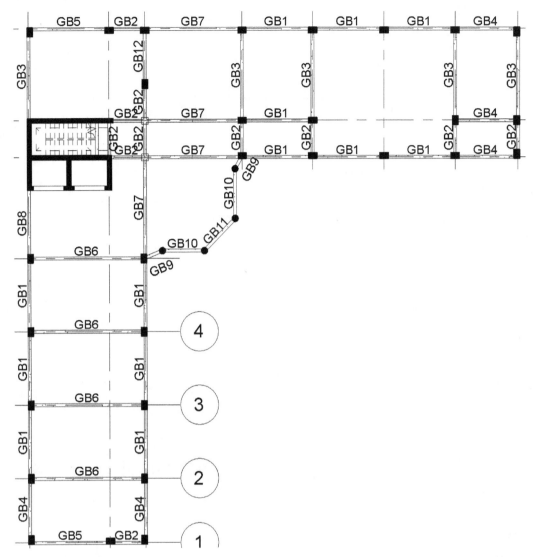

Fig. 13.7 – All Ground Beams

13.3 Slab on Grade

Slab on grade is a insitu concrete floor 100mm thick. It has a slab edge on all sides.

1. Structural Plans → 01 GF Framing → Right-click → Duplicate View → Duplicate with Detailing.
2. 01 GF Framing Copy 1 is created → Right-click → Rename = 01 GF Slab (Fig. 13.3).
3. Structural Plans → 01 GF Slab.
4. Select any beam tag → Right-click → Hide in View → Category (Fig. 13.8).
5. All beam tags are hidden.

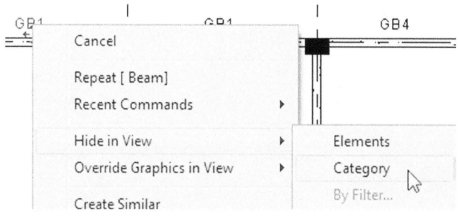

Fig. 13.8 – Hide selected type

6. Zoom to area between grids E-G and 6-8.
7. On Structure tab → Structure panel → click Floor tool.
8. In Properties palette, select type = Insitu Concrete 330mm.
9. Edit Type → Duplicate → Name = Insitu Concrete 100mm → OK (Fig. 13.9).

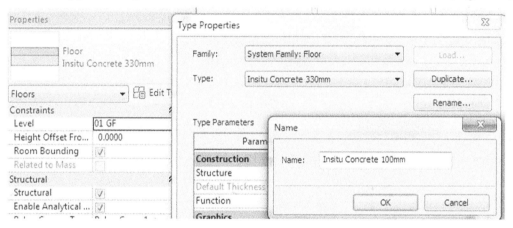

Fig. 13.9 – Edit Floor type

10. In Type Properties dialog box, under Parameter, in Construction group, Structure → Edit.
11. Make changes as shown in Fig. 13.10.

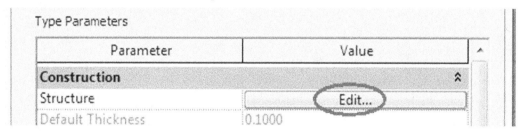

Type Parameters	
Parameter	Value
Construction	
Structure	Edit...
Default Thickness	0.1000

	Function	Material	Thickness	Wraps	Structur Materi
1	Core Boundary	Layers Above Wrap	0.0000		
2	Structure [1]	Concrete - Cast In Situ	0.1000		
3	Core Boundary	Layers Below Wrap	0.0000		

Fig. 13.10 – Edit Floor structure

12. Similarly make floor type Insitu Concrete 260mm
- Function = Structure
- Material = Concrete - Cast in Situ.
- Thickness = 0.2600

13. Similarly make floor type Insitu Concrete 200mm
- Function = Structure
- Material = Concrete - Cast in Situ.
- Thickness = 0.2000

14. Similarly make floor type Insitu Concrete 400mm
- Function = Structure
- Material = Concrete - Cast in Situ.
- Thickness = 0.4000

15. Similarly make floor type Insitu Concrete 120mm
- Function = Structure
- Material = Concrete - Cast in Situ.
- Thickness = 0.1200

16. Similarly make floor type Lightweight Concrete 160mm.
- Function = Structure
- Material = Concrete - Lightweight.
- Thickness = 0.1600

17. In Properties palette, select type = Insitu Concrete 100mm.
18. On Draw panel, click on Pick Lines.
19. Pick lines as shown in Fig. 13.11 (Only one line on each side)..

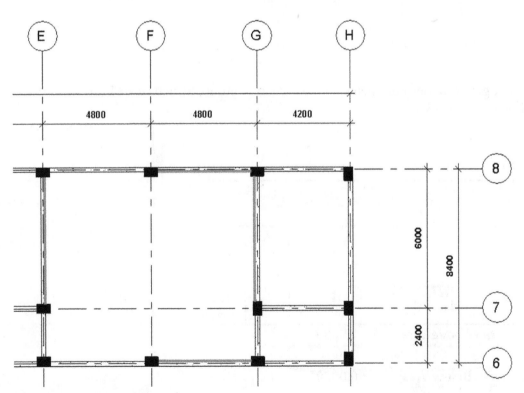

Fig. 13.11 – Pick Lines for Floor

20. Trim on all sides to make rectangle.
21. Mode panel → click Finish ✓ .
22. You will see a span symbol on the floor.
23. Select the span symbol.
24. In Properties palette, select type = M_Span Direction: Two Way Slab.

13.4 Slab Edge

Slab edge is placed around the slab inside the ground beams.

1. Structural Plans → 01 GF Slab.
2. Visual Style = Wireframe.
3. On Structure tab → Foundation panel → Slab Dropdown → click Floor: Slab Edge tool.
4. In Properties palette → Edit Type.
5. Make Type Parameters as shown in Fig. 13.12.

Parameter	Value
Construction	⌃
Profile	M_Slab Edge-Thickened : 600 x 300mm
Materials and Finishes	⌃
Material	Concrete - Precast Concrete - 35 MPa ⌄

Fig. 13.12 – Edit Slab Edge type

6. Click on all four sides of the slab. Slab edges will appear as shown in Fig. 13.12.

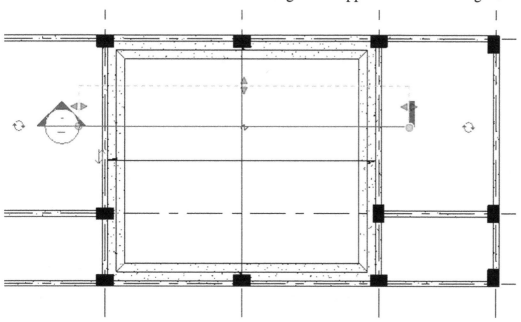

Fig. 13.12 – Slab Edge (Plan View)

7. The slab edges are placed on the slab level. They should be under the slab. You will make their vertical offset = − 0.10
8. Select all four slab edges.
9. In Properties palette → Vertical Profile Offset = − 0.10.
10. The section view looks as shown in Fig. 13.13.

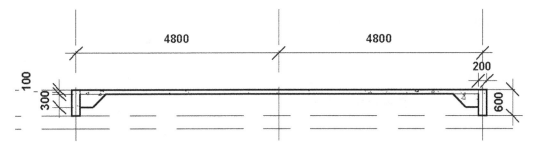

Fig. 13.13 – Slab Edge (Section View)

11. Repeat these steps to make slabs and slab edges in all spaces between ground beams.
12. In spaces between grids 6 - 7, (span < 3m) use span symbol type = M_Span Direction: One Way Slab and rotate it by 90º so that the one way span symbol is along the shorter dimension.
13. The complete floor looks as shown in Fig. 13.14.

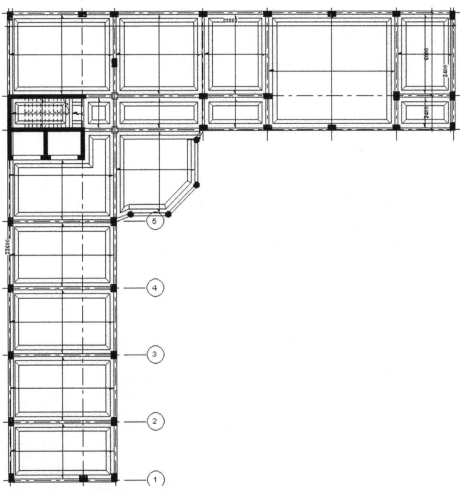

Fig. 13.14 – Slabs with Slab edges and Span directions

14. Structural Plans → 01 GF Framing.
15. Select all → Filter → Check None → Select Slab Edges and Floors → Right-click → Hide in View → Element.

16. Click ![save icon] to Save Project As **Str03**.

14 The First Floor Level

You will place drop beams, hourdi beams, slabs and other structural elements on First Floor level.

14.1 Drop Beams

Drop beams are concrete beams placed on outer sides on 02 FF level. You will create different types of drop beams.

1. Open Project **Str03.**
2. Save Project As **Str04.**
3. Structural Plans → 02 FF → Right-click → Duplicate View → Duplicate with Detailing (Fig. 13.3).
4. 02 FF Copy 1 is created → Right-click → Rename = 02 FF Framing.
5. Structural Plans → 01 GF Framing.
6. Select all → Filter → Check None → Select Structural Framing (Girder).
7. On Modify | Structural Framing contextual tab → Clipboard panel → click Copy tool.
8. Paste → Aligned to Selected Levels → 02 FF Framing → OK.
9. Structural Plans → 02 FF Framing.
10. On Annotate tab → Tag panel → click Tag All → Select as shown in Fig. 14.1.

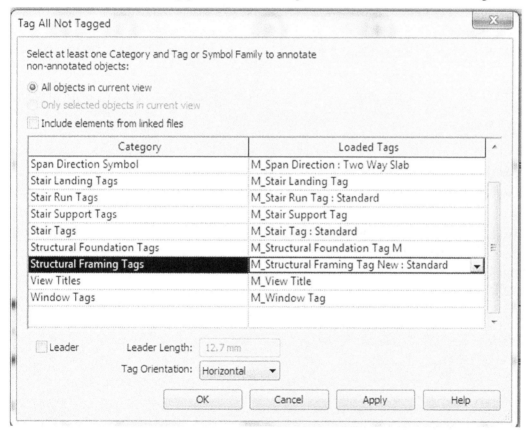

Fig. 14.1 –Beam Tag

11. Tags appear on all beams. Tags are GB1, GB2 etc. You will change them to DB1, DB2 etc.
12. Select a beam on **outer side** with tag GB1.
13. In Properties palette → Edit Type → Duplicate (Fig. 14.2).
14. Name = **200 x 600mm DB1**.
15. Type Mark = DB1 → OK → OK.

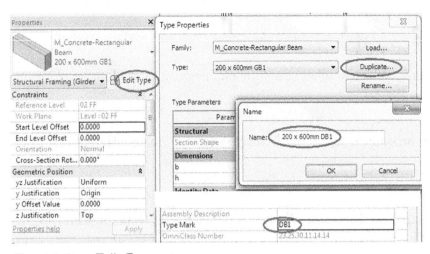

Fig. 14.2 – Edit Beam type

16. Select all other instances of GB1 (**on outer side only**) and select type = 200 x 600mm DB1.

17. Similarly change (**on outer side only**):

- GB2 → DB2
- GB3 → DB3
- GB4 → DB4
- GB5 → DB5
- GB7 → DB6
- GB8 → DB7
- GB9 → DB8
- GB10 → DB9
- GB11 → DB10

14.2 Hidden Beams

Hidden beams are concrete beams placed on 02 FF level. You will create different types of Hidden beams.

1. Select the beam on **inner side** on grid G with tag GB3.
2. In Properties palette → Edit Type → Duplicate(Fig. 14.3).
3. Name = **600 x 260mm HB1**.
4. b = 0.600, h = 0.2600, Type Mark = HB1 → OK → OK.

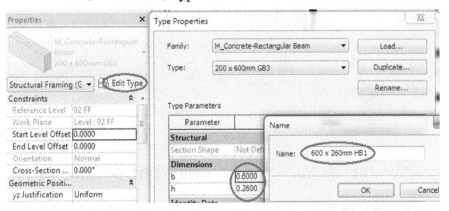

Fig. 14.3 – Edit Beam type

5. In the same way create other beams as shown in Fig. 14.4.

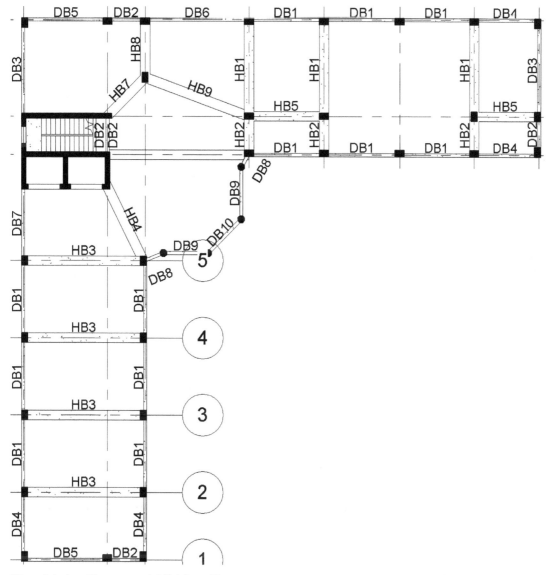

Fig. 14.4 –Drop and Hidden Beams

14.3 Hourdi Slab: Two-way

In hourdi slabs, hourdi blocks are used as a framework and a compression slab is cast over it. The overall structure of the floor is much lighter. It is an alternative to use steel framework.

14.3.1 Add Slab

1. Structural Plans → 02 FF Framing → Right-click → Duplicate View → Duplicate with Detailing (Fig. 13.3).
2. 02 FF Framing Copy 1 is created → Right-click → Rename = 02 FF Slab.
3. Structural Plans → 02 FF Slab.
4. Select any beam tag → Right-click → Hide in View → Category.
5. All beam tags are hidden.
6. Zoom to area between grids E-G and 6-8.
7. On Structure tab → Structure panel → click Floor tool.
8. In Properties palette, select type = Insitu Concrete 260mm.

9. On Draw panel, click on Pick Lines → Pick lines (inner side of beams in Fig 14.7) → Trim on all sides to make rectangle.
10. Mode panel → click Finish ✓ .
11. You will see a span symbol on the floor.
12. Select the span symbol.
13. In Properties palette, select type = M_Span Direction: Two Way Slab.

14.3.2 Add Voids

1. Structural Plans → 02 FF Slab. Zoom to area between grids E-G and 6-8.
2. Visual Style = Wireframe.
3. On Architecture tab → Build panel → Component dropdown → click Model-in-Place tool (Fig. 14.5).
4. From Family Category, select Floors → OK.
5. Name = Floor Ribs 1 → OK.

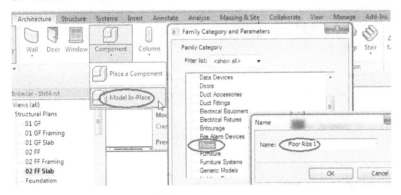

Fig. 14.5 – Model-in-Place

6. On Create tab → Forms panel → Void Forms dropdown → click Void Extrusion tool (Fig. 14.6).

Fig. 14.6 – Void Extrusion

7. On Draw panel → click Rectangle tool.
8. Draw a rectangle and adjust its dimensions as 0.6 x 0.6m.
9. Select the rectangle and move it in the center as shown in Fig. 14.7 (Move center of left line on horizontal span-direction and then move center of the top line on vertical span-direction).

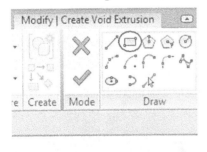

Fig. 14.7 – Rectangle in center

10. Select the rectangle.
11. On Modify panel → click Copy tool → On option bar → select ☑ Multiple (Fig. 14.8).
12. Click on any point on the rectangle and move the cursor vertically up.
13. Write 0.75 and press Enter. Do this many times until the rectangle reaches the upper end of the slab. Press Esc.

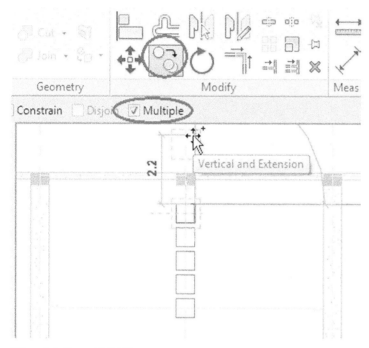

Fig. 14.8 – Edit Beam type

14. Select all upper rectangles except the central one.
15. On Modify panel → click Mirror - Pick Axis tool → click on horizontal span direction.
16. All upper rectangles are mirrored on lower side.

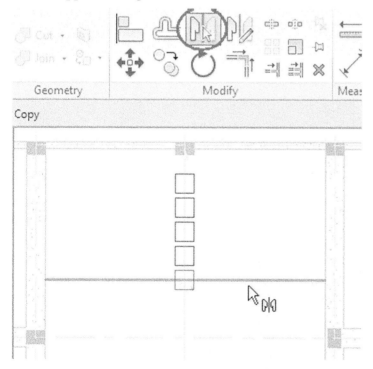

Fig. 14.9 – Edit Beam type

17. Select the whole vertical array of rectangles.
18. Repeat the steps 22-26 to copy and then mirror the array horizontally (Fig. 14.10).
19. In Properties palette, set Extrusion End = − 0.2600, Extrusion Start = − 0.1000.

20. Mode panel → click Finish ✓ .

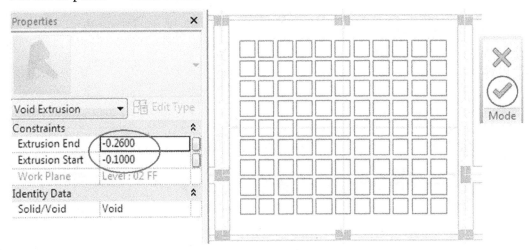

Fig. 14.10 – Voids in Two-way Hourdi slab

21. On Modify tab → Geometry panel → click Cut Geometry tool.
22. Click on slab and then on void.
23. In-Place Editor panel → Finish Model.

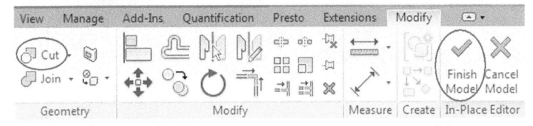

Fig. 14.11 – Cut Geometry

24. See 3D view from below. You will see voids cut in floor.

14.3.3 Fill Voids

You will fill these voids with lightweight concrete.

1. Structural Plans → 02 FF Slab. Zoom to area between grids E-G and 6-8.
2. Visual Style = Wireframe.
3. On Structure tab → Structure panel → click Floor tool.
4. In Properties palette, select

   - type = Lightweight Concrete 160mm.
   - Height Offset From Level = − 0.100

5. On Draw panel, click on Rectangle tool → Make a rectangle on lower left void.
6. Select this rectangle → Copy Multiple on all voids horizontally. Press Esc.
7. Select the horizontal array of rectangles → Copy Multiple on all voids vertically. Press Esc.

8. Mode panel → click Finish ✓ .
9. The slab will look as shown in Fig. 14.12.

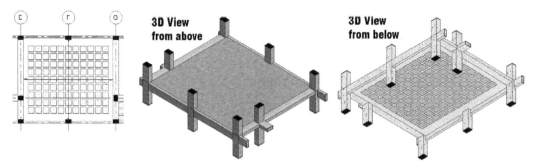

Fig. 14.12 – Two-way Hourdi slab

14.4 Hourdi Slab: One-way

One-way Hourdi slab is used where width of the area is small.

14.4.1 Add Slab

1. Structural Plans → 02 FF Slab. Zoom to area between grids G-H and 6-7.
2. On Structure tab → Structure panel → click Floor tool.
3. In Properties palette, select type = Insitu Concrete 260mm.
4. On Draw panel, click on Pick Lines → Pick lines → Trim on all sides to make rectangle.
5. Mode panel → click Finish ✓ .
6. You will see a span symbol on the floor.
7. Select the span symbol.
8. In Properties palette, select type = M_Span Direction: One Way Slab.
9. Rotate the span symbol so that it is along the shorter dimension of the slab.

14.4.2 Add Voids

1. Structural Plans → 02 FF Slab. Zoom to area between grids G-H and 6-7.
2. On Architecture tab → Build panel → Component dropdown → click Model-in-Place tool.
3. From Family Category, select Floors → OK.
4. Name = Floor Ribs 2 → OK.
5. On Create tab → Forms panel → Void Forms dropdown → click Void Extrusion tool.
6. Draw a line from center of span symbol.
7. Draw a rectangle and adjust its width as 0.48m. Move rectangle to bring it in center (Fig. 14.13).

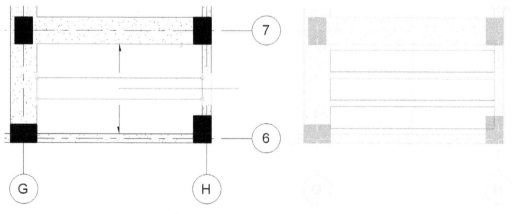

Fig. 14.13 – Voids in One-way Hourdi slab

8. Delete the line.

9. Copy the rectangle up and down at a distance of 0.63m.
10. In Properties palette, set Extrusion End = − 0.2600, Extrusion Start = − 0.1000.

11. Mode panel → click Finish ✔ .
12. On Modify tab → Geometry panel → click Cut Geometry tool.
13. Click on slab and then on void.
14. In-Place Editor panel → Finish Model.

14.4.3 Fill Voids

You will fill these voids with lightweight concrete.

1. Structural Plans → 02 FF Slab. Zoom to area between grids G-H and 6-7.
2. Visual Style = Wireframe.
3. On Structure tab → Structure panel → click Floor tool.
4. In Properties palette, select
5. type = Lightweight Concrete 160mm.
6. Height Offset From Level = − 0.100
7. On Draw panel, click on Rectangle tool → Make a rectangle on lower void.
8. Select this rectangle → Copy on other 2 voids.

9. Mode panel → click Finish ✔ .

14.4.4 Section View

You will make a section view of hourdi slab.

1. Structural Plans → 02 FF Slab. Zoom to area between grids G-H and 6-7.
2. Add a section as shown in Fig. 14.14.
3. Double-click on the head of the section. You will see the section view.
4. Detail Level = Fine.
5. On Annotate tab → Detail panel → click Detail Line tool.
6. Line Style panel → Line Style dropdown → Medium Lines.
7. Draw lines (cross inside rectangle) and copy as shown in Fig. 14.14.

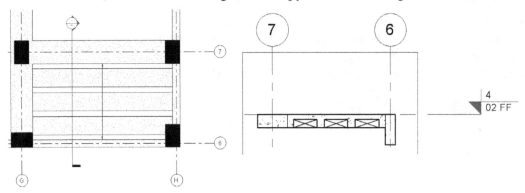

Fig. 14.14 – One-way Hourdi slab Section view

8. Make two-way or one-way hourdi slabs in other parts of the 02 FF level.

14.5 Solid Slab

In the area between grids A-D and 5-8, columns and beams are in an irregular arrangement. In this area, solid slab will be constructed.

1. Structural Plans → 02 FF Slab. Zoom to area between grids A-D and 5-8.

2. On Structure tab → Structure panel → click Floor tool.
3. In Properties palette, select type = Insitu Concrete 200mm.
4. On Draw panel, click on Pick Lines → Draw the boundary of the floor as shown in Fig. 14.15.

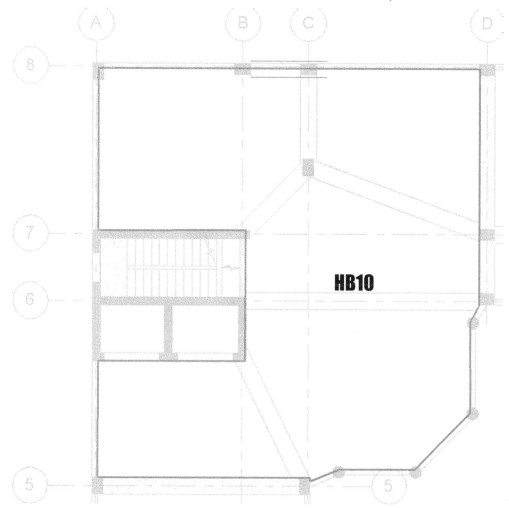

Fig. 14.15 – Solid Slab

5. Mode panel → click Finish ✓ .

14.6 Slab in Stair Area

In stair area, you will make Insitu Concrete 260mm floor.

1. Structural Plans → 02 FF Slab. Zoom to area between grids A-B and 6-7.
2. On Structure tab → Structure panel → click Floor tool.
3. In Properties palette, select type = Insitu Concrete 260mm.
4. On Draw panel, click on Rectangle → Draw a rectangle between the two beams.

5. Mode panel → click Finish ✓ .
6. Select floor and span symbol → Copy → Paste to level Roof.

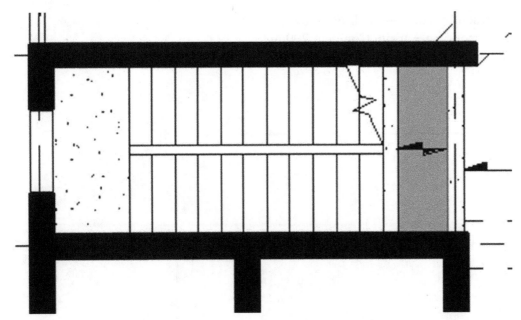

Fig. 14.16 – Slab in Stair Area

7. Click 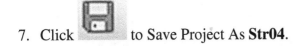 to Save Project As **Str04**.

15 The Roof Level

You will place drop beams, pre-cast hollow-core beams, waffle-slabs and other structural elements on Roof level.

15.1 Outer Beams

Some outer beams are drop beams and others are L beams. You will copy drop beams from 02 FF level and then make appropriate changes.

15.1.1 Copy Drop Beams

1. Open Project **Str04.**
2. Save Project As **Str05.**
3. Structural Plans → Roof → Right-click → Duplicate View → Duplicate with Detailing (Fig. 13.3).
4. Roof Copy 1 is created → Right-click → Rename = Roof Framing.
5. Structural Plans → 02 FF Framing.
6. Select drop beams (on outer side).
7. On Modify | Structural Framing contextual tab → Clipboard panel → click Copy tool.
8. Paste → Aligned to Selected Levels → Roof Framing → OK.
9. Structural Plans → Roof Framing.
10. On Annotate tab → Tag panel → click Tag All → Select Structural Framing Tags = M_Structural Framing Tag New: Standard.
11. Tags appear on all beams.

15.1.2 L Beams

1. Structural Plans → Roof Framing.
2. Select DB1 on grid A between grids 4 - 5.
3. In Properties palette, select Type = M_Precast-L Shaped Beam: 300 LB 400.
4. Edit Type → Duplicate → Name = 300 LB 400 LB1.
5. Make dimensions as shown in Fig. 15.1.
6. Type Mark = LB1.

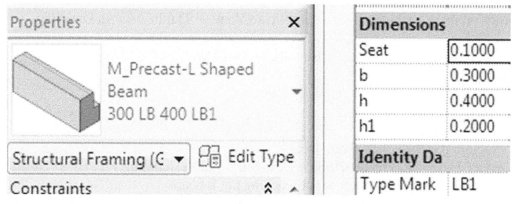

Fig. 15.1 – Edit Beam type

7. Some L beams need reflection → Click on the beam to be reflected → Click on the double-arrow in the middle of the beam.
8. Align outer side of the beams with outer side of the columns.
9. Similarly replace drop beams in area between grids 1 - 2 with L beams as follows:

- DB1 → LB1
- DB2 → LB2
- DB4 → LB4
- DB5 → LB5

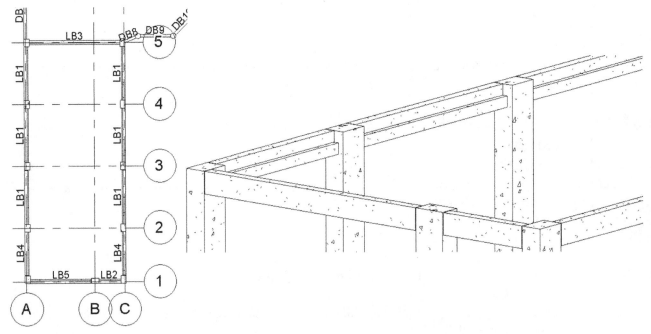

Fig. 15.2 – L Beams

10. Add LB3 on grid 5.

15.2 Pre-cast Hollow-core Slabs

Hollow-core slab is a pre-cast slab of pre-stressed concrete with tubular voids extending the full length of the slab. Width of the hollow core slab is fixed and it is cut for the required length. It is then placed on L shaped beams.

15.2.1 Place Hollow-core Slabs

1. Structural Plans → Roof Framing → Right-click → Duplicate View → Duplicate with Detailing (Fig. 13.3).
2. Roof Framing Copy 1 is created → Right-click → Rename = Roof Slab.
3. Structural Plans → Roof Slab.
4. Select any beam tag → Right-click → Hide in View → Category.
5. All beam tags are hidden.
6. Zoom to area between grids A-C and 1-2.
7. On Structure tab → Structure panel → click Beam tool.
8. In Properties palette, select Type = M_Precast-Hollow Core Slab: 1200 x 200mm.
9. Click on grid A then C. The slab is placed but it is not reaching the L beam.
10. Click on the slab. You will see dot and double-arrow on each end of the slab. Drag the arrow to inner side of the L beam. Do this on both sides (Fig. 15.3).

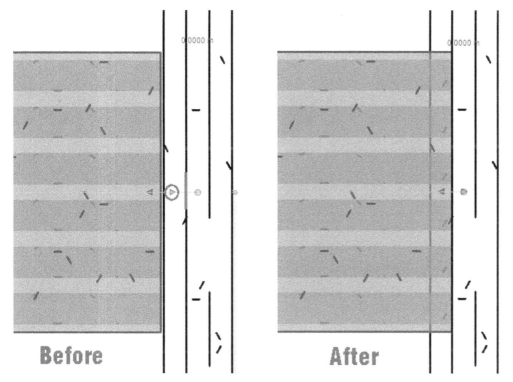

Fig. 15.3 – Place Hollow-core Slabs

11. Align edge of the slab (press Tab) with L beam on grid 1 (Fig. 15.4).

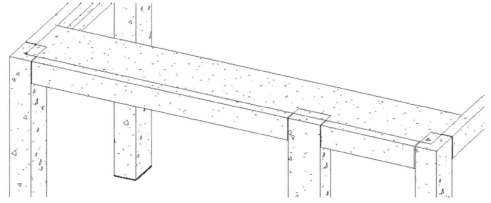

Fig. 15.4 – Align Beam Edge

12. Select the slab.
13. On Modify | Structural Framing contextual tab → Modify panel → click Array tool.
14. Select options on option bar as shown in Fig. 15.5.
15. Snap to a corner of the slab and move cursor vertically up.
16. Type 1.2 (for distance) → press Enter → type 10 (for number) → press Enter → array is not enough → type 15 (for number) → press Enter → now array is enough.

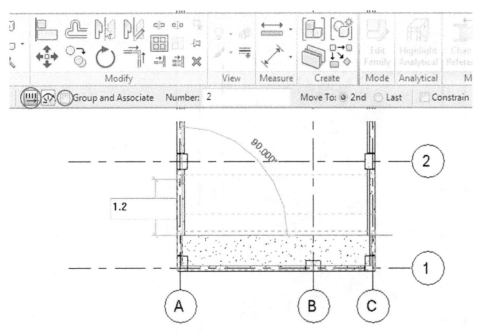

Fig. 15.5 – Array of Hollow-core slabs

17. At the end, a gap is left near grid 5. You will make a concrete floor here.
18. Slabs on grid 2, 3, 4 are not correct because of columns.
19. Select slab on grid 2. (You may hide the column temporarily by selecting the column and pressing HH).
20. Adjust length of the slab.
21. Do the same for slabs on grids 3 and 4.

15.2.2 Cut Hollow-core Slabs at Columns

You can see that in the structural model, hollow-core slabs and columns are overlapping. You should cut the slab to place them at columns.

1. Structural Plans → Roof Slab.
2. Zoom to area around column C1.
3. On Architecture tab → Opening panel → click By Face tool.
4. Select the hollow-core slab overlapping the column C1.
5. Draw panel click Rectangle tool.
6. Make a rectangle around the column.
7. Mode panel → click Finish ✓ .

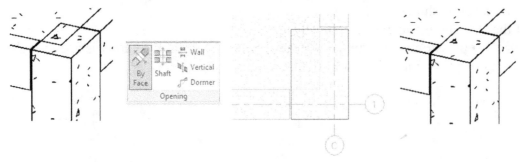

Fig. 15.6 – Cut Hollow-core Slabs at Columns

8. In the same way cut slabs overlapping other columns.

15.2.3 Fill the Gap

You can see that there is an empty space near grid 5. You will fill this space with a floor.

1. Structural Plans → Roof Slab.
2. Zoom to area around grid 5.
3. On Structure tab → Structure panel → click Floor tool.
4. In Properties palette, select

    *   Type = Insitu Concrete 100mm.
    *   Height Offset From Level = 0.000

5. On Draw panel, click on Pick Lines tool → Make a shape as shown in Fig. 15.7.

6. Mode panel → click Finish .

Fig. 15.7 – Floor Boundary

15.3 Waffle Slab

Waffle slab is a reinforced concrete slab on two-way pan joists. You will make:

*   solid head on columns.
*   floor along the beams.
*   Pan-Joist beam system.

Let Beam Spacing = BS

Width of Pan-joist beam = WP

To make middle of the waffle box on grids, make two direction lines for the beam system, one along a horizontal grid and other along vertical grid, each at distance of ½(BS) from the grids.

$$X = \frac{1}{2}(BS - WP)$$

All distances from axes = Y = X + n(BS)

In this project, you will keep beams spacing = BS = 0.6m and you will use pan-joist 150mm wide.

X = ½(0.6 − 0.15) = 0.225

Y = 0.225, 0.825, 1.425, 2.025 ...

15.3.1 Solid Head on Inner Columns

You will make a 400mm thick solid floor head on the columns to resist shear. Distance of floor edge from grids = 825mm.

1. Structural Plans → Roof.
2. Zoom to area around the column D7.
3. On Structure tab → Structure panel → click Floor tool.
4. In Properties palette, select

    *   Type = Insitu Concrete 400mm.
    *   Height Offset From Level = 0.000

5. On Draw panel, click on Pick Lines tool → Make a shape as shown in Fig. 15.8 (Pick lines → Offset = 0.825 → Click on grids D and 7 to make lines on both sides → Trim).

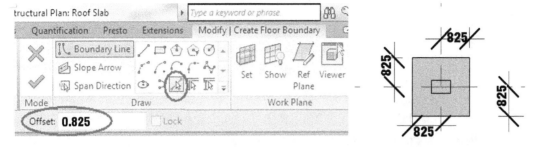

Fig. 15.8 – Solid Head on Inner Columns

6. Mode panel → click Finish ✓ .
7. Delete the span symbol.
8. Copy this floor to other inner column locations.

15.3.2 Solid Head on Outer Columns

You will make a 400mm thick solid floor head on the columns to resist shear.

Distance of floor edge from grids = 825mm.

1. Structural Plans → Roof Slab.
2. Zoom to area around the column A8.
3. On Structure tab → Structure panel → click Floor tool.
4. In Properties palette, select

    *   Type = Insitu Concrete 400mm.
    *   Height Offset From Level = 0.000

5. On Draw panel, click on Pick Lines tool → Make a shape as shown in Fig. 15.9 (Pick lines → Offset = 0.825 → Click on grids A and 8 → Offset = 0.0 → Click on outer sides of the column → Trim).

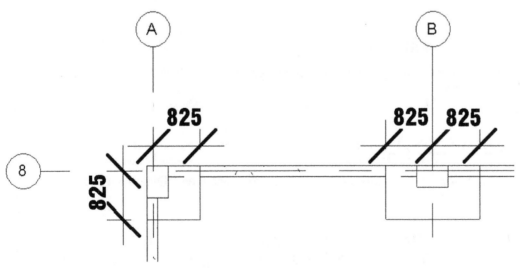

Fig. 15.9 – Solid Head on Outer Columns

6. Mode panel → click Finish ✓ .
7. Delete the span symbol.

8. Similarly make floor on column B8.
9. Copy this floor to other outer column locations.

15.3.3 Solid Floor Along the Beams

You will make a 400mm thick solid floor along the beams. Distance of floor edge from grids = 225mm.

1. Structural Plans → Roof Slab.
2. Zoom to area around the column A8.
3. Select the floor on the column A8.
4. On Modify | Floors contextual tab → Mode panel → click Edit Boundary.
5. On Draw panel, click on Pick Lines tool → Offset = 0.225 from grids.
6. Make a shape as shown in Fig. 15.10.

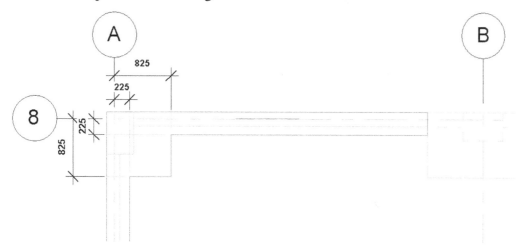

Fig. 15.10 – Solid Floor Along the Beams

7. Mode panel → click Finish .
8. Similarly make floor along other beams.

15.3.4 Solid Floor near Round Columns

You will make a 400mm thick solid floor head near the columns to resist shear.

1. Structural Plans → Roof Slab
2. Zoom to area around the column C5 and D6.
3. On Structure tab → Structure panel → click Floor tool.
4. In Properties palette, select
    *   Type = Insitu Concrete 400mm.
    *   Height Offset From Level = 0.000
5. On Draw panel, click on Pick Lines tool → Make a shape as shown in Fig. 15.11.
    *   Pick lines → Offset = 0.825 → Click on both sides of the grids
    *   Offset = 0.6 → Click on lines.
    *   Offset = 0.0 → Click on outer sides of the column
    *   Trim

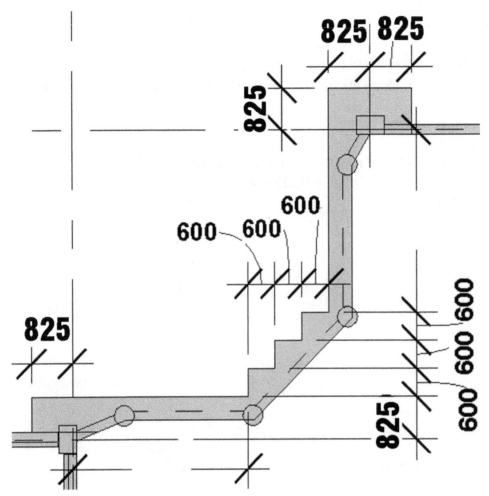

Fig. 15.11 – Solid Floor near Round Columns

6. Mode panel → click Finish ✓ .
7. Delete the span symbol.
8. The final shape of floor is as shown in Fig. 15.12.

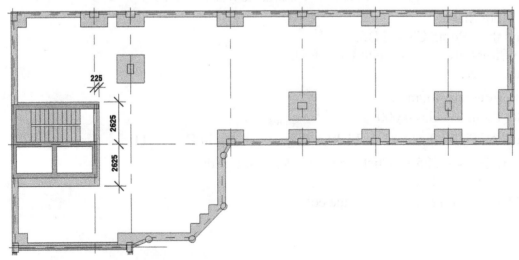

Fig. 15.12 – Final shape of floor

15.3.5 Two-way Pan Joist Beam System

You will make a Pan Joist beam system. Each beam is 150 x 400mm. The spacing between the beams is fixed distance = 0.60m. First you will make one-way beam system and align it with grids. Then you will copy it and paste it aligned to same place. After that, you will change beam direction of the pasted system. This will make a two-way beam system. (If you want to make ribbed slab, then just make one-way beam system).

1. Structural Plans → Roof Slab.
2. Zoom to area around between the grids A-H and 5-8.
3. On Structure tab → Model panel → click Model Line tool.
4. Draw two lines close to grid A and 8. Align them at distance 0.3m from the grids.
5. On Structure tab → Structure panel → click Beam System tool.
6. On Modify | Place Structural Beam System contextual tab → Beam System panel → Click Sketch Beam System.
7. Draw panel → Pick lines → Trim → Make the sketch as shown in Fig. 15.13.

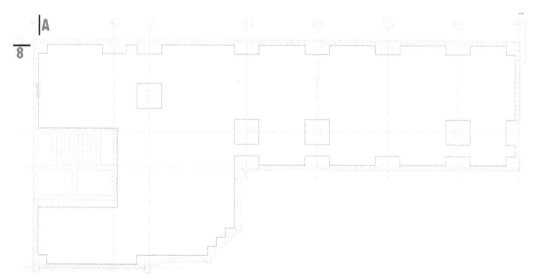

Fig. 15.13 – Pan Joist Beam System Boundary

8. In Properties palette, under Pattern group:
   - Layout Rule = Fixed Distance
   - Fixed Spacing = 0.60
   - Justification = Direction Line
   - Beam Type = M_Pan Joist: 150 x 400

9. On Modify | Create Beam System Boundary contextual tab → Draw panel → click Beam Direction then Line tool (Fig. 15.14).
10. Click on two ends of line 8.

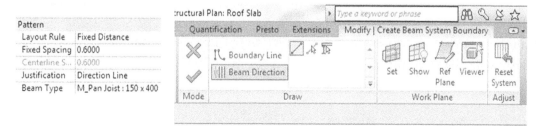

Fig. 15.14 – Set Beam direction

11. On Modify | Create Beam System Boundary contextual tab → Mode panel → click Finish ✓.
12. You see a beam system in one direction only (along line 8).
13. If you want to make ribbed slab, you will stop here.
14. To make waffle slab, select the beam system (Hover over the boundary until you see blue dotted lines on all the beams).
15. Clipboard panel → click on Copy to Clipboard → Paste dropdown → Aligned to Same Place. (You will see a message saying "There are identical instances at the same place ....". Close the message box).
16. Select the beam system (Hover over the boundary until you see blue dotted lines on all the beams One of the two instances will be selected).
17. On Modify | Structural Beam System contextual tab → Mode panel → click Edit Boundary.
18. Draw panel → click on Beam Direction.
19. Click on two ends of line A.
20. On Modify | Edit Boundary contextual tab → Mode panel → click Finish ✓.

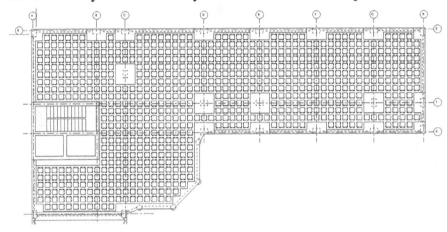

Fig. 15.15 – Two-way Pan Joist Beam System

15.3.6 Slab over the Beam System

You will make a 120mm slab over the beam system.

1. Structural Plans → Roof Slab.
2. Zoom to area around between the grids A-H and 5-8.
3. On Structure tab → Structure panel → click Floor tool.
4. In Properties palette, select
   • Type = Insitu Concrete 120mm.
   • Height Offset From Level = 0.000
5. On Draw panel, click on Pick Lines tool → Make a shape as shown in Fig. 15.13.
6. Mode panel → click Finish ✓.
7. Delete the span symbol.
8. In 3D view, different parts of floor are seen separately. You want to join the geometry.
9. On Modify tab → Geometry panel → click Join Geometry tool.
10. Join all floors.
11. Click 💾 to Save Project As **Str05**.

16 Presentation of Structural Design

Your structural Building Information Modeling (BIM) model is complete. You will print different views for presentation. Most of the views are already present in the model. But you may need to make some more views.

16.1 Sheet for the Foundation Level

You will make a sheet for Foundation level, showing information about isolated and wall foundations.

1. Open Project **Str05.**
2. Save Project As **Str06.**
3. Project Browser → Sheets → Right-click → New Sheet.
4. Load titleblock Arch A1.rfa.
5. From titleblocks, select Arch A1 → OK → Titleblock is added.
6. Select the Titleblock. In Properties palette, make:

   - Sheet Number = Str 101.
   - Sheet Name = Foundation Plan.

7. From Structural Plans node, drag the view Foundation on the sheet.
8. The sheet looks as shown in Fig. 16.1.

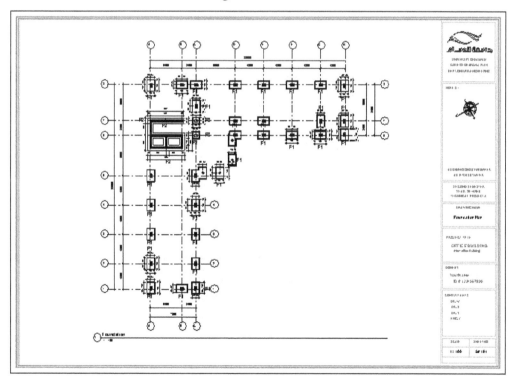

Fig. 16.1 – Sheet for Foundation Plan

16.2 Sheets for the Ground Floor Level

You will make sheets for Ground Floor level.

16.2.1 Ground Floor Columns-Axes Plan

You will make a view for Ground Floor Columns-Axes Plan and then make a sheet.

1. Structural Plans → 01 GF → Right-click → Duplicate View → Duplicate → Rename = 01 GF Columns-Axes.
2. Press VG → Model Graphics tab → Unselect:
    - Floors.
    - Structural Framing.
    - Stairs.
3. Press VG → Model Graphics tab → Clear overrides for columns and walls.
4. View Range → Edit (Fig. 16.2).

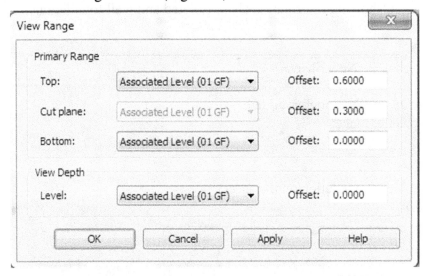

Fig. 16.2 – View Range for Ground Floor Plan

5. On View Control bar, set:
    - Detail Level = Coarse
    - Visual Style = Hidden Line
6. Add Column tags.
7. Add dimensions around columns and shear walls (Fig. 16.4).
8. Add a Structural Column Schedule and filter for Base Level = 01 GF (Fig. 16.3).

Structural Column Schedule 01 GF				
Type Mark	Family	Type	Length	Count
C1	M_Concrete-Rectangular-Column	400 x 600mm	4 m	29
C2	M_Concrete-Round-Column	450mm	4 m	4

Fig. 16.3 – Structural Column Schedule

9. Project Browser → Sheets → Right-click → New Sheet.
10. From titleblocks, select Arch A1 → OK → Titleblock is added.
11. Select the Titleblock. In Properties palette, make:
    - Sheet Number = Str 102.
    - Sheet Name = Ground Floor Columns-Axes Plan.
12. From Structural Plans node, drag the view 01 GF Columns-Axes on the sheet.
13. From Schedules node, drag the view Structural Column Schedule 01 GF on the sheet.

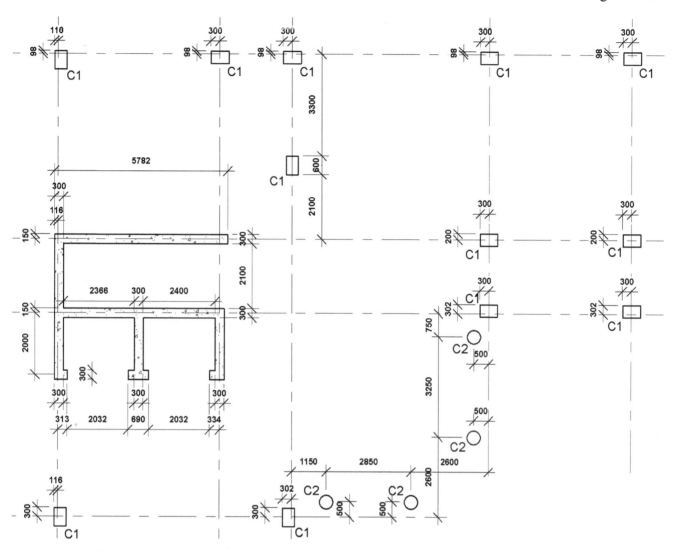

Fig. 16.4 – Dimensions for columns and shear walls

14. The sheet looks as shown in Fig. 16.5

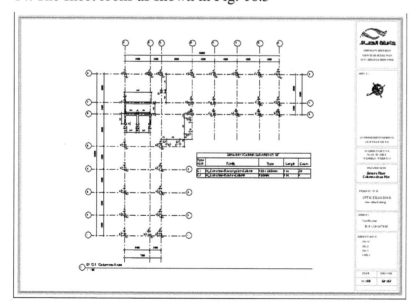

Fig. 16.5 – Sheet for Ground Floor Columns-Axes Plan

16.2.2 Ground Floor Framing Plan

You made a view for Ground Floor Framing Plan in § 13.2. Now you will make a sheet.

1. Structural Plans → 01 GF Framing.
2. Project Browser → Sheets → Right-click → New Sheet.
3. From titleblocks, select Arch A1 → OK → Titleblock is added.
4. Select the Titleblock. In Properties palette, make:
   - Sheet Number = Str 102.
   - Sheet Name = Ground Floor Framing Plan.
5. From Structural Plans node, drag the view 01 GF Framing on the sheet.
6. The sheet looks as shown in Fig. 16.6

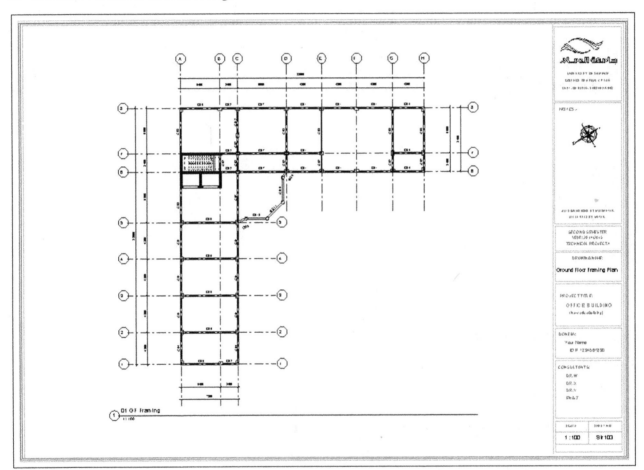

Fig. 16.5 – Sheet for Ground Floor Framing Plan

7. Similarly you can add sheets for other views of other levels.

8. Click ![save] to Save Project As **Str06**.

Part 3 . MEP

17 New MEP Project

You have completed the architectural design of your Revit project. Now you will start the MEP project with architectural model as linked model. You will make air-conditioning, electrical and plumbing systems. Each system consists of many sub-systems e.g., plumbing system consists of sanitary, cold water, hot water and vent systems.

17.1 Starting a New MEP Project

You will start your work with a project mep_project.rvt. You will download this file from the Download Folder (page v).

1. Open Revit → Projects → Open.
2. Select **mep_project.rvt** → Open
3. Save Project As **AC01.**
4. In the Project Browser, under Views node, you can see nodes for HVAC, Lighting, Plumbing and Power.
5. Same level can be seen in different views under different nodes depending on the view properties.
6. In Project Browser → Design → HVAC → Elevations → South - Mech → You see two levels viz., Level 1 and Level 2.
7. In Project Browser → Design → Level 1 floor plan is present as:

   - HVAC → Floor Plans → 1 - Mech.
   - Lighting → Floor Plans → 1 - Lighting.
   - Plumbing → Floor Plans → 1 - Plumbing.
   - Power → Floor Plans → 1 - Power.

8. Each view has different Discipline, Sub-Discipline and visibility properties.

17.2 Link with Architectural Project

You will link your MEP project with the architectural project you finished before.

1. In Project Browser → Mechanical → HVAC → Floor Plans → 1 - Mech.
2. On Insert tab → Link panel → click Link Revit tool.
3. Browse to Arch05.rvt (You saved this project at the end of chapter 5. You can take any project you saved at the end of chapter 5 to Chapter 10. If you didn't save it, then download it from the Download Folder (page v). **Keep this file in same folder where you saved AC01**). (Fig. 17.1).

File name:	Arch05.rvt
Files of type:	RVT Files (*.rvt)
Positioning:	Auto - Center to Center

Fig. 17.1 – Link with Architectural Project

4. Click on Open. The architectural project is inserted.
5. Select Linked Model → Edit Type → Room Bounding = ☑ (Fig. 17.2).

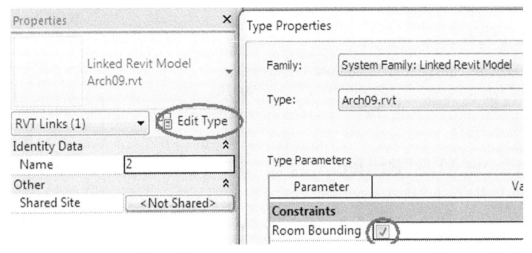

Fig. 17.2 – Room Bounding

6. On Manage tab → Settings panel → click Project Information
7. Enter all the information. (You will make Energy Settings later) (Fig. 17.3).

Parameter	Value
Identity Data	⌃
Organization Name	My Organization
Organization Description	Building Material Traders
Building Name	Sales Office
Author	My Name
Energy Analysis	⌃
Energy Settings	Edit...
Other	⌃
Project Issue Date	01/01/2015
Project Status	Under Construction
Client Name	My Client
Project Address	Edit...
Project Name	My Project
Project Number	PRJ - 123

Fig. 17.3 – Project Information

8. Architecture → Room and Area (Fig. 17.4).
9. Area and Volume Computations
10. Select ⊙Area and Volume ⊙At Wall Finish

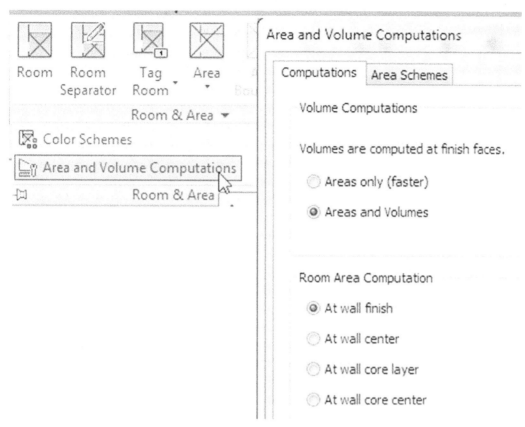

Fig. 17.4 – Area and Volume Computations

17.3 View Settings

In a view, you may want to hide elements disturbing the view and unhide elements needed for the view. This is done through the Visibility/Graphics dialog box.

17.3.1 View Settings for view 1 - Mech

1. In Project Browser → Mechanical → HVAC → Floor Plans → 1 – Mech.
2. Press VG → Model Graphics tab → Unselect:
   - Generic Models.
   - Plumbing Fixtures.
3. Press VG → Model Graphics tab → Expand Spaces → Select All (Fig. 17.5).

Visibility	Projection/Surface		
	Lines	Patterns	Transparency
☑ Spaces			
☑ Color Fill			
☑ Interior			
☑ Reference			

Fig. 17.5 – Space visibility

4. Press VG → Revit Links tab → By Host View (Fig. 17.6).
5. Basic tab → Custom radiobutton.
6. Model Categories tab → Model Categories = <Custom> → Unselect:

- Furniture.
- Furniture System.

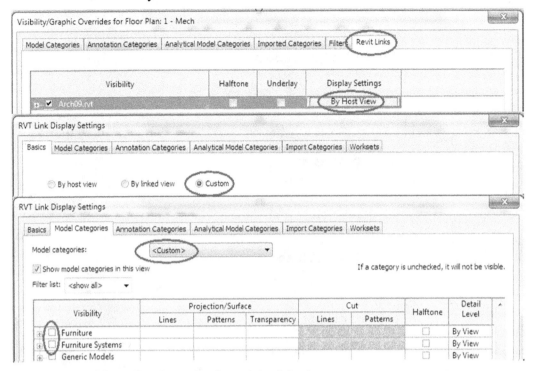

Fig. 17.6 – View Settings for Level 1 - Mech

17.3.2 View Settings for view 2 - Mech

These view settings in § 17.3.1 are for the view 1 - Mech. If you want to make the same view settings for the view 2 - Mech also, then you will repeat the step in § 17.3.1. Another way is that you make a view template from 1 - Mech and apply it to 2 - Mech.

1. In Project Browser → Mechanical → HVAC → Floor Plans → 1 – Mech.
2. On View tab → Graphics panel → View Templates dropdown → click Create Template from Current View (Fig. 17.7).
3. Name = AC Floor Plan → OK.

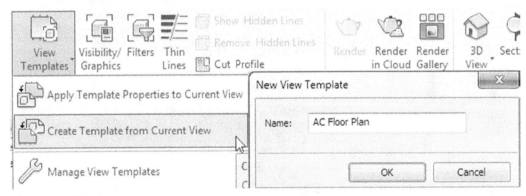

Fig. 17.7 – New View Template

4. In Project Browser → Mechanical → HVAC → Floor Plans → 2 – Mech.
5. On View tab → Graphics panel → View Templates dropdown → click Apply Template Properties to Current View.
6. Select AC Floor Plan → OK.

17.4 Add Levels and Adjust View Properties

You will add one more level for Roof. Also you will add Plenum levels for Level 1 and Level 2. Corresponding views will be added. You will adjust properties of different views.

1. In Project Browser → Mechanical → HVAC → Elevations → South - Mech.
2. Level 1 corresponds to 01 GF. Select Level 12. In Properties palette, set Elevation = 0.
3. Level 2 corresponds to 02 FF. Select Level 2. In Properties palette, set Elevation = 4000.
4. On Architecture tab → Datum panel → click Level tool.
5. On Option Bar:
6. Select ☑ Make Plan View (Fig. 17.8).
7. Click Plan View Types and select Floor Plan and Ceiling Plan.
8. On Draw panel, select Pick Lines and on Option Bar, set Offset = 4000.

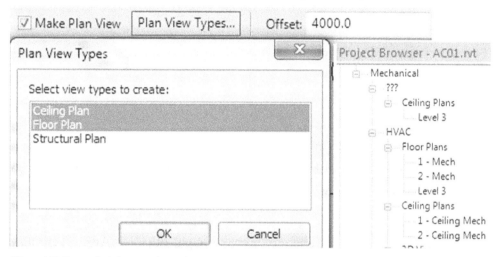

Fig. 17.8 – Add new level

9. In Properties palette, select type = 8mm Head
10. Hover over Level 2. When see a dashed blue level line above, click.
11. A level at elevation 8000 will be added. Rename this level to 3 - Mech.
12. In Project Browser, under Mechanical node, you will see ??? node.
13. In Mechanical → ??? → Ceiling Plans → Select 3 - Mech → Change properties as shown in Fig. 17.9.

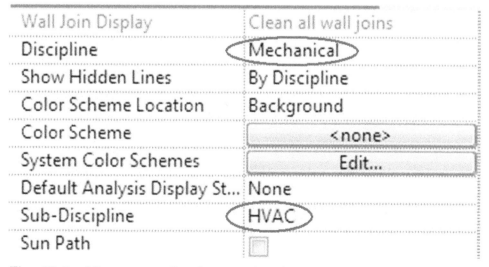

Fig. 17.9 – View properties for new level

14. In Project Browser, the 3 - Mech views move from ??? node to HVAC node.

17.5 Add Plenum Levels

You will add two plenum levels above Level 1 and Level 2. Plenum levels are placed at ceiling elevation. AC Terminals (diffusers) and lighting fixtures are placed on plenum level. AC ducts, VAV units, water pipes, electrical wires are placed in the plenum space (space between plenum level and the slab above).

In your architectural model, you have placed ceiling at elevation = 2.7m above the level. Now you will place plenum level at 2700mm above the level.

1. In Project Browser → Mechanical → HVAC → Elevations → South - Mech.
2. On Architecture tab → Datum panel → click Level tool.
3. On Option Bar:
    - Select ☑ Make Plan View.
    - Click Plan View Types and select Floor Plan only.
    - Set Offset = 2700.
4. On Draw panel, select Pick Lines.
5. In Type selector, select type = Plenum.
6. Hover over Level 1. When see a level line above, click.
7. Hover over Level 2. When see a level line above, click.
8. A level at elevation 2700mm will be added. Rename this level to 1 - Mech Plenum. In Properties palette, set Computation Height = 150.
9. A level at elevation 6700mm will be added. Rename this level to 2 - Mech Plenum. In Properties palette, set Computation Height = 150.
10. In Mechanical → HVAC → Floor Plans → Select a Plenum view → Right-click → Apply Template Properties ... → Select AC Floor Plan → OK.
11. In Mechanical → HVAC → Floor Plans → Select a Plenum view → Change Sub- Discipline = Plenum.
12. In Project Browser, the Plenum views move from HVAC to Plenum.

13. Click  to Save Project As **AC01**.

18 Spaces and Zones

Spaces contain information about the location where you will place them. This information will be used to calculate heating and cooling loads, lighting requirements etc. This calculation will be used to place diffusers, lighting fixtures etc.

A zone consists of a group of spaces with similar Construction properties. The spaces in a zone can be adjacent or non-adjacent, even on different levels.

18.1 Place Spaces

You will add spaces in different areas of the building

18.1.1 Spaces on Level 1 - Mech

You can place spaces automatically. Spaces will be created within the elements whose room-bounding property is True (Selected).

1. Open Project **AC01**.
2. Save Project As **AC02.**
3. In Project Browser → Mechanical → HVAC → Floor Plans → 1 – Mech
4. On Analyze tab → Spaces & Zones panel → Click Space tool
5. Tag panel → Tag on Placement = Blue (Fig. 18.1).
6. On Option Bar:

    - Upper Limit = 1 - Mech Plenum
    - Offset = 0
    - Horizontal
    - Unselect Leader
    - Space = New

7. Spaces panel → Click Place Spaces Automatically.
8. You will see a Messagebox showing the number of spaces created. You will also see the newly created spaces.

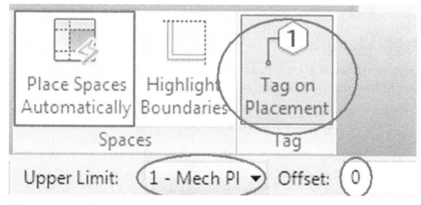

Fig. 18.1 – Creating Spaces

18.1.2 Spaces on Level 2 - Mech

For level 2 - Mech, you will repeat the steps in § 17.6.1. The only difference is that on Option Bar, you will select Upper Limit = 2 - Mech Plenum.

18.1.3 Spaces on Level 1 - Mech Plenum

1. In Project Browser → Mechanical → MEP Plenum → Floor Plans → 1 – Mech Plenum.
2. In Properties palette → Extents group → View Range → Edit → Set as shown in Fig. 18.2. Make sure that Computation Height for 1 – Mech Plenum is 150mm (Step 8-9 in § 17.5).

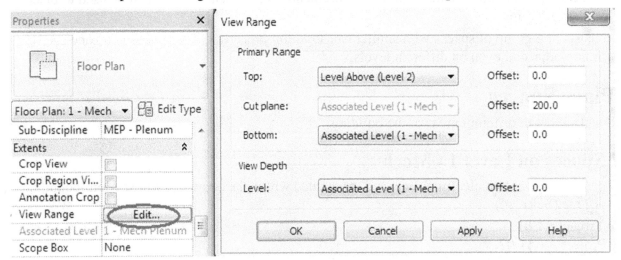

Fig. 18.2 – View Range for Plenum Levels

3. On Analyze tab → Spaces & Zones panel → Click Space tool
4. Tag panel → Tag on Placement = Blue
5. On Option Bar:
   - Upper Limit = Level 2
   - Offset = 0
   - Horizontal
   - Unselect Leader
   - Space = New
6. Spaces panel → Click Place Spaces Automatically.
7. 5 spaces will be placed, 1 in stair area, 1 in elevator area, 2 in shaft areas and 1 in remaining large area.

18.1.4 Spaces on Level 2 - Mech Plenum

For level 2 - Mech Plenum, you will repeat the steps in § 17.6.3. The only difference is that on Option Bar, you will select Upper Limit = 3 - Mech. 5 spaces will be placed.

18.2 Space Naming

The spaces you added have been assigned a name = Space and a number. But in architectural model, you have assigned names and numbers to the rooms. The room names and numbers can be transferred to spaces using a utility from Autodesk® called Autodesk Revit Space Naming Utility (SNU). Download and install it.

1. On Add-Ins tab → Space Naming Utility panel → Click Launch SNU (Fig. 18.3).
2. A dialog box appears. Select as shown in the Fig. 18.3. OK.

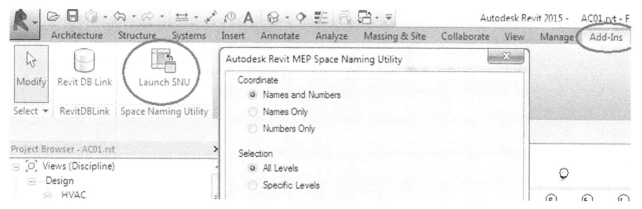

Fig. 18.3 – Using Space Naming Utility

3. Names and numbers of all rooms at all levels are transferred to the spaces.
4. You will notice that large spaces in plenum area have same name and number because there is no corresponding room in the architectural model. Also Shaft 105 (and some other names and numbers) have been assigned to 2 spaces, first to the space on the respective level and second to the space in plenum area.

18.3 Modify Spaces

Some spaces need modification.

18.3.1 Space in Shaft Area

With automatic space placement, a shaft area is divided in four spaces. Actually there should be only one long vertical space here. You will delete three spaces and modify the properties of one remaining space. A space must be deleted in **System Browser only**.

1. In Project Browser → Mechanical → HVAC → Floor Plans → 1 – Mech.
2. Draw section passing through Shaft 105 and double-click section head to see the section view.
3. VG → Model Graphics tab → Expand Spaces → Select all three.
4. Press F9 to see the System Browser. View = Zones.
5. Select Shaft-2 105-2. It will be highlighted in the System Browser. Right-click on the highlighted space **in the System Browser** and click Delete (Fig. 18.4).
6. *Note: Do not delete a space in a view otherwise it will remain in the System Browser as an unassigned space.*

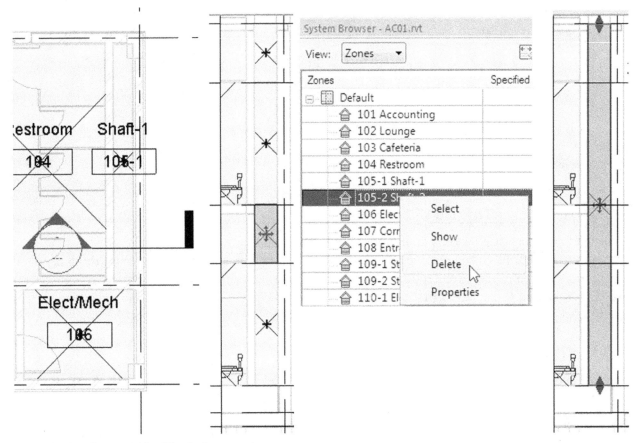

Fig. 18.4 – Spaces in Shaft Area

7. Similarly delete Shaft-1 207-1 and Shaft-2 207-2.
8. Select Shaft-1 105-1.
9. In Properties palette, change Upper Limit = 3 - Mech.
10. In HVAC floor plan view 1 - Mech, change name = Shaft, number = 105.
11. Do the same for Shaft 114.

18.3.2 Space in Stairs and Elevator Area

There is no ceiling in the Elevator and Stair area. Extra spaces in plenum levels need to be deleted.

1. In Project Browser → Mechanical → HVAC → Floor Plans → 1 – Mech.
2. Draw section passing through Stairs 109 and Elevator 110. Double-click section head to see the section view.
3. VG → Model Graphics tab → Expand Spaces → check all three.
4. Delete spaces Stairs-2 109-2, Elevator-2 110-2, Stairs-2 211-2, Elevator-2 212-2 (Fig. 18.5).
5. Select Stairs-1 109-1.
6. In Properties palette, change Upper Limit = Level 2.
7. In HVAC floor plan view 1 - Mech, change name = Stairs, number = 109.

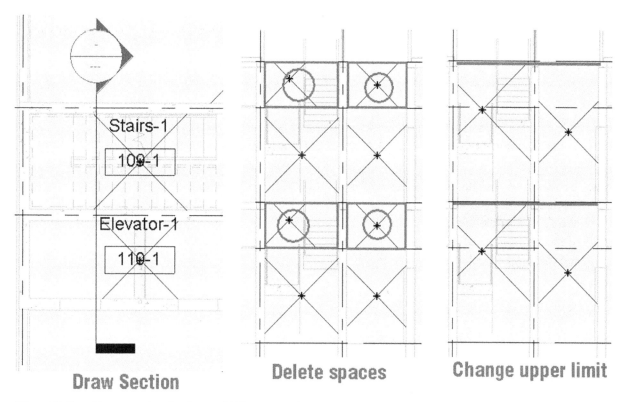

Draw Section   **Delete spaces**   **Change upper limit**

Fig. 18.5 – Spaces in Stair and Elevator Area

8. Do the same for Elevator-1 110-1, Stairs-1 211-1, Elevator-1 212-1

18.3.3 Space in Elect/Mech Area

There is no ceiling in the Elect/Mech area. The spaces in plenum levels need to separated and deleted.

1. In Project Browser → Mechanical → MEP Plenum → Floor Plans → 1 – Mech Plenum.
2. Zoom to area above Elect/Mech 106.
3. On Analyze tab → Spaces & Zones panel → Click Space Separator tool (Fig. 18.6).
4. Draw 2 space separators as shown in Fig. Volume above Elect/Mech 106 will be empty.

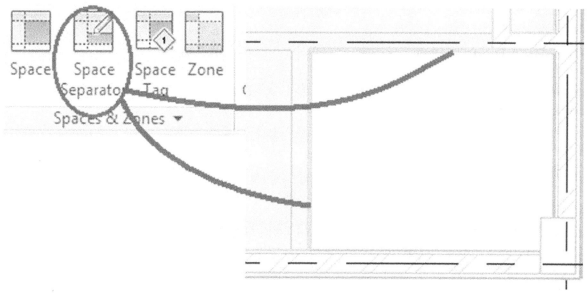

Fig. 18.6 – Spaces in Elect/Mech Area

5. In Project Browser → Mechanical → HVAC → Floor Plans → 1 – Mech.
6. Select Elect/Mech 106.
7. In Properties palette, change Upper Limit = Level 2.
8. Do the same for Elect/Mech 113, Elect/Mech 208, Elect/Mech 217.

18.3.4 Space in Entrance/Lobby Area

You will divide the space in Entrance/Lobby area in to two parts so that each part could be include in a different zone.

1. In Project Browser → Mechanical → HVAC → Floor Plans → 1 – Mech.
2. Zoom to Entrance 108.
3. Draw a space separator as shown in Fig. 18.7.
4. On Analyze tab → Spaces & Zones panel → Click Space tool.
5. Place a space manually as shown in Fig. 18.7.

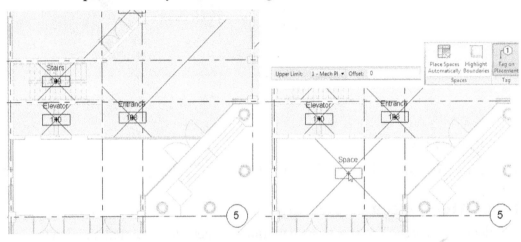

Fig. 18.7 – Spaces in Entrance/Lobby Area

6. Change name = Entrance, number = 108B.
7. For the other space named Entrance, change number = 108A.
8. Do the same for Lobby 210.

18.3.5 Spaces in Plenum Area

Rename and renumber the spaces in plenum areas manually because the names and numbers of these areas were not present in the architectural model.

1. In Project Browser → Mechanical → MEP Plenum → Floor Plans → 1 – Mech Plenum.
2. Select the large space.
3. Change name = Plenum 1, number = 115.
4. Select the large space in 2 – Mech Plenum.
5. Change name = Plenum 2, number = 219.

18.4 Zones

A zone consists of a collection of spaces. You can control the spatial environment of a zone. Through zoning, you can perform heating and cooling load analysis of the building more accurately.

When you place spaces in the building, they are automatically included in a zone named Default (as shown in the System Browser). Later on, when you create new zones and add spaces, they are removed from the Default zone.

18.4.1 Zones Consisting of Spaces on the Same Level

To add spaces on same level to a new zone, you will open the floor plan view of that level so that you can select the spaces.

1. In Project Browser → Mechanical → HVAC → Floor Plans → 1 – Mech.
2. On Analyze tab → Spaces & Zones panel → Click Zone tool.
3. In Mode panel, Add Space tool is selected (Fig. 18.8).
4. Click on spaces 101, 102, 103, 104, 106, 107, 108A, 109 to add.
5. In Properties palette, change Name = GF North.
6. Edit Zone panel → Click Finish Editing Zone.

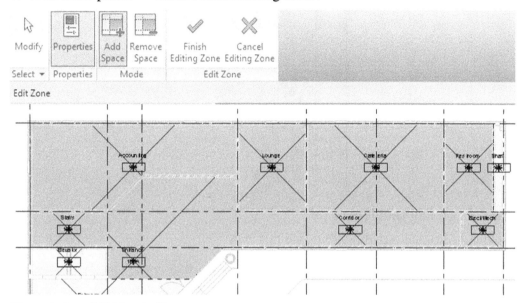

Fig. 18.8 – GF North Zone

7. In the System Browser, all spaces selected in step 4 are transferred from Default to GF North zone.
8. Similarly make a zone GF South consisting of spaces 108B, 111, 112, 113.
9. Similarly make a zone FF North consisting of spaces 201, 202, 203, 204, 205, 206, 208, 209, 210A, 211.
10. Similarly make a zone FF South consisting of spaces 210B, 213, 214, 215, 216, 217, 218.

18.4.2 Zones Consisting of Multiple Level Spaces

To add spaces on different levels to a new zone, you will open the floor plan views of all the levels containing required spaces so that you can select the spaces from different views.

1. In Project Browser → Mechanical → HVAC → Floor Plans → 1 – Mech.

2. On Quick Access Toolbar, click on Close Hidden Windows .
3. In Project Browser → Mechanical → HVAC → Floor Plans → 2 – Mech.
4. Press WT (Windows Tile). Floor plans 1 – Mech and 2 – Mech are shown side by side (Fig. 18.9).
5. On Analyze tab → Spaces & Zones panel → Click Zone tool.
6. In Mode panel, Add Space tool is selected.
7. From floor plan 1 – Mech, click on spaces 105, 110, 114.
8. From floor plan 2 – Mech, click on space 212.
9. In Properties palette, change Name = Shafts.
10. Edit Zone panel → Click Finish Editing Zone.

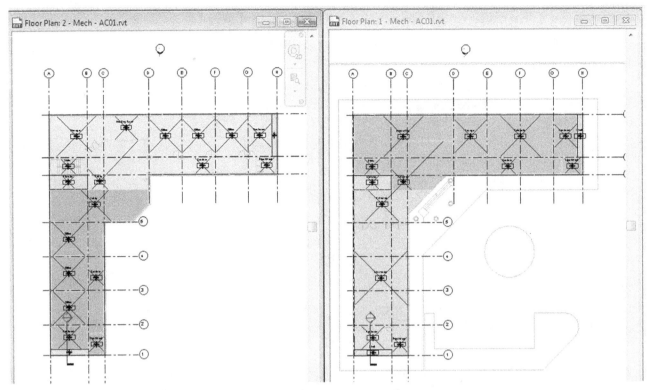

Fig. 18.9 – Zone with Spaces on different levels

11. Similarly make a zone Plenum Area consisting of spaces 115, 219.
12. No space is left in Default zone.

18.5 Space Schedule

To perform heating and cooling load analysis, you need to set properties of spaces. This can be done through a space schedule.

18.5.1 Add Fields

You will make a space schedule and select required fields from available fields.

1. On View tab → Create panel → Schedules dropdown → click Schedule/Quantities
2. From Categories select Spaces. Name = Space Schedule
3. On Fields tab, add Number, Name, Space Type, Occupiable, Number of People, Area, Construction Type, Condition Type, Zone to Scheduled Fields in the same order as listed. (To adjust the order, click Move Up or Move Down buttons) (Fig. 18.10).
4. On Sorting/Grouping tab, Sort by Number (⦿ Ascending) (☑ Itemize every instance).
5. Click OK to see the space schedule.

18.5.2 Space and Condition Type

You will make settings for space and condition type according to the room or space usage.

1. In the Space Schedule, in the row for space number 101, space type is <Building>. Click on 🔲 in this cell. In Space Type Settings dialog box, select Office - Enclosed. (Fig. 18.11) You will see Parameters for Energy Analysis. Some default values are written. You can change any value e.g. value for Parameter Occupancy Schedule is given as Common Office Occupancy - 8 AM to 5 PM.
2. If you click on this value, you will see Schedule Settings. You can make a new schedule, modify, duplicate or rename a schedule or even delete a schedule.

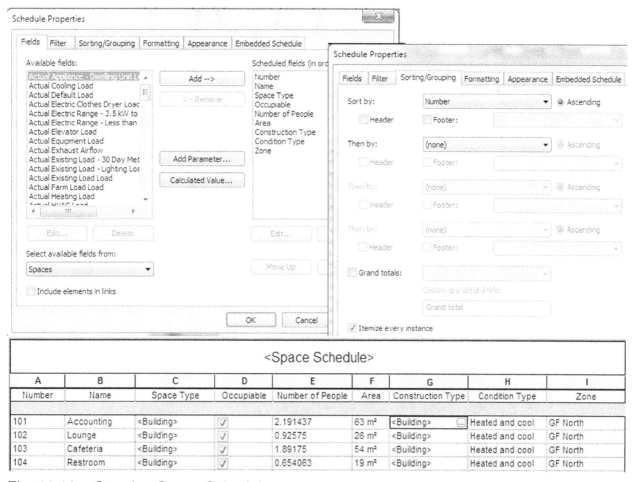

Fig. 18.10 – Creating Space Schedule

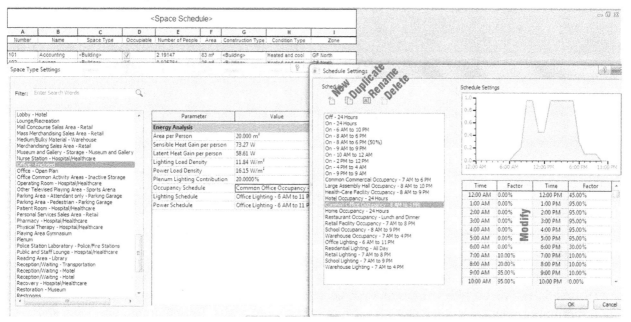

Fig. 18.11 – Creating Spaces

3. In the same way you can edit other values.
4. For Condition Type, you can select:
   - Heated.

- Cooled.
- Heated and cooled.
- Unconditioned.
- Vented.
- Naturally vented only.

5. You will select a Space Type and Condition Type for each space as shown in Fig. 18.12.

				<Space Schedule>				
A	B	C	D	E	F	G	H	I
Number	Name	Space Type	Occupiable	Number of People	Area	Construction Typ	Condition Type	Zone
101	Accounting	Office - Enclosed	☑	3.130624	63 m²	<Building>	Heated and cooled	GF North
102	Lounge	Lounge/Recreation	☑	6.6125	26 m²	<Building>	Heated and cooled	GF North
103	Cafeteria	Dining Area	☑	37.823653	54 m²	<Building>	Heated and cooled	GF North
104	Restroom	Restrooms	☑	1.86875	19 m²	<Building>	Vented	GF North
105	Shaft	Plenum	No	0	3 m²	<Building>	Unconditioned	Shafts
106	Elect/Mech	Electrical/Mechanical	☐	0.177377	6 m²	<Building>	Cooled	GF North
107	Corridor	Corridor/Transition	☑	3.3325	33 m²	<Building>	Heated and cooled	GF North
108A	Entrance	Lobby - Hotel	☑	16.021236	53 m²	<Building>	Heated and cooled	GF North
108B	Entrance	Lobby - Hotel	☑	11.815654	39 m²	<Building>	Heated and cooled	GF South
109	Stairs	Stairway	☑	1.127245	11 m²	<Building>	Heated and cooled	GF North
110	Elevator	Elevator Lobbies	☑	0.89565	9 m²	<Building>	Naturally vented only	Shafts
111	Showroom	Merchandising Sales	☑	16.346273	109 m²	<Building>	Heated and cooled	GF South
112	Restroom	Restrooms	☑	1.671475	17 m²	<Building>	Vented	GF South
113	Elect/Mech	Electrical/Mechanical	☐	0.177377	6 m²	<Building>	Cooled	GF South
114	Shaft	Plenum	No	0	3 m²	<Building>	Unconditioned	Shafts
115	Plenum 1	Plenum	No	0	426 m²	<Building>	Unconditioned	Plenum Area
201	Manager	Office - Enclosed	☑	2.041831	41 m²	<Building>	Heated and cooled	FF North
202	Meeting Room	Conference Meeting/	☑	10.8875	22 m²	<Building>	Heated and cooled	FF North
203	Office	Office - Enclosed	☑	1.3225	26 m²	<Building>	Heated and cooled	FF North
204	Office	Office - Enclosed	☑	1.3225	26 m²	<Building>	Heated and cooled	FF North
205	Office	Office - Enclosed	☑	1.3225	26 m²	<Building>	Heated and cooled	FF North
206	Restroom	Restrooms	☑	1.86875	19 m²	<Building>	Vented	FF North
208	Elect/Mech	Electrical/Mechanical	☐	0.177377	6 m²	<Building>	Cooled	FF North
209	Corridor	Corridor/Transition	☑	3.3325	33 m²	<Building>	Heated and cooled	FF North
210A	Lobby	Lobby - Hotel	☑	17.290836	58 m²	<Building>	Heated and cooled	FF North
210B	Lobby	Lobby - Hotel	☑	17.676095	59 m²	<Building>	Heated and cooled	FF South
211	Stairs	Stairway	☑	1.127245	11 m²	<Building>	Heated and cooled	FF North
212	Elevator	Elevator Lobbies	☑	0.89565	9 m²	<Building>	Naturally vented only	Shafts
213	Office	Office - Enclosed	☑	1.18289	24 m²	<Building>	Heated and cooled	FF South
214	Office	Office - Enclosed	☑	1.18289	24 m²	<Building>	Heated and cooled	FF South
215	Office	Office - Enclosed	☑	1.18289	24 m²	<Building>	Heated and cooled	FF South
216	Corridor	Corridor/Transition	☑	3.3325	33 m²	<Building>	Heated and cooled	FF South
217	Elect/Mech	Electrical/Mechanical	☐	0.177377	6 m²	<Building>	Cooled	FF South
218	Restroom	Restrooms	☑	1.671475	17 m²	<Building>	Vented	FF South
219	Plenum 2	Plenum	No	0	450 m²	<Building>	Unconditioned	Plenum Area

Fig. 18.12 – Space Type and Condition Type

18.5.3 Construction Type

You will make settings for construction type according to the types of constructions used in different parts of the model. The default Construction Type selected in the Space Schedule is <Building>. This means that thermal properties of the materials used in structure of walls, floors, doors, windows and other components of the building used in the architectural model will be used for energy analysis.

But sometimes you want to use a type of construction different from the one used in the architectural model. For instance, you want to make energy analysis of the building using different types of materials available in the market and then select the best materials. In this case, you can override default construction and use construction with materials of different type of thermal properties selected from a dropdown list.

1. In the Space Schedule, in the row for space number 101, construction type is <Building>. Click on ⊡ in this cell. In Construction Types dialog box, you will see <Building> and Construction1 (Fig. 18.13).
2. Select Construction1 (or make a new Construction Type and rename it).
3. Keep Override True ☑.
4. For each Category, select appropriate Analytic Construction.
5. You can also enter a shading factor for the exterior windows.
6. Click OK to save the settings.
7. You can make more than one construction types to be used for different spaces.
8. Assign a construction type to each space.

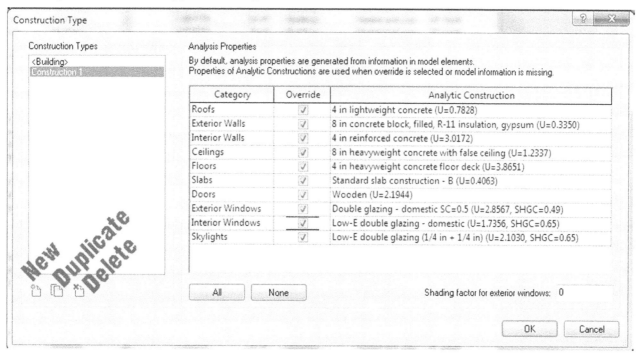

Fig. 18.13 – Construction Type

18.6 Energy Analysis Properties of HVAC Zones

All spaces with similar energy analysis properties are grouped in an HVAC zone. These properties control and affect all the spaces in a zone. You can adjust their values before performing the energy analysis.

1. Select a zone in Project Browser.
2. In the Properties palette, under Energy Analysis group, you will see properties shown in Fig. 18.14.

Fig. 18.14 – Zone Properties

3. For Service Type, you can select the air-conditioning system you will use for your building.
4. For Coil Bypass, you can enter a Coil Bypass factor given by the manufacturer of the system you selected in Service Type.
5. For Cooling Information, set the Cooling Set Point, Cooling Air Temperature and Dehumidification Set Point.

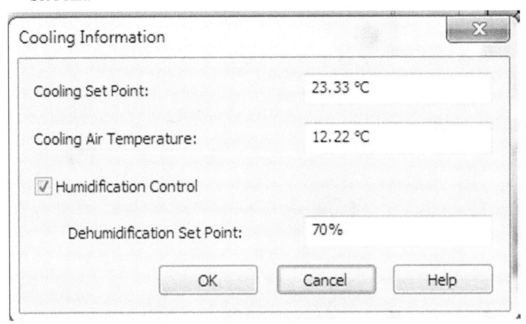

Fig. 18.16 – Zone Cooling Information

6. For Cooling Information, set the Cooling Set Point, Cooling Air Temperature and Dehumidification Set Point.

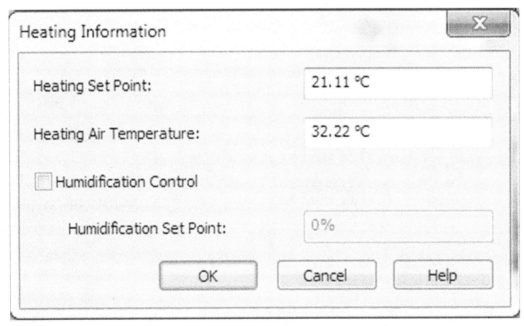

Fig. 18.17 – Zone Heating Information

7. For Outdoor Air Information, set the Outdoor Air per Person, Outdoor Air per Area and Air Changes per Hour.

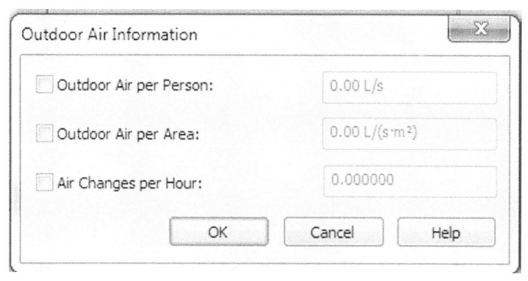

Fig. 18.18 – Zone Outdoor Air Information

8. In the same way, you can set energy analysis properties of all zones.

9. Click to Save Project As **AC02**.

19 Air Terminal Layout

Air terminals are placed on the reflected ceiling plan. But before you place the air terminals, you have to perform energy analysis

The calculation of heating and cooling load of the building depends on the external weather conditions, thermal properties of the walls, floors and other building components through which heat energy flows and other energy settings.

19.1 Energy Settings

You can make energy settings through the Energy Settings dialog box.

1. Open Project **AC02**. (You can get AC02 and Arch05 from Download Folder (page v). Keep both files in the same folder).
2. Save Project As **AC03**.
3. On Manage tab → Settings panel → click Project Information.
4. Energy Settings → Edit.
5. The Energy Settings dialog box opens.

19.1.1 Building Type

In Building Type dropdown, you have many choices to select. Building Type determines at what times of the day air-conditioning, lighting and other services will be used in the building. For example most of the services are used for 24 hours per day in a hospital but same services are used from 8 AM to 7 PM in an office.

You can override Building Type settings as explained in § 18.5.2.

You select Building Type = Office.

19.1.2 Location

External weather conditions depend on the location of the building on earth. When you set the location, hourly weather data from the nearest weather station will be used to perform energy analysis.

1. Click on ⬚ in Value column of Location parameter (Fig. 19.1).
2. On Location tab, you can set the location in two ways:
   - Select from Default City List.
   - Internet Mapping Service.

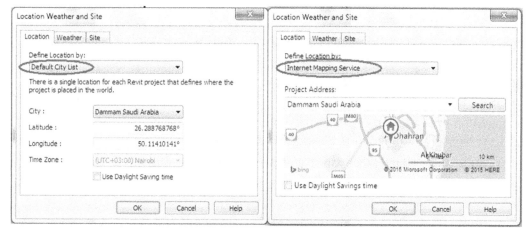

Fig. 19.1 – Set Project Location

3. On Weather tab (Fig. 19.2), you can select ☑ to use the Dry Bulb, Wet Bulb and Mean Daily Range of temperature from the nearest weather station. Otherwise you can enter the values manually.
4. You will set a value for Heating Design Temperature.
5. You will write a Clearness Number for the location. According to the 2007 ASHRAE Handbook - HVAC Applications, Section 33.4, clearness is specified as:

- Clear and Dry - greater than 1.2
- Average - 1.0
- Hazy, humid - less than 0.8

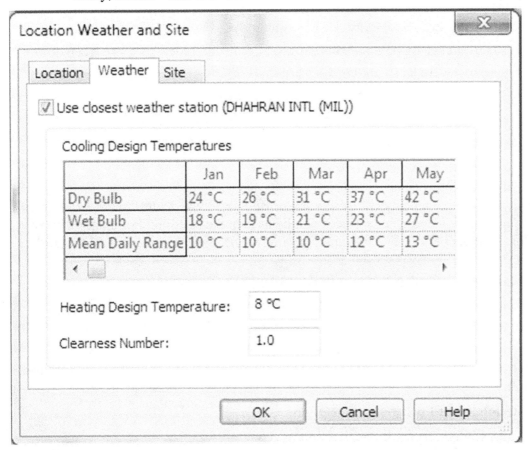

Fig. 19.2 – Location Weather

19.1.3 Sliver Space Tolerance

A sliver space is like a gap between two parallel walls e.g. a narrow shaft where you have not created a room.

When performing energy analysis, a wall is considered as interior if there is a room (or space) on both sides and exterior if there is a room (or space) on one side.

If a wall has a room (or space) on one side and a sliver space on the other side such that the width of the sliver space is less than Sliver Space Tolerance, it is considered as interior.

In this way, you will get accurate energy analysis even if you don't place a room in sliver spaces.

You select Sliver Space Tolerance = 300

19.1.4 Building Infiltration Class

Outdoor air may infiltrate into the building through windows, doors or other leaks.

1. You will select a value from the Building Infiltration Class dropdown with following choices.

    - Loose: 0.386 liter/m^2 s of outside air.
    - Medium: 0.193 liter/m^2 s of outside air.
    - Tight: 0.097 liter/m^2 s of outside air.
    - None: Air infiltration is excluded from energy analysis.

2. On Manage tab → Settings panel → click Project Information.
3. Energy Settings → Edit.
4. Building Infiltration Class = Medium (Fig. 19.3).

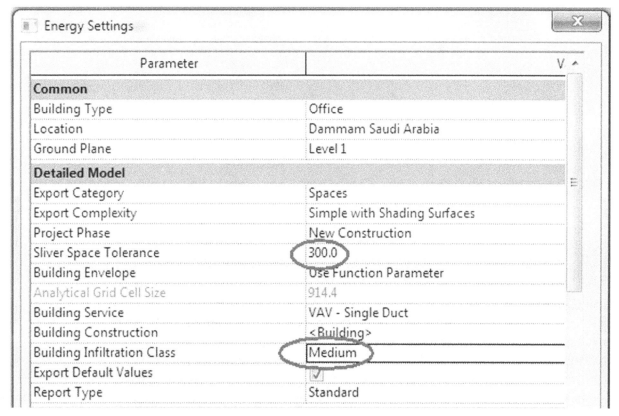

Fig. 19.3 – Energy Settings

19.2 Heating and Cooling Load Calculations

Now you are ready to make Heating and Cooling Load Calculations.

1. On Analyze tab → Reports & Schedules panel → click Heating and Cooling Loads.
2. You will see the Heating and Cooling Loads dialog box (Fig. 19.4).
3. On General tab, you will see the energy setting you made before.
4. On Detail tab, with Spaces selected, you will see a treeview with zones as nodes.
5. If you expand a zone node, you will see a list of all the spaces in that zone.
6. If you select any node of the treeview, its information is displayed below. You can modify this information. Also you can highlight or isolate the view of that node in the 3D view on left side.

7. There is a symbol to the left of each space name. ⌂ means Occupiable space, ⌂ means Unoccupiable space, ⌂ means Plenum space

8. ⚠ indicates a warning. Select the space and click on Show Related Warning button to see the warning. If this warning cannot be ignored then fix the problem. (For Shafts 105 and 114, ignore warning).

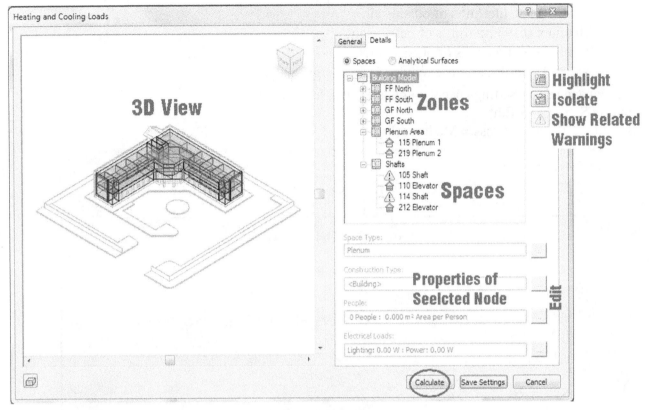

Fig. 19.4 – Heating and Cooling Load Calculations

9. Click on Calculate.
10. Loads Report (1) will appear. (It is present in Project Browser → Reports → Loads Reports node).
11. It shows Project Summary, Building Summary, Zone Summary, Space Summary.
12. In Building Summary, you can find the Peak Cooling and Heating Loads in watts.
13. You can change building orientation (by changing angle for True North), change building construction, change shading factor for exterior windows etc. and run the calculation many times to compare the Peak Cooling and Heating Loads for different building parameters.

19.3 Selecting Air Terminals

The ceiling you used in the architectural model is 600 x 600mm therefore you select air terminals of same size. When air flows through the terminals, it produces noise. This noise should be less than the recommended Noise Criteria (NC). For an office building, the recommended Noise Criteria (NC) values (taken from 2011 ASHRAE Handbook—HVAC Applications) are:

- Executive and Private Offices: 30
- Conference Rooms: 30
- Teleconference Rooms: 25
- Open-Plan Offices: 40
- Corridors and Lobbies: 40

You will use M_Supply Diffuser - Hosted: Workplane-based Supply Diffuser. You will check manufacturer's data to find the airflow for recommended NC values. For this project, you may buy two types of terminals, one with airflow of 100 L/s (NC = 28) for offices and the other with air flow of 160 L/s (NC = 40) for corridors and lobbies.

19.4 Placing Air Terminals

You will place air terminals on the reflected ceiling plan. The ducts will be placed at an offset of 3300mm from the associated level. View range will be little more.

1. Project Browser → Mechanical → HVAC → Ceiling Plans → 1 – Ceiling Mech
2. In Properties palette (Fig. 19.5), set:

    - Underlay = Level 1
    - Underlay Orientation = Reflected Ceiling Plan
    - View Range → Edit (Top and View Depth: Associated Level, Offset = 3400, Cut Plane Offset = 0)

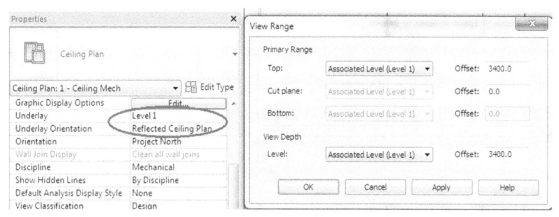

Fig. 19.5 – Reflected Ceiling Plan Settings

3. VG → Revit Links tab → Click under Display Settings.
4. Basics tab → select ⊙Custom (Fig. 19.6).
5. Model Categories tab → Model categories → <Custom>.
6. In Visibility column, unselect:

    - Entourage.
    - Furniture.
    - Furniture Systems.
    - Plumbing Fixtures

7. OK → OK.
8. On System tab → HVAC panel → click Air Terminal.
9. Load Family → Mechanical → MEP → Air-Side Components → Air Terminals → M_Supply Diffuser - Hosted.rfa
10. In Properties palette, select M_Supply Diffuser - Hosted: Workplane-based Supply Diffuser → Flow = 100 L/s
11. On Modify | Place Air Terminal contextual tab → Placement panel → click Place on Face.
12. Place air terminals as shown in Fig. 19.7.
13. Air flow of terminals in Entrance area is 160 L/s. Air flow of all other terminals is 100 L/s.
14. Repeat steps 1-12 for 2 – Ceiling Mech. Use all terminals with air flow = 100 L/s (Fig. 19.15).
15. Each terminal should be placed exactly in the 600 x 600mm box of the ceiling. Align all Air Terminals with the ceiling lines by using Align tool.
16. Add M_Exhaust Diffuser - Hosted: Workplane-based Exhaust Diffuser in the Restrooms 104 and 112.

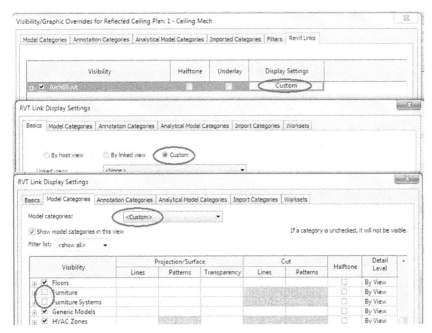

Fig. 19.6 – Visibility Settings for Linked Model

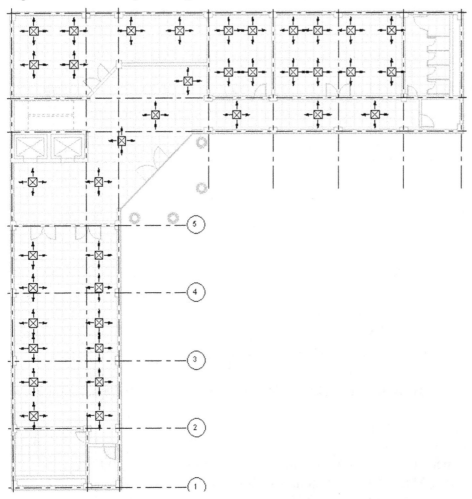

Fig. 19.7 – Air Terminals on 1 - Ceiling Mech

19.5 Air System Schedule

You have already calculated cooling load of each room (space) which also gives required airflow. Now you will make an air system schedule to find out number of air terminals needed in a room.

1. On View tab → Create panel → Schedules dropdown → Schedule/Quantities → Air Terminals.
2. In Category listbox, select Air Terminals → OK.
3. Fields tab → Select available fields from: **Air Terminals**. Select Mark, System Classification and Flow (Fig. 19.8).

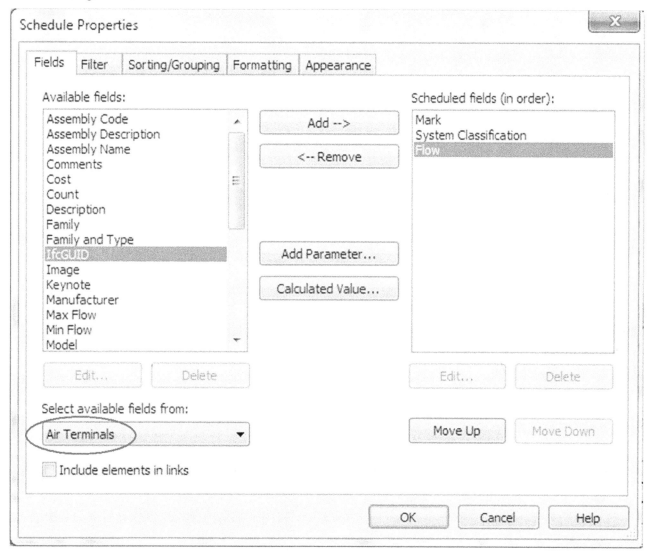

Fig. 19.8 – Air Terminal Schedule

4. Select available fields from: **Space**. Select Name, Number, Actual Supply Airflow, Calculated Supply Airflow.

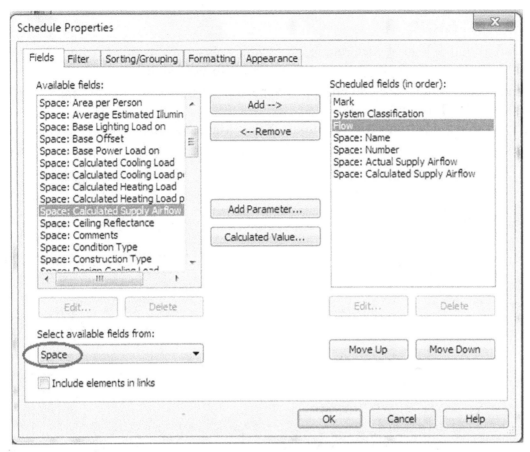

Fig. 19.9 – Air Terminal Schedule - Space Fields

5. By pressing Move Up and Move Down buttons, arrange all fields as shown in Fig. 19.9.
6. Press Calculated Value button (Fig. 19.10).
7. In the Calculated Value dialog box, set as:
   - Name = Delta Airflow.
   - ⊙Formula.
   - Discipline = HVAC.
   - Type = Air Flow.
   - Formula = Space: Actual Supply Airflow - Space: Calculated Supply Airflow → OK.

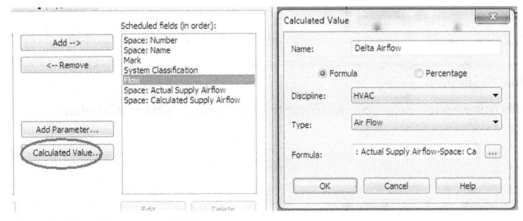

Fig. 19.10 – Calculated Field

8. On Filter tab → Filter by: Space: System Classification - equals - Supply Air (Fig. 19.11).

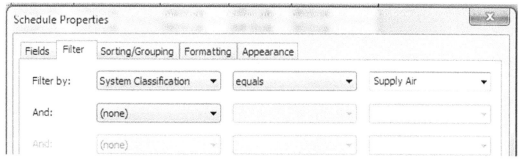

Fig. 19.11 – Air Terminal Schedule - Filter Fields

9. On Sorting/Grouping tab → Sort by: Space: Number ◉Ascending. ☑Itemize every instance (Fig. 19.12).

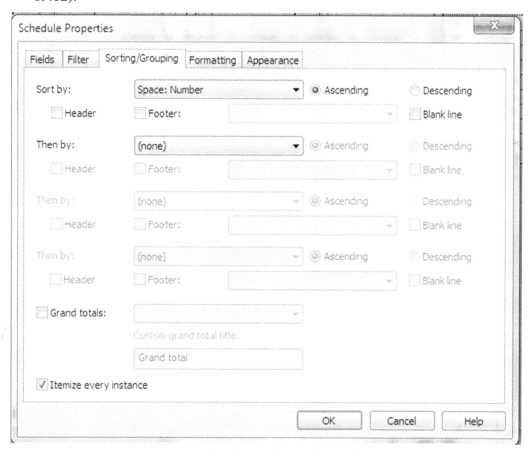

Fig. 19.12 – Air Terminal Schedule - Sort Fields

10. On Formatting tab → Fields listbox → select Delta Airflow (Fig. 19.13).
11. Press Conditional Formatting button.
12. On Conditional Formatting dialog box, select:
   - Field = Delta Airflow.
   - Test = Not Between.
   - Value = -35 L/s and 65 L/s.
   - Background Color = RED.
13. OK → OK

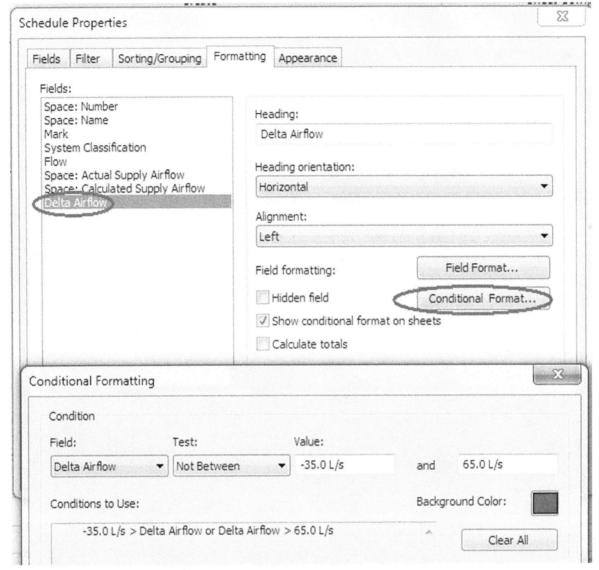

Fig. 19.13 – Air Terminal Schedule - Format Fields

14. You will see the Air Terminal Schedule.

19.6 Adjust Air Flow

You can see that in many rows of the Air Terminal Schedule, the cells in Delta Airflow column are red. This needs adjustment.

1. Project Browser → Schedules/Quantities → Air Terminal Schedule.
2. On Quick Access Toolbar, click on Close Hidden Windows.
3. Project Browser → Mechanical → HVAC → Ceiling Plans → 1 – Ceiling Mech
4. Press WT. You can see the 1 – Ceiling Mech plan and Air Terminal Schedule in tiled windows.
5. Space 101 is OK.
6. In Space 102, Actual Air Flow is 400 L/s while Calculated Air Flow is 235.1. Delete one Air Terminal. The delta cells become white.
7. Delete one Air Terminal in Space 103.
8. There is no Supply Air Terminal in Spaces 104, 105, 106.
9. Space 107 is OK.
10. Place one more Air Terminal in Space 108A.

11. Space 108B is OK.
12. Delete one Air Terminal in Space 111.
13. Add some M_Return Diffuser - Hosted: Workplane-based Return Diffuser.
14. 1 – Ceiling Mech plan will look as shown in Fig. 19.14.

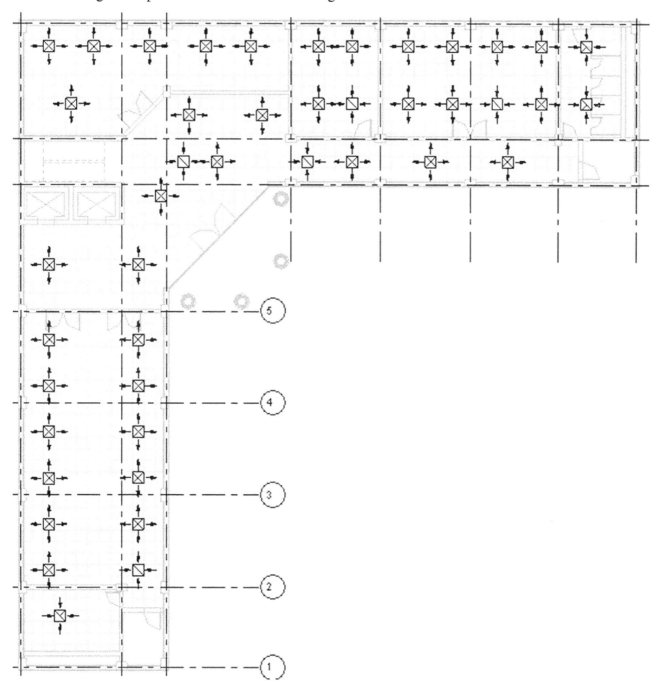

Fig. 19.14 – Air Terminals on 1 - Ceiling Mech

15. Do the same for 2 – Ceiling Mech.
16. 2 – Ceiling Mech plan will look as shown in Fig. 19.15.

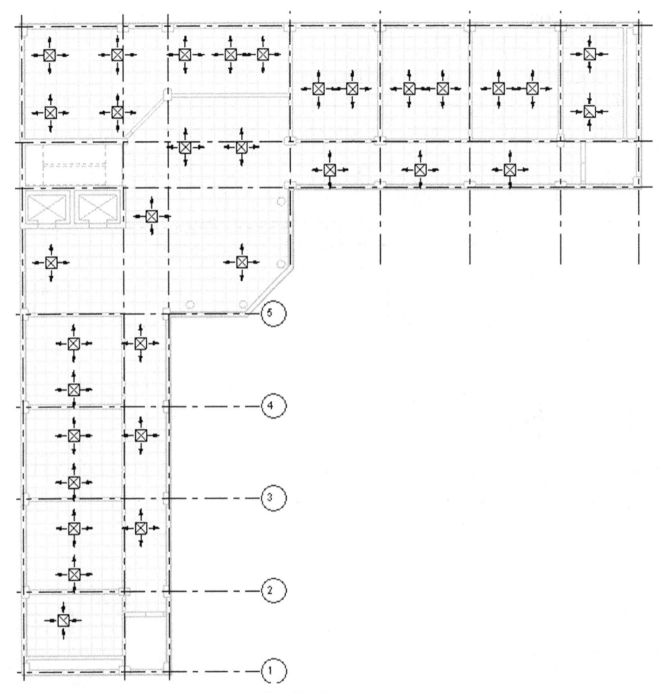

Fig. 19.15 – Air Terminals on 2 - Ceiling Mech

17. All the air terminals belong to a system named Unassigned. Later on, when you create duct systems, the air terminals will be removed from Unassigned and added to the duct systems you will create. You can view this in System Browser (Press F9) under View = Systems.

18. Click [save icon] to Save Project As **AC03**.

20 Supply Air Ductwork

After placing the supply air terminals, you will connect a set of terminals to a VAV (Variable Air Volume) box with ducts. This will be a low pressure secondary Air Supply System.

Later on, you will create a high pressure primary Air Supply System, in which you will connect VAV boxes to the air-conditioner with the main duct.

20.1 Duct Settings

Ducts come in different sizes, in different cross-sectional shapes, with different elbow shapes and connection methods.

For duct settings, you select a duct's cross-sectional shape (square, rectangular, round, elliptical), elbow shape (radius or mitered), and connection method (tee or tap).

1. Open Project AC03.
2. Save Project As AC04.
3. Press MS.
4. Under Duct Settings node, click on Conversion (Fig. 20.1).
5. For System Classification = Supply Air, make settings as :
6. Main Duct Type = Rectangular Duct : Mitered Elbows / Taps
7. Offset = 3300
8. Brach Duct Type = Rectangular Duct : Mitered Elbows / Taps
9. Offset = 3300
10. Flex Duct Type = Flex Duct Round : Flex - Round
11. Maximum Flex Duct Length = 900

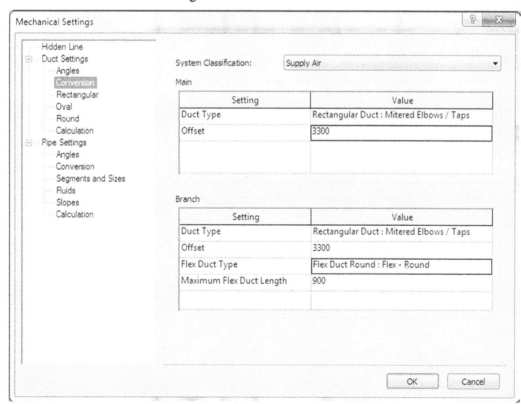

Fig. 20.1 – Duct Settings

20.2 Air Supply System in Zone GF North

First you will create a secondary Air Supply System, which consists of a VAV box and one or more air terminals. The ductwork of the system will be created automatically. Actually you will select one out of many layouts.

Later on you will create a primary Air Supply System, for which you will draw the main duct manually and connect VAV boxes and air terminals into it.

20.2.1 Secondary Air Supply System in Zone GF North

From the Load Report or Air Terminal Schedule, you can see that peak cooling air flow for Cafeteria 103 is 646.8 L/s. You have placed seven supply air terminals each giving 100 L/s (total 700 L/s).

You will place a Parallel Fan Powered VAV box. It mixes variable amount of recirculated air from plenum (secondary air) with the conditioned air from main duct (primary air). You will keep the primary to supply airflow ratio = 0.5 (which means that when supply airflow is 100 L/s then primary airflow will be 50 L/s and secondary airflow will be 50 L/s). Actually its fan runs intermittently and damper opens or closes according to the need.

1. Project Browser → Design → HVAC → Floor Plans → 1 –Mech.
2. VG → Model Graphics tab → Unselect:

    • HVAC Zones.
    • Spaces.

3. On System tab → Mechanical panel → click Mechanical Equipment.
4. In the Type Selector, select M_VAV Unit Parallel Fan Powered: M_Size 3 - 300mm Inlet.
5. In Properties palette, set

    • Offset = 3300 (Same as duct offset).
    • PrimaryTosupplyRatio = 0.5000.

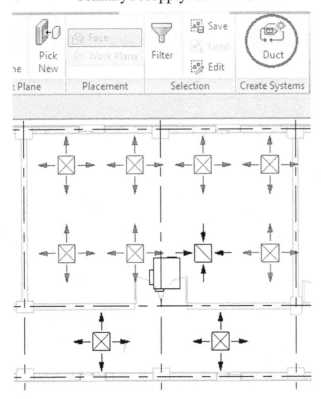

Fig. 20.2 –Duct tool

6. Hover over the door of Cafeteria 103. Press space bar to rotate the image of VAV box such that the Inlet is towards the corridor and Outlet is towards the interior of the room 103 as shown in Fig. 20.2. Click to place VAV box.
7. Select the seven supply air terminals (by pressing CTRL).
8. On Modify | Air Terminals contextual tab → Create Systems panel → Click Duct tool (Fig. 20.2).
9. *Note: Duct tool appears only when all the air terminals you select belong to an Unassigned system. If one or more terminals belong to an already created duct system, Duct tool will not appear and you must remove the terminals from the system. An easy way is to delete that duct system. Open System Browser → View = Systems → Expand nodes to reach the duct system → Right-click → Delete. This will only delete the system, not the air terminals or other equipment.*
10. *Another way to delete a duct system is to Select an Air Terminal in the system → Click on Duct Systems contextual tab (Fig. 20.3) → On System Tools panel, click Edit System → On Edit Duct System panel, click Remove from System → Select Air Terminals → On Mode panel, click Finish Editing System. The terminals will be removed from the system. You can start from step 7 again.*

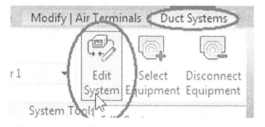 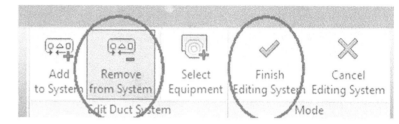

Fig. 20.3 – Duct System Editing

11. Create Duct System dialog box will appear (Fig. 20.3). You can change the name of the system. On Create Duct System dialog box, click OK. A duct system with given name will be created. You can see this in System Browser.
12. On Modify | Air Terminals contextual tab → System Tools panel → Click Select Equipment.
13. Select the VAV box.
14. On Modify | Air Terminals contextual tab → Layout panel → Click Generate Layout.

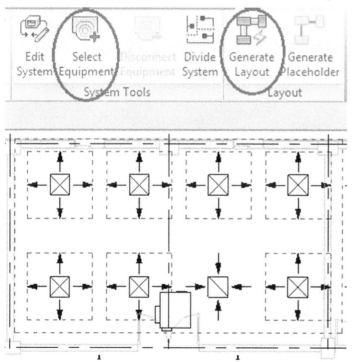

Fig. 20.4 – Create Duct System dialog box

15. On Option Bar, there is an option of six solutions.

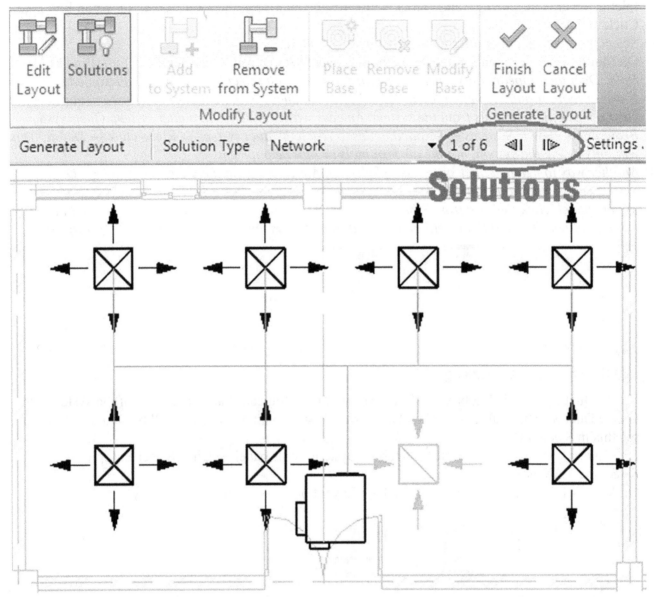

Fig. 20.5 – Set Project Location

16. Keep solution 1.
17. On Generate Layout panel → click Finish Layout ✓ .
18. Duct layout will appears.
19. The ducts are blue but the central duct is orange. A warning box also appears with warning that this element has an open connection. Actually the central duct has open end on both sides. You must cap the open ends.
20. Select the central duct.
21. On Edit panel → click Cap Open Ends (Fig. 20.6).
22. The other way is to right-click on the open end and click on Cap Open End (Fig. 20.6).
23. Another way is: System tab → HVAC panel → Duct Fitting → From Type selector, select M_Rectangular Endcap : Standard → Place Endcap on both open duct ends.

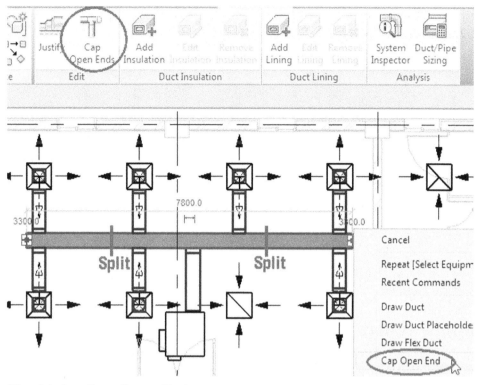

Fig. 20.6 – Cap Open Ends

24. On Modify tab → Modify panel → click Split Element tool.
25. Touch the knife at places shown in Fig. 20.6.
26. Bring cursor on the VAV box and press Tab twice. VAV box, ducts and terminals are highlighted.
27. On Analysis panel → click Duct/Pipe Sizing (Fig. 20.7).
28. On Duct Sizing dialog box, choose sizing method as
    • Friction = 0.82 Pa/m
    • ⊙only
    • Branch Sizing = Calculated Size Only → OK.

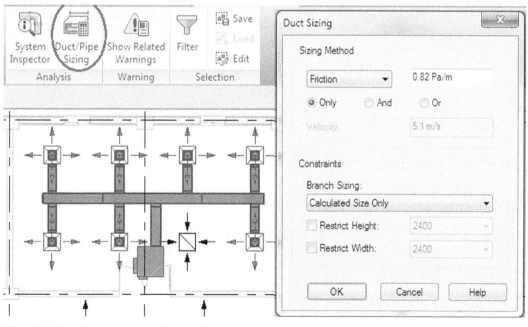

Fig. 20.7 – Secondary Duct Sizing

29. Duct sizes change at the split points.
30. Do the same for Lounge 102 and Accounting 101.

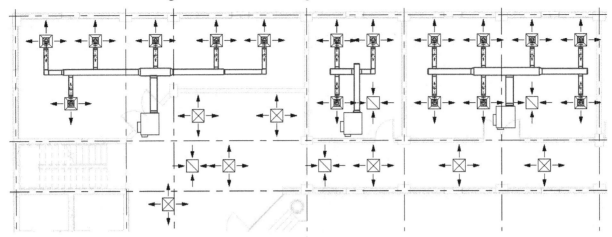

Fig. 20.8 – Secondary Air Supply System

20.2.2 Primary Air Supply System in Zone GF North

You will draw a main duct from Elect/Mech 106 to Entrance 108A over the air terminals in the Corridor 107.

1. Project Browser → Mechanical → HVAC → Floor Plans → 1 –Mech.
2. On System tab → HVAC panel → click Duct.
3. In the Type Selector, select Rectangular Duct : Radius Elbows / Taps (Fig. 20.9).
4. In Properties palette or on Option Bar, set:

   - Width = 400.
   - Height = 400.
   - System Type = Supply Air.
   - Offset = 3300.0 mm.

5. On Placement Tools panel → select Automatically Connect.

Fig. 20.9 – Primary Duct Properties

6. Hover over the air terminal in Corridor 107 close to Elect/Mech 106. When a circle in the center is highlighted, move cursor inside Elect/Mech 106 with blue dashed line showing. Draw duct up to the VAV box of Accounting 101 (Fig. 20.10).

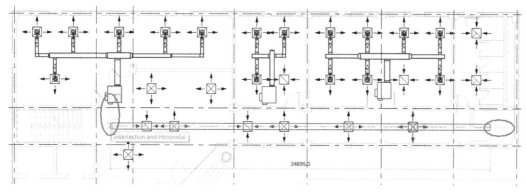

Fig. 20.10 – Draw main duct

7. Select a VAV box → On Layout panel → click Connect Into → select Supply Air connector → click on the primary duct (Fig. 20.11). VAV box will connect to the main duct.

Fig. 20.11 – Connect Into

8. Do the same for other VAV boxes.
9. Do the same for the remaining air terminals in the GF North zone.
10. Split the main duct at three places.
11. Bring cursor at the start of the main duct → Press Tab 3 times → Make duct sizing as explained in step 27 of § 20.2.1 (Fig. 20.12).

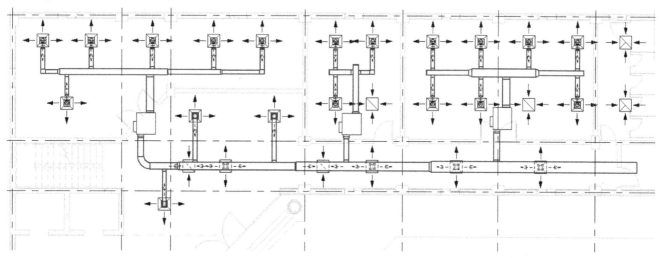

Fig. 20.12 – Primary Duct Sizing

20.3 Air Supply System in Zone GF South

In zone GF South, you will connect all air terminals directly to the main duct without a VAV box. But first you will place a VAV box and create an air system automatically. Then you will delete the VAV box and draw the main duct up to the Elect/Mech 113.

1. Project Browser → Mechanical → HVAC → Floor Plans → 1 –Mech.
2. On System tab → Mechanical panel → click Mechanical Equipment.
3. In the Type Selector, select M_VAV Unit Parallel Fan Powered: M_Size 3 - 300mm Inlet.

4. In Properties palette, set Offset = 3300 (Same as duct offset).
5. Place VAV box in Restroom 112 and press space bar to rotate it such that the outlet is towards Showroom 111.
6. Select the 11 supply air terminals in Showroom 111 and two terminals in Entrance 108B (by pressing CTRL).
7. On Modify | Air Terminals contextual tab → Create Systems panel → Click Duct tool. (If Duct tool does not appear, see steps 9-10 of § 20.2.1).
8. Create Duct System dialog box will appear. You can change the name of the system. On Create Duct System dialog box, click OK. A duct system with given name will be created. You can see this in System Browser.
9. On Modify | Air Terminals contextual tab → System Tools panel → Click Select Equipment (Fig. 20.4).
10. Select the VAV box.
11. On Modify | Air Terminals contextual tab → Layout panel → Click Generate Layout.
12. On Option Bar, there is an option of six solutions. Select a solution.

13. On Generate Layout panel → click Finish Layout ✓ .
14. Duct layout will appears.
15. Delete the VAV box and other unnecessary elements (Fig. 20.13).
16. Select the main duct.
17. Right click at the end in the Restroom 112 → click Draw Duct.
18. Draw duct up to Elect/Mech 113.
19. Cap the main duct at the end in the Entrance, split and resize.

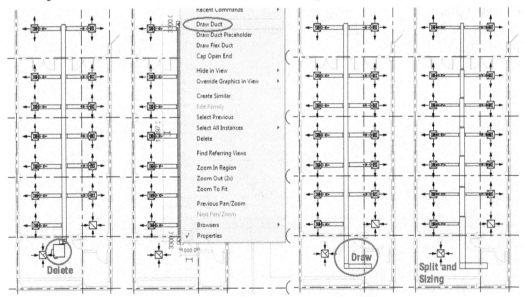

Fig. 20.13 – Air Supply System in Zone GF South

20.4 Air Supply System in Zone FF North

Similar to zone GF North, place VAV boxes and make secondary air supply systems. Draw main duct and connect VAV boxes and remaining air terminals into the main duct. Cap ducts, split and resize. The layout looks as shown in Fig. 20.14.

20.5 Air Supply System in Zone FF South

Similar to zone GF South, place VAV box and make secondary air supply systems. Delete VAV box and draw main duct. Cap main duct at far end, split and resize. The layout looks as shown in Fig. 20.14.

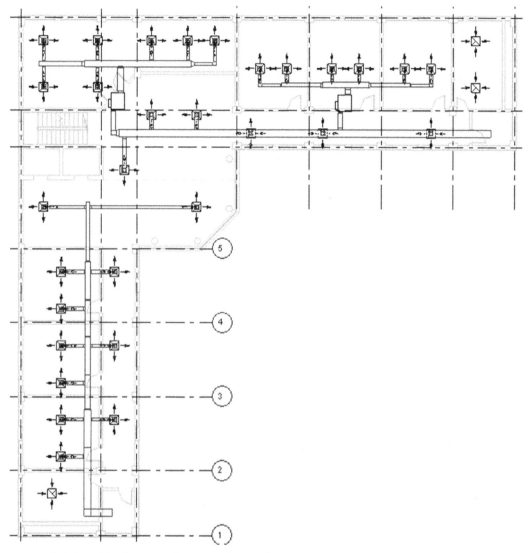

Fig. 20.14 – Air Supply System in 2 - Mech

20.6 Air-Conditioner for South Zones

From the Load Report, we see that peak cooling load for the zone GF South is 20.838 kW and for the zone FF South is 21.849 kW. For both zones, an air-conditioner of about 43 kW is needed.

Click on the start of the main duct on zone GF South. In Properties palette, under Mechanical - Flow group, note that Flow = 1300.00 L/s

Click on the start of the main duct on zone FF South. In Properties palette, under Mechanical - Flow group, note that Flow = 1220.00 L/s

Total airflow needed for South zones is 2520 L/s

1. Project Browser → Mechanical → HVAC → Floor Plans → 3 –Mech.
2. On System tab → Mechanical panel → click Mechanical Equipment.
3. On Mode panel → click Load Family.

4. Mechanical → MEP → Air-Side Components → Air Conditioners → M_Rooftop AC Unit - 11-44 kW - Bottom Connection.rfa

5. In the Type Selector, select M_Rooftop AC Unit - 11-44 kW - Bottom Connection: 44 kW.

6. In Properties palette, set

   - Offset = 300.
   - AirFlow - Supply = 2550.00 L/s.
   - AirFlow - Return = 2550.00 L/s.

7. Place the air-conditioner above the Elect/Mech rooms 113, 217.

8. Draw a section. Double-click on section head (Fig. 20.15).

9. In section view, select the air-conditioner.

10. Right-click on Out connection and click on Draw Duct (In Type selector, select type = Rectangular Duct : Mitered Elbows/Taps).

11. Draw duct up to Plenum1 115.

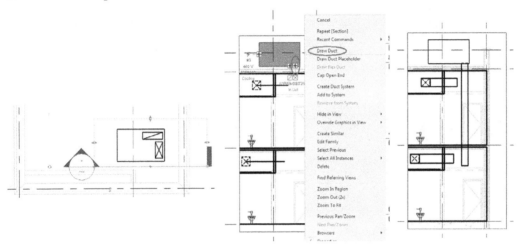

Fig. 20.15 – Draw AC Duct

12. Project Browser → Mechanical → HVAC → Floor Plans → 1 – Mech.

13. Click on the main duct in Elect/Mech 113.

14. With Up/Down arrows, adjust the position of the duct. Drag the main duct to join with AC duct.

15. Do the same for main duct on 2 – Mech in Elect/Mech 217.

16. See the 3D view.

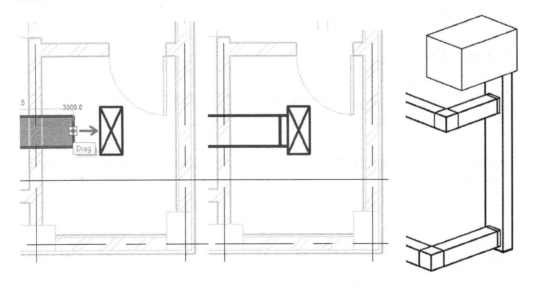

Fig. 20.16 – Join Main Duct to AC Duct

20.7 Air-Conditioner for North Zones

From the Load Report, we see that peak cooling load for the zone GF North is 34.460 kW and for the zone FF North is 34.698 kW. For both zones, an air-conditioner of about 70 kW is needed.

Click on the start of the main duct on zone GF South. In Properties palette, under Mechanical - Flow group, note that Flow = 1500.00 L/s

Click on the start of the main duct on zone FF South. In Properties palette, under Mechanical - Flow group, note that Flow = 1430.00 L/s

Total airflow needed for South zones is 2930 L/s

1. Project Browser → Mechanical → HVAC → Floor Plans → 3 –Mech.
2. On System tab → Mechanical panel → click Mechanical Equipment.
3. On Mode panel → click Load Family.
4. Mechanical → MEP → Air-Side Components → Air Conditioners → M_Rooftop AC Unit - 53-88 kW - Bottom Return Connection.rfa
5. In the Type Selector, select M_Rooftop AC Unit - 53-88 kW - Bottom Return Connection.rfa: 70 kW.
6. In Properties palette, set

    - Offset = 300.
    - AirFlow - Supply = 3500.00 L/s.
    - AirFlow - Return = 3500.00 L/s.

7. Place the air-conditioner above the Elect/Mech rooms 106, 208.
8. Draw a section. Double-click on section head.
9. In section view, select the air-conditioner.
10. Right-click on Out connection and click on Draw Duct.
11. Draw duct up to Plenum1 115.
12. Project Browser → Mechanical → HVAC → Floor Plans → 1 – Mech.
13. Click on the main duct in Elect/Mech 106.
14. With Up/Down arrows, adjust the position of the duct. Drag the main duct to join with AC duct.

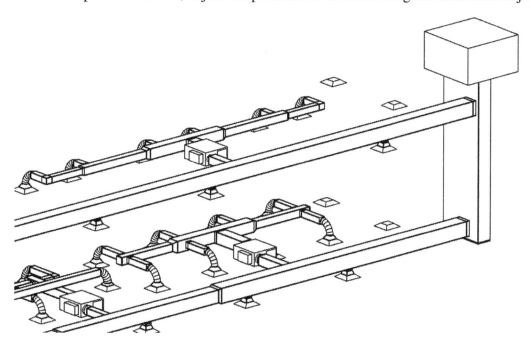

BIM Project by Imtaar

Fig. 20.17 – Air-Conditioner for North Zones

15. Do the same for main duct on 2 – Mech in Elect/Mech 208.
16. See the 3D view (Fig. 20.17).
17. The AC system is now complete.

18. Click to Save Project As **AC04**.

21 Presentation of AC System

Information about AC system can be displayed in the form of schedules. Different view can be presented on sheets.

21.1 Sheets for the AC System Layout

You will make sheets showing air terminals, ducts, VAV boxes and other information.

1. Open Project **AC04.**
2. Save Project As **AC05.**
3. Project Browser → Mechanical → HVAC → Floor Plans → 1 – Mech.
4. You see that many unwanted elements are visible in the view. You will crop the view.
5. On the View Control bar, press Show Crop Region ⬚ and Crop View ⬚.
6. A rectangular boundary appears around the view. Click on this boundary. Move the crop handles (blue dots) on left and right side to crop.
7. When crop handles are adjusted, press Hide Crop Region (Same for Show).

21.2 Sheet with Air Terminals Information

You will duplicate the view and add tags for air terminals.

1. In Project Browser, Right-click on Air Terminal Schedule → Duplicate.
2. In Project Browser, double-click on Air Terminal Schedule Copy 1.
3. In Properties palette, click on Filter - Edit.
4. Filter by - Space: Number - is less than - 200
5. And - System Classification - Equals - Supply Air → OK.
6. Project Browser → Mechanical → HVAC → Floor Plans → 1 – Mech → Right-click → Duplicate View → Duplicate.
7. You will get another view 1 – Mech Copy 1.
8. Floor Plans → 1 – Mech Copy 1→ Right-click → Rename = 1 – Mech Diffusers.
9. On Annotate tab → Tag panel → click Tag All tool.
10. From Category, select Air Terminal Tags with tag = M_Diffuser Tag → OK.
11. Tags appear on all air terminals.
12. Project Browser → Sheets → Right-click → New Sheet.
13. Click on Load.
14. Navigate to Arch A1.rfa.
15. OK.
16. Titleblock is added.
17. From Project Browser → Mechanical → HVAC → Floor Plans, drag 1 – Mech Diffusers to the sheet.
18. From Project Browser → Schedules/Quantities, drag Air Terminal Schedule Copy 1 to the sheet.
19. In the Viewport Properties palette, change View Scale = 1:100.
20. Adjust Column widths of the schedule.
21. Select the Titleblock. In Properties palette, make:
    - Sheet Number = AC 101.
    - Sheet Name = 1-Mech Diffuser.
22. You can see the changes on the sheet (Fig. 21.1).

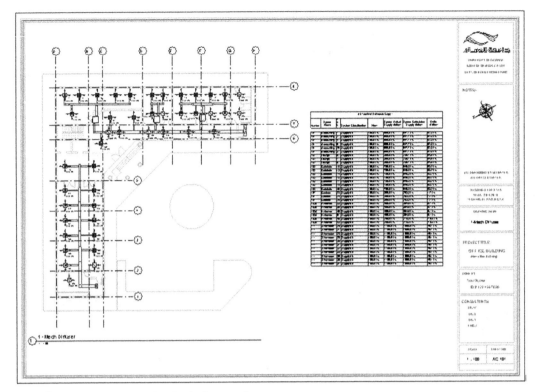

Fig. 21.1 – Air Terminals Information

21.3 Sheet with Duct Mark

You will duplicate the view and add tags for duct marks.

1. Project Browser → Mechanical → HVAC → Floor Plans → 1 – Mech → Right-click → Duplicate View → Duplicate → Rename = 1 – Mech Duct Mark.
2. On Annotate tab → Tag panel → click Tag All tool.
3. From Category, select Duct Tags with tag = M_Duct Mark Tag → OK.
4. Similarly make a view 2 – Mech Duct Mark.
5. Project Browser → Sheets → Right-click → New Sheet → Select titleblock Arch A1 → OK.
6. Select the Titleblock. In Properties palette, make:

    • Sheet Number = AC 102.
    • Sheet Name = Duct Mark.

7. Drag the views 1 – Mech Duct Mark and 2 – Mech Duct Mark on the sheet.
8. Select a viewport. In Properties palette, set:

    • View Scale = Custom.
    • Scale Value = 1:150.

9. The sheet looks as shown in Fig. 21.2.

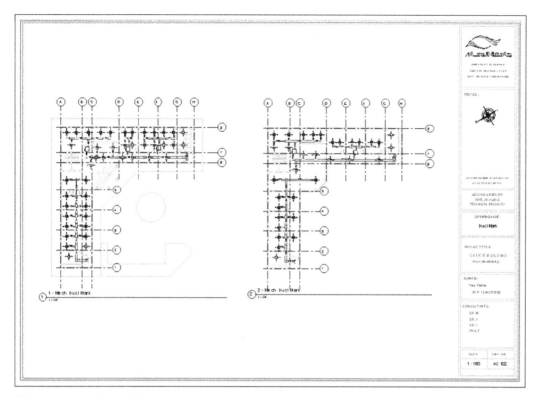

Fig. 21.2 – Duct Mark

21.4 Sheet with Duct Schedule

You will make a schedule containing information about ducts.

1. On View tab → Create panel → Schedules dropdown → click Schedules/Quantities tool.
2. In New Schedule dialog box → Category listbox → click Ducts.
3. Name = Duct Schedule → OK.
4. On Fields tab, from Available Fields listbox, select the following fields and add them (double-click or press Add →) to Schedule Fields listbox.

   - Mark.
   - Family and Type.
   - Flow.
   - Length.
   - Velocity.
   - System Name.
   - System Type.
   - System Classification.
   - Size.
   - Pressure Drop.
   - Bottom Elevation.

5. On Sorting/Grouping tab, Sort by = Mark (Ascending).
6. Unselect Header, Footer, Grand Totals checkboxes → OK.
7. You will get the duct schedule.
8. There are more than 100 rows. You will divide it in two parts.
9. Right-click on duct schedule → Duplicate two times.
10. In Project Browser, double-click on Duct Schedule Copy 1.

11. In Properties palette, click on Filter - Edit.
12. Filter by - Mark - is less than - 215 → OK.
13. In Project Browser, double-click on Duct Schedule Copy 2.
14. In Properties palette, click on Filter - Edit.
15. Filter by - Mark - is greater than - 214 → OK.
16. Project Browser → Sheets → Right-click → New Sheet → Select titleblock Arch A1 → OK.
17. Select the Titleblock. In Properties palette, make:

- Sheet Number = AC 103.
- Sheet Name = Duct Schedule.

18. Drag Duct Schedule Copy 1 and Duct Schedule Copy 2.
19. Adjust column widths of the two schedule parts (Fig. 21.3).

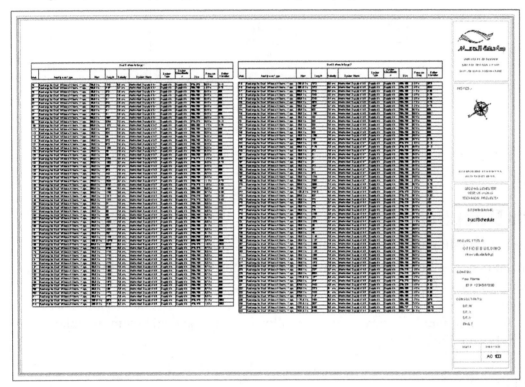

Fig. 21.3 – Duct Schedule

21.5 Sheet with Duct Size

You will duplicate the view and add tags for duct sizes.

1. Project Browser → Mechanical → HVAC → Floor Plans → 1 – Mech → Right-click → Duplicate View → Duplicate → Rename = 1 – Mech Duct Size.
2. On Annotate tab → Tag panel → click Tag All tool.
3. From Category, select Duct Tags with tag = M_Duct Size Tag → OK.
4. Crop the view to see only the zone GF North.
5. Select the linked model → Right-click → Hide in View → Element.
6. Project Browser → Sheets → Right-click → New Sheet → Select titleblock Arch A1 → OK.
7. Select the Titleblock. In Properties palette, make:

- Sheet Number = AC 104.
- Sheet Name = Duct Size.

8. Drag the views 1 – Mech Duct Mark and 2 – Mech Duct Mark on the sheet.

9. Select a viewport. In Properties palette, set View Scale = 1:50.
10. The sheet looks as shown in Fig. 21.4.

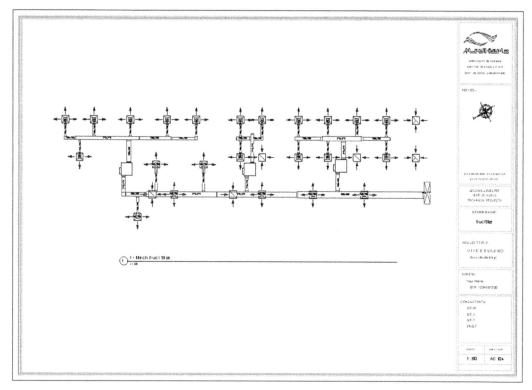

Fig. 21.4 – Duct Size

21.6 Sheet with 3D AC System

You will duplicate the 3D view and using section box, you will separate the views level-wise.

1. Project Browser → Mechanical → HVAC → 3D Views → {3D} → Right-click → Duplicate View → Duplicate two times → Rename = 3D 1 – Mech and 3D 2 – Mech.
2. Project Browser → Mechanical → HVAC → 3D Views → 3D 1 – Mech.
3. Select the linked model → Right-click → Hide in View → Element.
4. In Properties palette → Extents group → Section Box ☑ (Fig. 9.24).
5. If you don't see the section box then press VG → Annotation Categories tab → Select Section Boxes ☑.
6. You will see six handles on six invisible surfaces of the section box. You can move these handles to change the size of the section box. Anything inside the section box will be visible (Fig.21.5).
7. Adjust handles to see elements on 1 – Mech level only.
8. VG → Annotation Categories tab → Unselect Section Boxes ☐.
9. Project Browser → Mechanical → HVAC → 3D Views → 3D 2 – Mech.
10. Use section box to see elements on 2 – Mech level only.
11. Add a new sheet → Add title block → Drag 3D 1 – Mech and 3D 2 – Mech.
12. Select a viewport for 3D 1 – Mech. In Properties palette, set View Scale = 1:100.
13. Select a viewport for 3D 2 – Mech. In Properties palette, set View Scale = 1:50.
14. Project Browser → Sheets → Right-click → New Sheet → Select titleblock Arch A1 → OK.

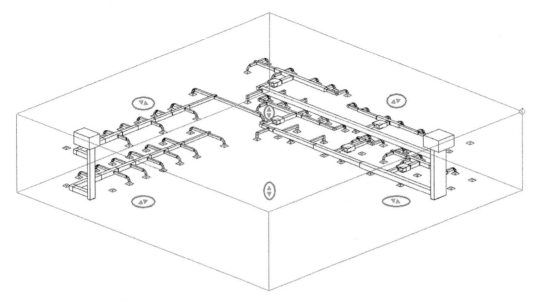

Fig. 21.5 – 3D Section

15. Select the Titleblock. In Properties palette, make (Fig. 21.6) :

  • Sheet Number = AC 105.
  • Sheet Name = 3D AC System.

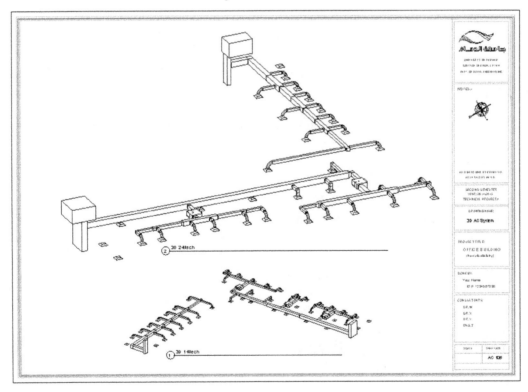

Fig. 21.6 – 3D AC System

16. Click [save icon] to Save Project As **AC05**.

22 Lighting Design

Before placing the lighting fixtures in different spaces, you will analyze the building for lighting requirements. You will make a schedule showing difference between average estimated illumination due to lighting fixtures and the required lighting level. Using this schedule, you will place lighting fixtures in all the spaces.

22.1 Key Schedule for Required Lighting Levels

A key schedule is a schedule of keys which can be used in other schedules. The key can be bound to an element category. It is also used to setup a number of styles for an object type.

Here you will make a space key schedule and bind the keys to spaces in another schedule.

1. Open Project **AC05.** (You can start with AC02. You can get AC02 and Arch05 from Download Folder (page v). **Keep both files in the same folder**).
2. Save Project As **EL01.**
3. On View tab → Create panel → Schedules dropdown → click Schedule/Quantities.
4. From Categories select Spaces (Fig. 22.1).
5. Write Name = Space Lighting Requirements and Key Name = Lighting Levels → Press OK.

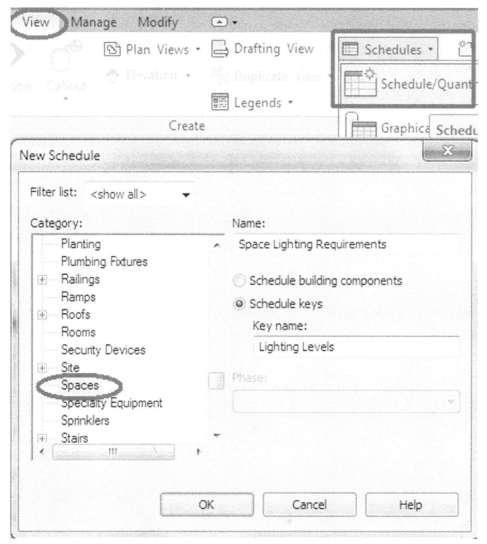

Fig. 22.1 – Key Schedule

6. On Fields tab → from Available Fields listbox → add Required Lighting Level → Press OK
7. On Modify Schedule/Quantities contextual tab → Rows panel → Insert dropdown → click Data Row tool 9 times to insert 9 rows.
8. Fill the rows as shown in table 22.1.

Space Lighting Requirements	
Key Name	Required Lighting Level
Cafeteria	215 lx
Corridor	215 lx
Entrance	485 lx
Lounge	325 lx
Mech/Elec	215 lx
Office	540 lx
Show Room	805 lx
Stairs	225 lx
Toilet	215 lx

Table 22.1 – Required Lighting Levels

22.2 Assign Space Keys to the Spaces

1. Project Browser → Electrical → Lighting → Floor Plans → 1 – Lighting.
2. Press VG → Model Graphics tab → Unselect:

- Entourage.
- Generic Models.
- HVAC Zones.
- Parking.
- Planting.
- Plumbing Fixtures.
- Roads.
- Site.
- Topography.

3. Press VG → Model Graphics tab → Expand Spaces → Select All (Fig. 22.2).

Visibility	Projection/Surface		
	Lines	Patterns	Transparency
☑ Spaces			
☑ Color Fill			
☑ Interior			
☑ Reference			

Fig. 22.2 – Visibility of Spaces

4. Press VG → Revit Links tab → By Host View (Fig. 22.3).
5. Basic tab → Custom radiobutton.

6. Model Categories tab → Model Categories = <Custom> → Unselect:
   • Furniture.
   • Furniture System.

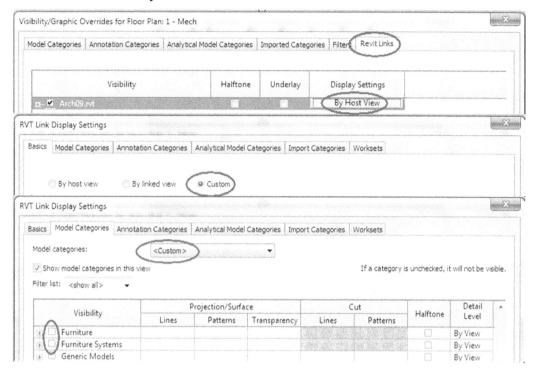

Fig. 22.3 – Visibility of Linked Model

7. Annotate → Tag All → Space Tags
8. Select Accounting 101 (Fig. 22.4).
9. In Properties palette, under Identity Data group, set Lighting Levels = Office.

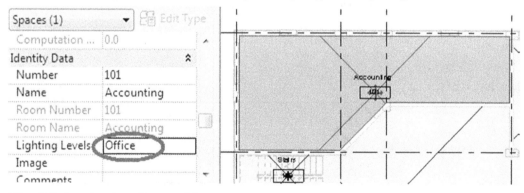

Fig. 22.4 – Assign Space Keys

10. Similarly set Lighting Levels property for all spaces.
11. Do the same for 2 – Lighting. (Select Manager 201 + all offices and set Lighting Levels = Office).

22.3 Space Lighting Analysis Schedule

1. On View tab → Create panel → Schedules dropdown → click Schedule/Quantities.
2. From Categories select Spaces.
3. Write Name = Space Lighting Analysis → Press OK.
4. On Fields tab, add following fields

- Number
- Name
- Required Lighting Level
- Average Estimated Illumination

5. Add Calculated Value (Fig. 22.5):
   - Name = Delta Light.
   - ⊙ Formula.
   - Discipline = Electrical.
   - Type = Illuminance.
   - Formula = Estimated Illumination - Required Lighting Level.

6. OK.

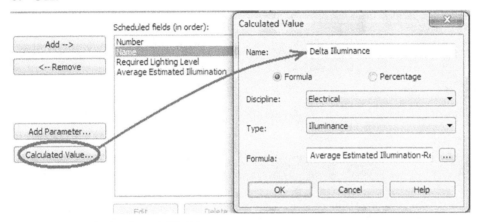

Fig. 22.5 – Calculated Field

7. On Sorting/Grouping tab, Sort by: Number
8. On Formatting tab → select Delta Light → press Conditional Format…
9. In Conditional Formatting dialog box, Condition frame, set (Fig. 22.6):
   - Field: Delta Illuminance.
   - Test: Not Between.
   - Value: – 55 lx and 55 lx.
   - Background Color: RED.

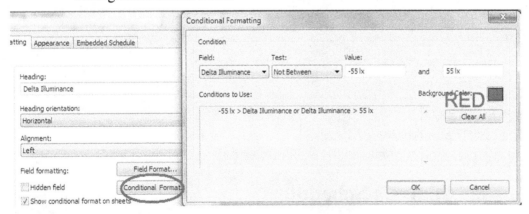

Fig. 22.6 – Conditional Format

10. Space Lighting Analysis schedule appears.
11. Delta Illuminance column is red.

22.4 Place Lighting Fixtures

1. Project Browser → Electrical → Lighting → Ceiling Plans → 1 - Ceiling Elec.
2. In Properties palette, Extents group, View Range: Edit.
3. In View Range, set:

   - Top = Level 2, Offset = 0.0.
   - Cut Plane Offset = 1200.
   - View Depth: Level = Level 2, Offset = 0.0.

4. Press VG → Model Graphics tab → Select Air Terminals → Unselect:

   - Entourage.
   - Generic Models.
   - HVAC Zones.
   - Parking.
   - Planting.
   - Plumbing Fixtures.
   - Roads.
   - Site.
   - Spaces.
   - Topography.

5. Close Hidden → Space Lighting Analysis → WT.
6. Set focus on 1 - Ceiling Elec.
7. On System tab → Electrical panel → click Lighting Fixture tool.
8. On Modify | Place Fixture contextual tab → Mode panel → Click Load Family → Lighting → MEP → Internal → M_Recessed Parabolic Light.rfa
9. Select 600 x 1200mm 4 Lamp 120v.
10. On Modify | Place Fixture contextual tab → Placement panel → Place on Face.
11. Zoom to Accounting 101.
12. Place lighting fixtures (not conflicting with air terminals) until Delta Illuminance cell changes from red to white as shown in Fig. 22.7

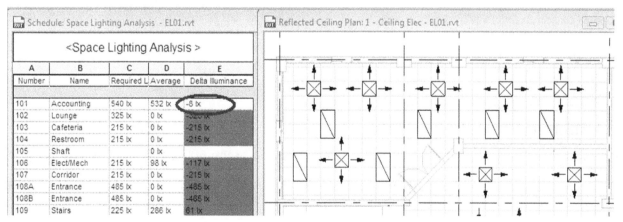

Fig. 22.7 – Placing Lighting Fixtures

13. Place lighting fixtures in all rooms until all Delta Illuminance cells change from red to white.
14. Place M_Celing Light – Flat Round: 100W – 120V in Restrooms.
15. Place M_Wall Lamp – Bracket: 100W – 120V in Stairs (Fig. 22.8).

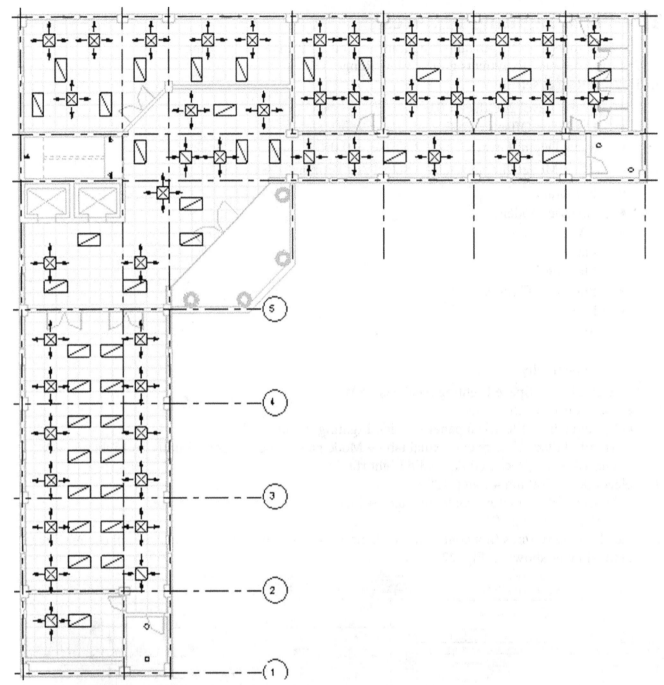

Fig. 22.8 – Lighting Fixtures on 1 - Lighting

16. Do the same for 2 - Ceiling Elec. (Use M_Recessed Parabolic Light: 600 x 1200mm 3 Lamp 120v) (Fig. 22.9).

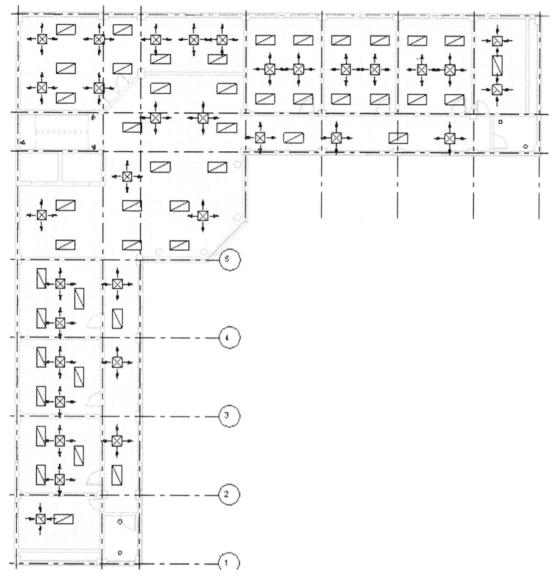

Fig. 22.9 – Lighting Fixtures on 2 - Lighting

22.5 Color Scheme for Lighting

1. Project Browser → Electrical → Lighting → Floor Plans → 1 – Lighting → Right-click → Duplicate View → Rename = 1 – Lighting Color.
2. In Properties palette, Graphics group, click on <None> in front of Color Scheme.
3. Edit Color Scheme dialog box appears (Fig. 22.10).
4. In Schemes frame, click on Schema 1 and Rename = Illumination.
5. In Scheme Definition frame, set:

   - Title = Illumination.
   - Color: Average Estimated Illumination.
   - ◉ By Range.

6. Add ranges (Press ✚ several times. Modify from **last** entry in At Least column).
7. Select colors
8. On Annotate tab → Color Fill panel → click Color Fill Legend → Click anywhere in the view.
9. Press VG → expand Spaces → select Color Fill only.
10. The view looks as shown in Fig. 22.11.

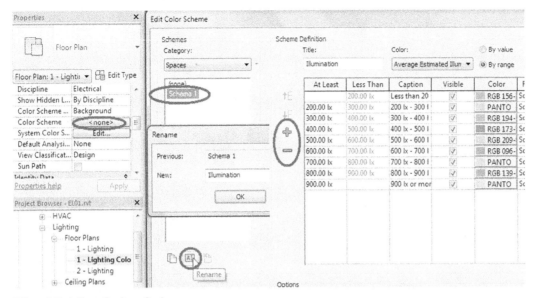

Fig. 22.10 – Color Scheme

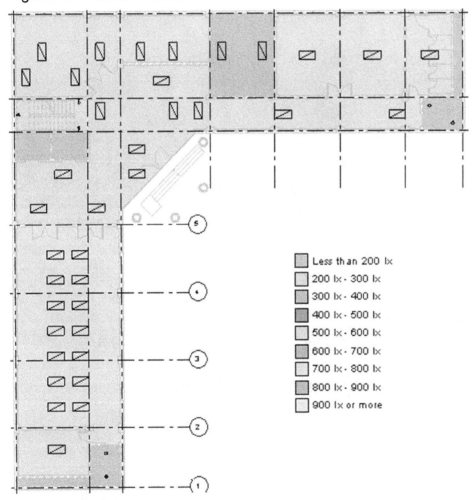

Fig. 22.11 – Color Scheme for Lighting

11. Click [icon] to Save Project As **EL01**.

23 Electrical Power Design

You have placed the lighting fixtures in the building. You will connect them to Panel boards through switches. You will also place power receptacles in different rooms and connect them to the Panel boards.

23.1 Place Panel Boards

Panel boards are used to control light, heat or power circuits. They divide the main electric power supply into branch circuits with protective devices such as fuses or circuit breakers.

1. Open Project **EL01.**
2. Save Project As **EL02.**
3. Project Browser → Electrical → Power → Floor Plans → 1 – Power.
4. Zoom to Elect/Mech 106.
5. On System tab → Electrical panel → click Electrical Equipment.
6. On Modify | Place Equipment contextual tab → Mode panel → click Load Family → Electrical → MEP → Electric Power → Distribution → M_Lighting and Appliance Panelboard - 208V MLO - Surface.rfa.
7. In Properties palette → type selector → select type = M_Lighting and Appliance Panelboard - 208V MLO - Surface: 100 A.
8. On Modify | Place Equipment contextual tab → Placement panel → click Place on Vertical Face.
9. Place a panel board on north side wall of Elect/Mech 106 (Fig. 23.1).
10. In Properties palette → set Panel Name = DP106.
11. On Option Bar, set Distribution System = 120/208 Wye.

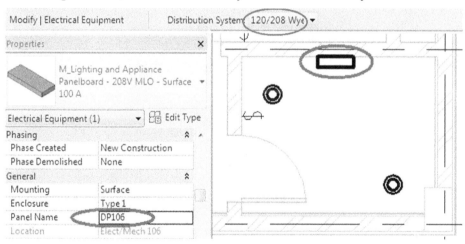

Fig. 23.1 – Place Panel Board

12. In the same way, place a panel board in Elect/Mech 113, 208, 217.
13. In Properties palette → set Panel Name = DP113, DP208, DP217.
14. On Option Bar, set Distribution System = 120/208 Wye.

23.2 Lighting Switches

Electrical switches are hosted by walls of the linked model. You will place switches in the rooms to control the lights. A single pole switch controls the lights from one location only. Multi-pole switches e.g. three-way switches can control same lights from more than one locations.

1. On System tab → Electrical panel → click small arrow to open Electrical Settings dialog box (or just press ES).
2. Click Load Calculations node and select ☑ Run calculations for loads in spaces (Fig. 23.2).

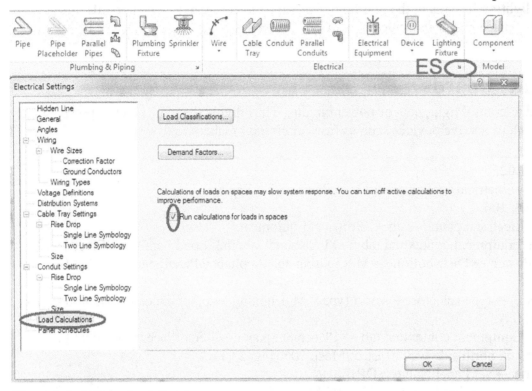

Fig. 23.2 – Electrical Settings

3. Project Browser → Electrical → Lighting → Floor Plans → 1 – Lighting.
4. On View Control tollbar, set scale = 1:100.
5. Press VG → Model Graphics tab → Unselect:
   - Data Devices.
   - Electrical Fixtures.
   - Entourage.
   - Generic Models.
   - Furniture.
   - Furniture System.
   - HVAC Zones.
   - Parking.
   - Planting.
   - Plumbing Fixtures.
   - Roads.
   - Site.
   - Spaces.
   - Topography.
   - Elevations (Annotation Categories).
   - Grids.

6. Zoom to Accounting 101.
7. On System tab → Electrical panel → Device dropdown → click Lighting tool.
8. In Properties palette → type selector → select type = M_Lighting Switches: Single Pole.

9. On Modify | Place Lighting Device contextual tab → Placement panel › click Place on Vertical Face.
10. Place a switch on left side of the door (Fig. 23.3).
11. In Properties palette, write Switch ID = 101 A.
12. Place another switch on right side of the door and write Switch ID = 101 B.

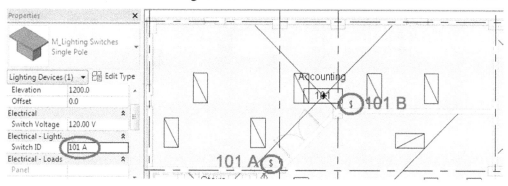

Fig. 23.3 – Switch ID

13. In Corridor 107 and Showroom 111, place switches of type = M_Lighting Switches: Three Way.
14. In this way, place all switches in all other rooms and set their Switch ID as shown in Fig. 23.4.

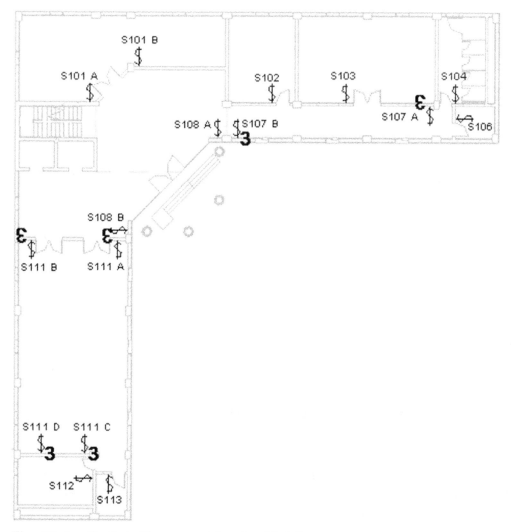

Fig. 23.4 – Switch Placement for 1 – Lighting

15. Do the same for 2 – Lighting (Fig. 23.5).

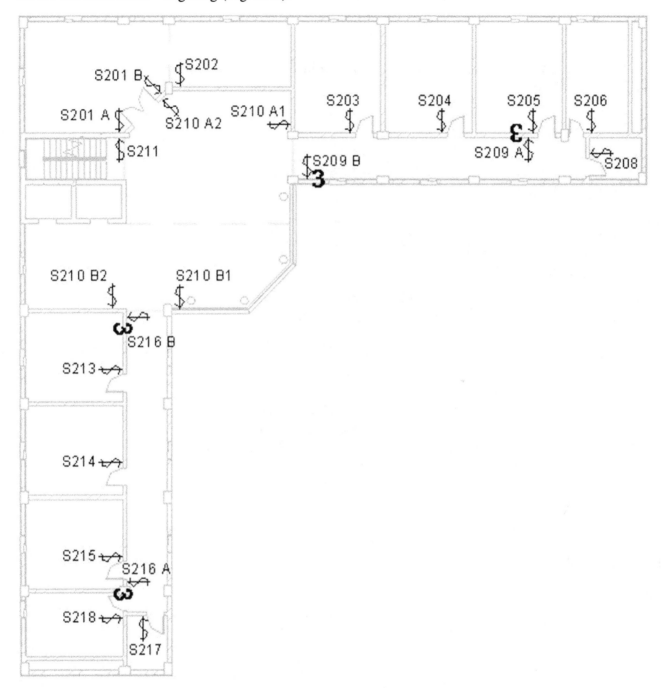

Fig. 23.5 – Switch Placement for 2 – Lighting

23.3 Switch and Power Systems for Lighting

1. Project Browser → Electrical → Lighting → Floor Plans → 1 – Lighting.
2. Zoom to Accounting 101.
3. Select four lighting fixtures on west side of Accounting 101 (Fig. 23.6).
4. On Modify | Lighting Fixtures contextual tab → Create Systems panel → click Switch. (If you do not see Switch tool, try steps 9-10 in § 20.2.1).

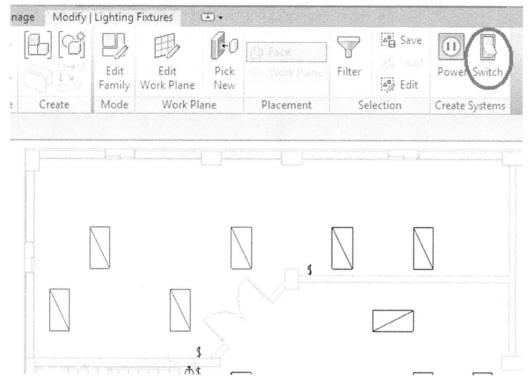

Fig. 23.6 – Selecting Lighting Fixture for Switch System

5. On Modify | Switch System contextual tab → System Tools panel → click Select Switch (Fig. 23.7).
6. Select switch S101 A. Blue dashed lines show connections.

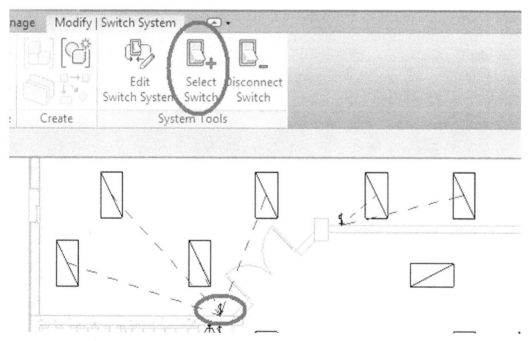

Fig. 23.7 – Switch System

7. Similarly make a switch system, connecting switch S101 B with two lighting fixtures on east side of Accounting 101.
8. Select all six lighting fixtures and two switches (S101 A and S101 B) (Fig. 23.8).
9. On Modify | Multi-Select contextual tab → Create Systems panel → click Power. (If you do not see Power tool, try steps 9-10 in § 20.2.1).

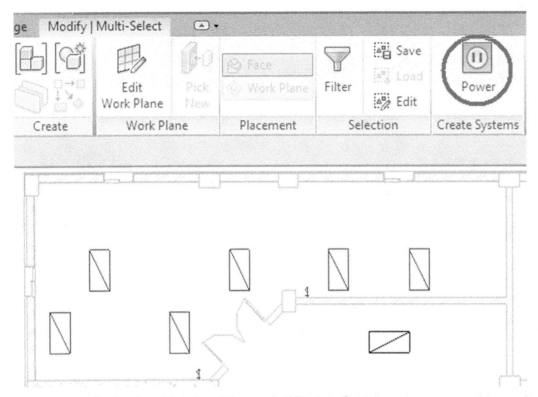

Fig. 23.8 – Selecting Lighting Fixture for Power System

10. On Modify | Electric Circuits contextual tab → System Tools panel → click Select Panel (Fig. 23.9).
11. Select panel DP106.
12. Blue dashed temporary wiring lines appear.
13. On Modify | Electric Circuits contextual tab → Convert to Wire panel → click Arc Wire. (You can select Chamfered Wire also).
14. Permanent wiring lines appear.

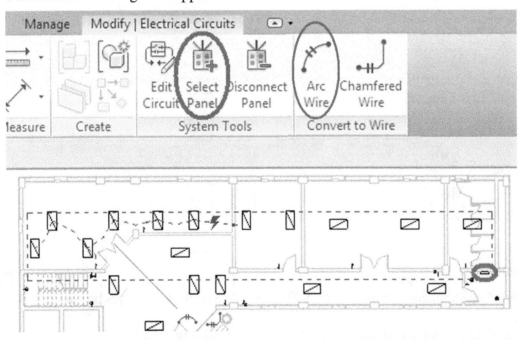

Fig. 23.9 – Connect to Panel Board

15. In the same way, make Switch System and Power System for all rooms (Fig. 23.10).

16. *Note: For Lounge 102, Cafeteria 103 and Restroom 104, make separate switch systems but one power system.*
17. *In Corridor 107, there are two lighting fixtures and two three way switches S107 A and S107 B. For switching system select only S107 A because only one switch can be used in switching system, but select both lighting fixtures and both three way switches for power system.*

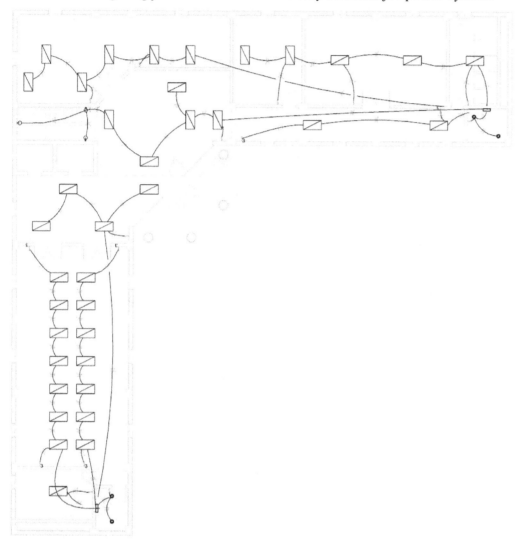

Fig. 23.10 – Wiring for 1 - Lighting

23.4 Multi-circuit Wire Runs

1. Project Browser → Electrical → Lighting → Floor Plans → 2 – Lighting.
2. Make switch systems as explained in § 23.3.
3. Zoom to west side offices 203 and 204.
4. Make electric power system for each office (Fig. 23.11).

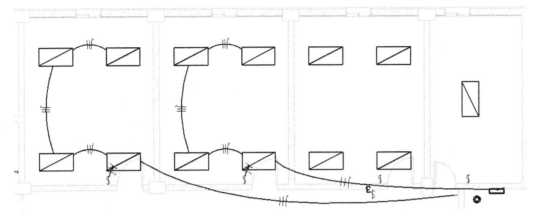

Fig. 23.11 – Wiring for offices 203 and 204

5. Each system has its own wire running to panel board. You will connect both circuits with one wire.
6. Select the wire running from room 203 to panel board. Press Delete.
7. On System tab → Electrical panel → Wire dropdown → click Arc Wire tool.
8. Connect the two lighting fixtures as shown in Fig. 23.12.

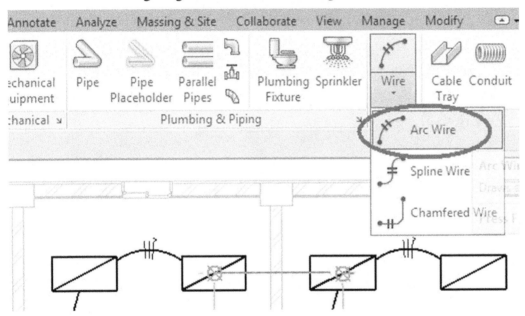

Fig. 23.12 – Multi-circuit Wire Run

9. To check connection, bring cursor on wire connecting to the panel board. When it is highlighted, press Tab and check that all wires, lighting fixtures and switches are highlighted.
10. Complete the electric wiring for 2 – Lighting as shown in Fig. 23.13.

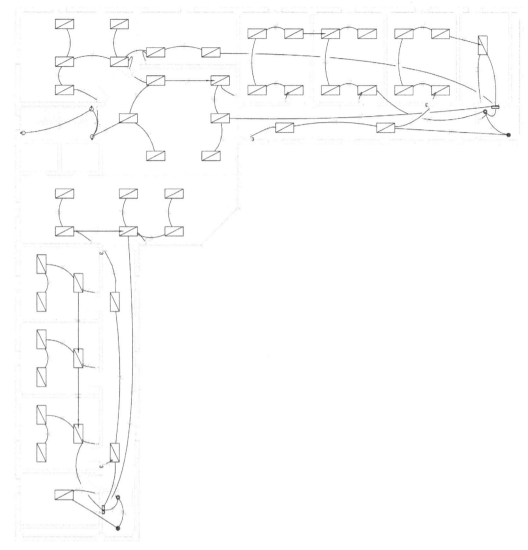

Fig. 23.13 – Wiring for 2 - Lighting

23.5 Power Receptacles

1. Project Browser → Electrical → Power → Floor Plans → 1 – Power.
2. Press VG → Model Graphics tab → Unselect:

- Entourage.
- Generic Models.
- Furniture.
- Furniture System.
- HVAC Zones.
- Parking.
- Planting.
- Plumbing Fixtures.
- Roads.
- Site.
- Spaces.
- Topography.

3. Zoom to Accounting 101.

4. On System tab → Electrical panel → Device dropdown → click Electrical Fixtures tool.
5. In Properties palette → type selector → select type = M_Duplex Receptacle: Standard.
6. On Modify | Place Devices contextual tab → Placement panel → click Place on Vertical Face.
7. Place receptacles in Accounting 101 (Fig. 23.14).

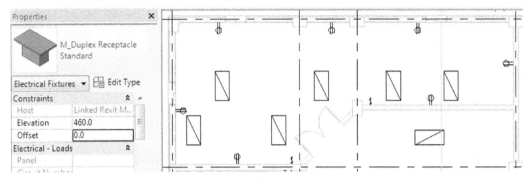

Fig. 23.14 – Power Receptacles in Accounting 101

8. In this way, place receptacles in all other rooms.
9. In Showroom 111, place receptacles on floor also. (On Modify | Place Devices contextual tab → Placement panel → click Place on Face) (Fig. 23.15).

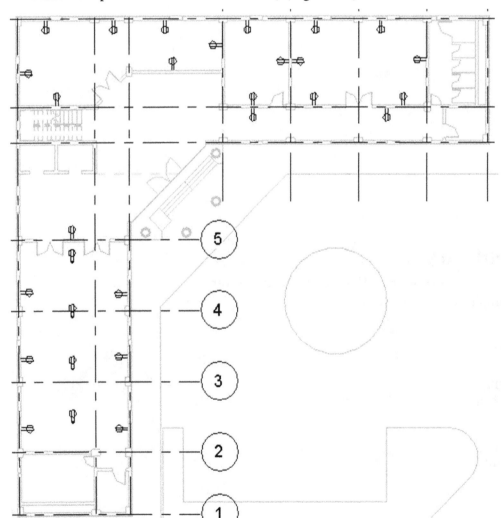

Fig. 23.15 – Power Receptacles in 1 - Power

10. Do the same for 2 – Power.

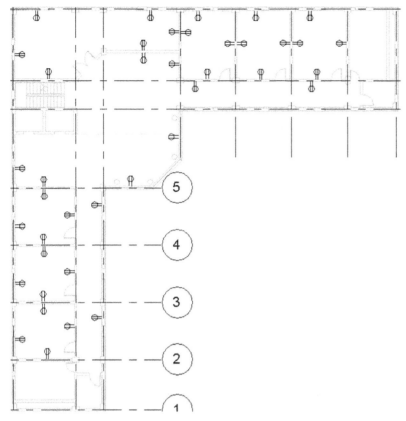

Fig. 23.16 – Power Receptacles in 2 - Power

23.6 Power Systems for Receptacles

11. Project Browser → Electrical → Power → Floor Plans → 1 – Power.
12. Zoom to Accounting 101.
13. Select all seven receptacles (Fig. 23.17).
14. On Modify | Electrical Fixtures contextual tab → Create Systems panel → click Power. (If you do not see Power tool, try steps 9-10 in § 22.2.1).

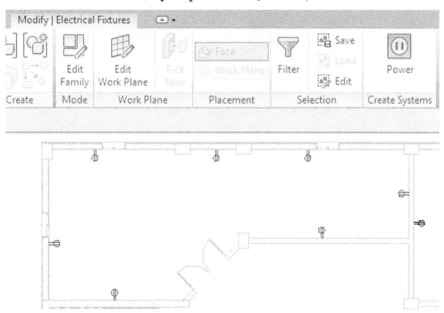

Fig. 23.17 – Selecting Receptacles for Power System

15. On Modify | Electric Circuits contextual tab → System Tools panel → click Select Panel.
16. Select panel DP106.
17. Blue dashed temporary wiring lines appear.
18. On Modify | Electric Circuits contextual tab → Convert to Wire panel → click Arc Wire. (You can select Chamfered Wire also).
19. Permanent wiring lines appear.

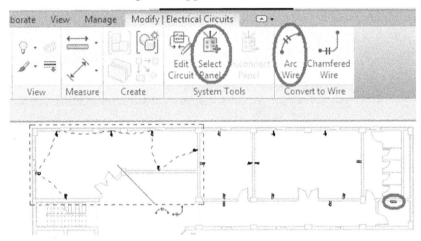

Fig. 23.18 – Creating Power System for Accounting 101

20. In the same way, complete wiring on 1 – Power (Fig. 23.19). Make multi-circuit wire runs where you want as explained in § 23.4.

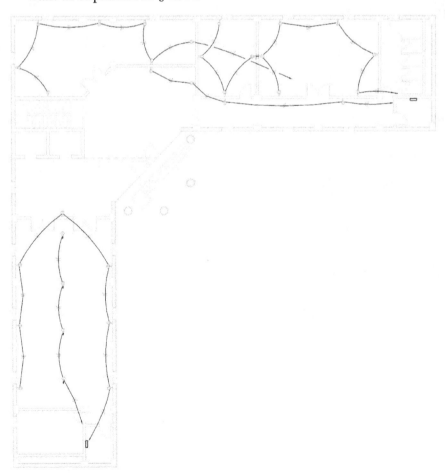

Fig. 23.19 – Power System in 1 - Power

21. Do the same for 2 – Power (Fig. 23.20).

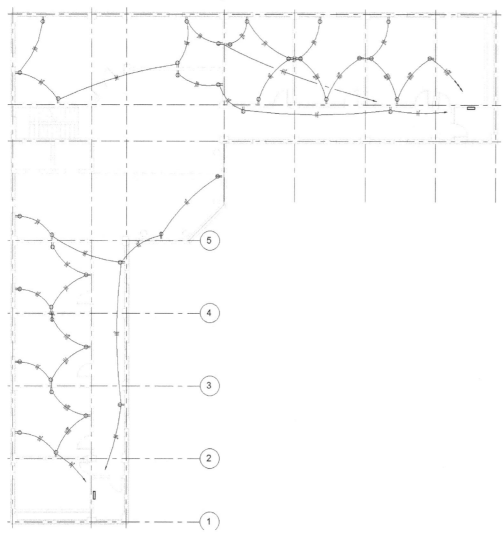

Fig. 23.20 – Power System in 2 - Power

23.7 Electrical System Documentation

You will extract different types of information from the model in the form of schedules.

23.7.1 Lighting and Power Load

You will make a schedule showing lighting and power load in different rooms.

1. On View tab → Create panel → Schedules dropdown → click Schedule/Quantities.
2. From Categories select Spaces.
3. Write Name = Lighting and Power Load → Press OK.
4. On Fields tab, add following fields

- Number
- Name
- Actual Lighting Load
- Actual Power Load
- Zone
- Level

5. On Filters tab, set as:

| Filter by: | Zone | does not equal | Shafts |
| And: | Zone | does not equal | Plenum Area |

6. On Sorting/Grouping tab, set as:

Sort by:	Level	◉ Ascending	○ Descending
☐ Header	☐ Footer:		☐ Blank line
Then by:	Zone	◉ Ascending	○ Descending
☑ Header	☑ Footer:	Title, count, and totals	☐ Blank line
Then by:	Number	◉ Ascending	○ Descending
☐ Header	☐ Footer:		☐ Blank line

7. On Formatting tab, select:
   - Calculate Totals for Actual Lighting Load.
   - Calculate Totals for Actual Power Load.
   - Hidden Field for Zone.
   - Hidden Field for Level.
8. Press OK.

23.7.2 Electrical Power Load on Panel Boards

You will make repots showing electrical load on different Panel Boards.

1. Project Browser → Electrical → Power → Floor Plans → 1 – Power.
2. Zoom to Elect/Mech 106.
3. Select the panel board DP106.
4. On Modify | Electrical Equipment contextual tab → Electrical panel → Create Panel Schedules dropdown → Click Use Default Template.
5. You will see load report for DP106.
6. In the same way, make load reports for other panels.

23.7.3 Schedule for Lighting Switch Systems

You will make a schedule showing information about switch systems.

1. On View tab → Create panel → Schedules dropdown → click Schedule/Quantities.
2. From Categories select Spaces.
3. Write Name = Lighting Switch Systems → Press OK.
4. On Fields tab, add following fields
   - Number
   - Name
   - Zone
5. On Sorting/Grouping tab,
   - Sort by Number

- ⊙ Ascending
- ☑ Header
- ☑ Itemize every instance

6. On Formatting tab, select Hidden Field for Zone.
7. On Embedded Schedule tab, Select Category = Lighting Fixtures and press Embedded Schedule Properties (Fig. 23.21).
8. On Fields tab, add following fields

   - Switch ID
   - Type
   - Panel
   - Circuit Number

9. OK → OK

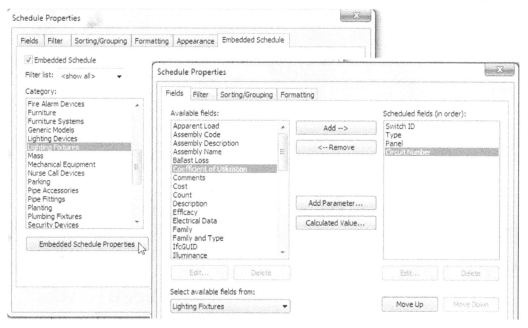

Fig. 23.21 – Switch Systems Schedule

23.8 Electrical System Presentation

You will present electrical system information on sheets.

23.8.1 Lighting Switches Layout Sheet

1. Project Browser → Sheets → Right-click → New Sheet → Select titleblock Arch A1 → OK.
2. Select the Titleblock. In Properties palette, make:

   - Sheet Number = Elect 101.
   - Sheet Name = Lighting Switches Layout.

3. Drag the views 1 - Lighting Switches and 2 - Lighting Switches on the sheet. (Set scale of the views = 1:100. If there are blank spaces around the views, crop the views before dragging on the sheet).
4. The sheet looks as shown in Fig. 23.22

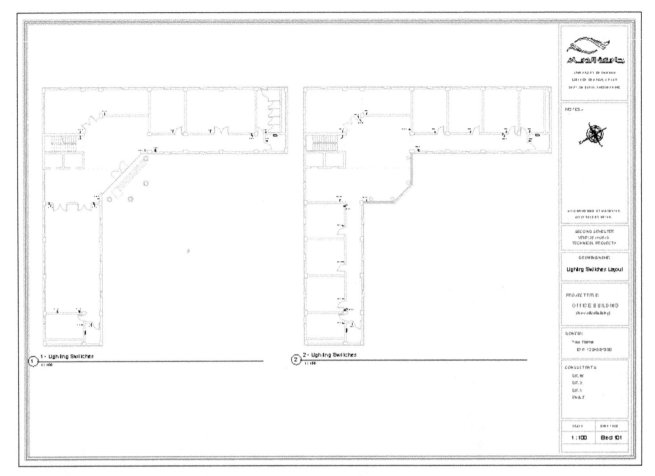

Fig. 23.22 – Lighting Switches

23.8.2 Lighting Wiring Layout Sheet

1. Project Browser → Sheets → Right-click → New Sheet → Select titleblock Arch A1 → OK.
2. Select the Titleblock. In Properties palette, make:
   - Sheet Number = Elect 102.
   - Sheet Name = Lighting Wiring Layout.
3. Drag the views 1 - Lighting and 2 - Lighting on the sheet. (Set scale of the views = 1:100. If there are blank spaces around the views, crop the views before dragging on the sheet).
4. The sheet looks as shown in Fig. 23.23.

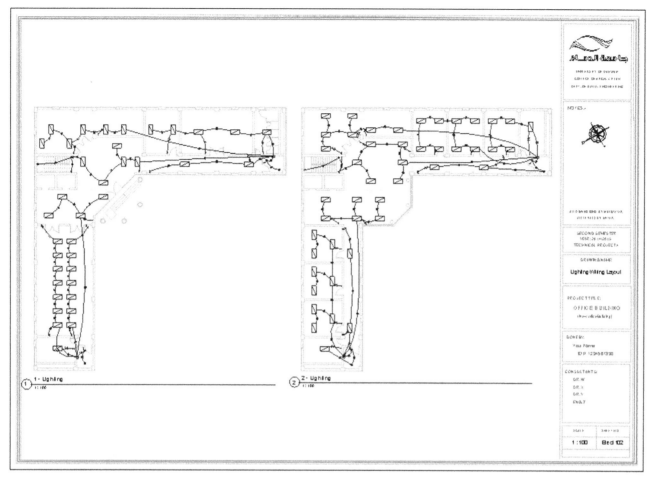

Fig. 23.23 – Lighting Wiring

23.8.3 Power Receptacles Wiring Layout Sheet

1. Project Browser → Sheets → Right-click → New Sheet → Select titleblock Arch A1 → OK.
2. Select the Titleblock. In Properties palette, make:
   - Sheet Number = Elect 103.
   - Sheet Name = Power Receptacles Wiring Layout.
3. Drag the views 1 - Power and 2 - Power on the sheet. (Set scale of the views = 1:100. If there are blank spaces around the views, crop the views before dragging on the sheet).
4. The sheet looks as shown in Fig. 23.24.

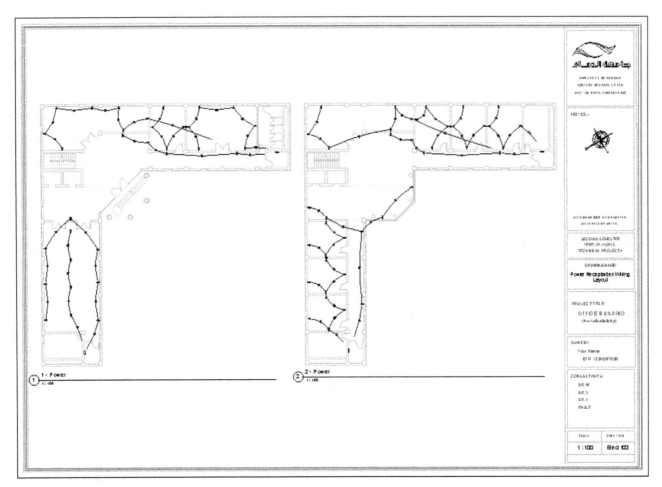

Fig. 23.24 – Power Receptacles Wiring

23.8.4 Power Load and Switch Systems Sheet

1. Project Browser → Sheets → Right-click → New Sheet → Select titleblock Arch A1 → OK.
2. Select the Titleblock. In Properties palette, make:
   - Sheet Number = Elect 104.
   - Sheet Name = Power Load and Switch Systems.
3. Drag the Lighting and Power Load schedule (which you created in § 23.7.1) on upper left corner of the sheet.
4. Drag the Lighting Switch Systems schedule (which you created in § 23.7.3) on the sheet. This schedule is very long and does not fit on the sheet, therefore delete it.
5. Right-click on Lighting Switch Systems schedule and duplicate four times. Rename them as:
   - Lighting Switch Systems GF North
   - Lighting Switch Systems GF South
   - Lighting Switch Systems FF North
   - Lighting Switch Systems FF South
6. Double-click Lighting Switch Systems GF North.
7. In Properties palette → Filer → Edit → Set:

8. Similarly set filter for other three schedules also.

9. Drag all four schedules on the sheet.
10. The sheet looks as shown in Fig. 23.25.

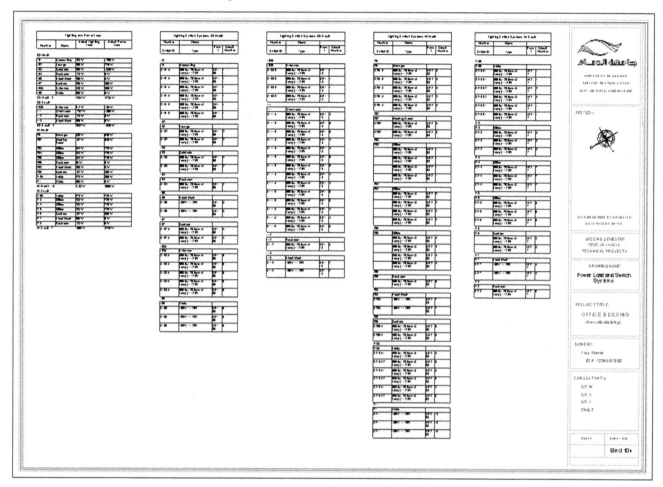

Fig. 23.25 – Power Load

23.8.5 Panel Schedules Sheet

11. Project Browser → Sheets → Right-click → New Sheet → Select titleblock Arch A1 → OK.
12. Select the Titleblock. In Properties palette, make:
    - Sheet Number = Elect 105.
    - Sheet Name = Panel Schedules.

13. Drag the panel schedules (which you created in § 23.7.2) on the sheet from Panel Schedules node of the Project Browser.
14. The sheet looks as shown in Fig. 23.26.

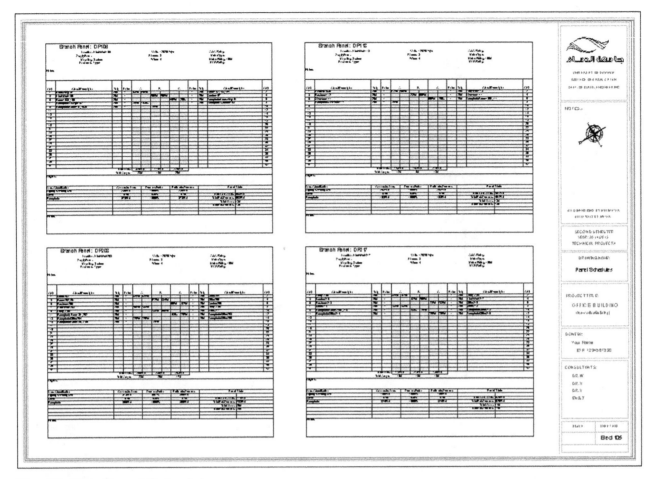

Fig. 23.26 – Panel Schedules

15. Click ![save icon] to Save Project As **EL02**.

24 Plumbing Design

You placed some plumbing fixtures in architectural model in § 3.9. You will copy them from architectural model to MEP model and make sanitary, cold water, hot water and vent systems.

24.1 Plumbing Fixtures

You will copy the plumbing fixtures from the linked model. The sanitary pipes are laid below the level, therefore you will set the view depth to -500mm.

1. Open Project **EL02.** (You can start with AC02. You can get AC02 and Arch05 from Download Folder (page v). **Keep both files in the same folder**).
2. Save Project As **PL01.**
3. Project Browser → Mechanical → Plumbing → Floor Plans → 1 – Plumbing.
4. Zoom to Restroom 104.
5. In Properties palette, View Range → Edit. Set values as shown in Fig. 24.1.

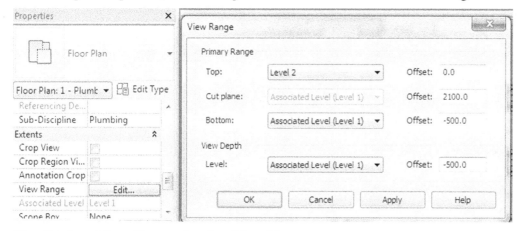

Fig. 24.1 – View Range for 1 – Plumbing

6. On Collaborate tab → Coordinate panel → Copy/Monitor dropdown → click Select Link (Fig. 24.2).

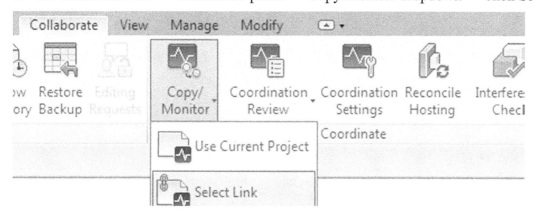

Fig. 24.2 – Select Link

7. Click on the linked model.
8. On Copy/Monitor contextual tab → Tools panel
9. Click Copy (Fig. 24.3).
10. Select ☑Multiple.
11. Select all the plumbing fixtures (5 toilets, 4 sinks, 3 drains).

12. Click Finish on Copy/Monitor option bar.

13. On Copy/Monitor contextual tab → Tools panel → click Finish ✓ .

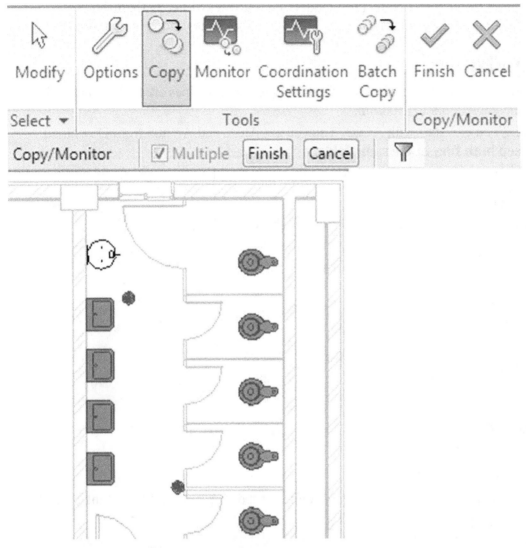

Fig. 24.3 – Copy plumbing fixtures

14. On System tab → Plumbing & Piping panel → click Plumbing Fixture.
15. From Type Selector, select Water_Heater.
16. Place it as shown in Fig. 24.3. In Properties palette set Offset = 2000.

24.2 Sanitary System

You will use PVC pipes for sanitary system. The pipes are laid at an offset of –300 mm with slope 1.000%.

24.2.1 Sanitary System for Toilets

You will make sanitary system for toilets. Main pipe and base are placed in Shaft 105.

1. Project Browser → Mechanical → Plumbing → Floor Plans → 1 – Plumbing.
2. Select a toilet.
3. In Properties palette, click Edit Type.
4. In Type Properties dialog box, under Dimensions group, set:

- Sanitary Diamctcr = 100 mm.
- Cold Water Diameter = 25 mm.

5. On View Control bar, set:
   - Detail Level = Fine
   - Visual Style = Wireframe

6. On Quick Access Toolbar, press Thin Lines ▀▟ .
7. Select all toilets.
8. On Modify | Plumbing Fixtures contextual tab → Create Systems panel → Click Piping (Fig. 24.4). (If you do not see Piping tool, try steps 9-10 in § 20.2.1).

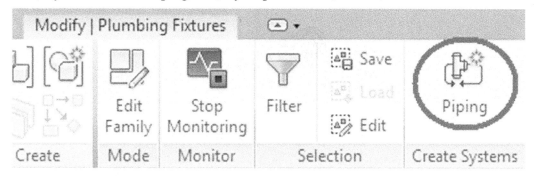

Fig. 24.4 – Piping

9. On Create Piping System dialog box, set System Type = Sanitary. (Change System Name if you want to). Press OK.
10. On Modify | Piping Systems contextual tab → Layout panel → click Generate Layout (Fig. 24.5).

Fig. 24.5 – Generate Layout

11. On Generate Layout contextual tab → Slope panel → set Slope Value = 1.000% (Fig. 24.6).
12. On Generate Layout contextual tab → Modify Layout panel → click Place Base (Fig. 24.6).

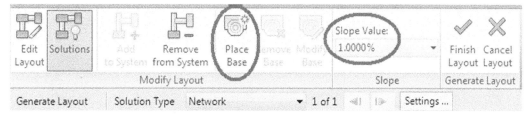

Fig. 24.6 – Set Slope Value

13. Place Base in north side of Shaft 105 (Fig. 24.7) with Offset = -900, Diameter = 100.
14. On Generate Layout contextual tab → Modify Layout panel → click Solutions (Fig. 24.7).

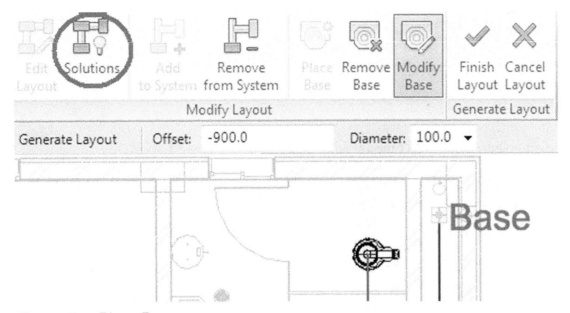

Fig. 24.7 – Place Base

15. Click on Solution arrows until you get the solution shown in Fig. 24.8.

16. On Generate Layout contextual tab → Generate Layout panel → click Finish Layout ✓.

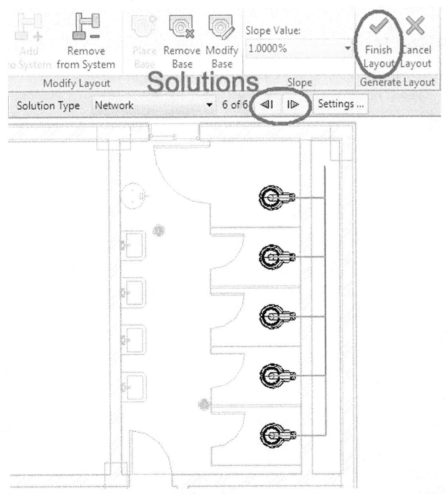

Fig. 24.8 – Solution for Toilets Sanitary

24.2.2 Cleanout in Shaft 105

There are two cleanouts in the Restroom 104 and one in Shaft 105.

1. Project Browser → Mechanical → Plumbing → Floor Plans → 1 – Plumbing.
2. On Modify tab → Modify panel → click Align tool.
3. Click on center line of cleanout then on center line of pipe to align pipe with the cleanout.
4. Select the bend. Click on **+** to change elbow to tee. Connect it to the Floor Drain.
5. **Method 1**. Select the tee. Right-click on the open end. From floating menu, select Draw Pipe (Fig. 24.9).
6. On Sloped Piping panel, select Slope Up ⬜. Select Slope Value = 1.000%.
7. Click on center of the cleanout. The cleanout connects with the main pipe.

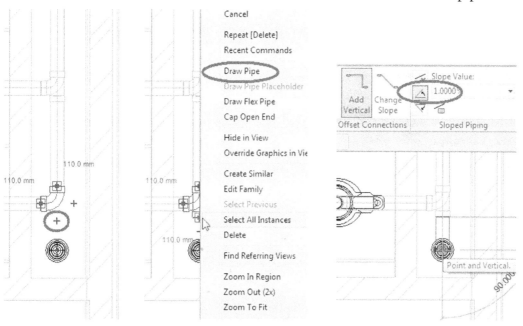

Fig. 24.9 – Connect Pipe with Floor Drain

8. **Method 2**. Select the tee. Right-click on the open end. From floating menu, select Draw Pipe.
9. On Sloped Piping panel, select Slope Up. Draw a small pipe (Fig. 24.10).

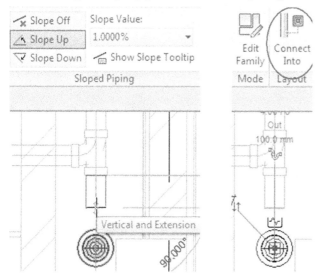

Fig. 24.10 – Connect Floor Drain into Pipe

10. Select the Floor Drain. On Layout panel, click on Connect Into (Fig. 24.10).
11. Click on small pipe.
12. **Method 3**. Draw Pipe from Tee as explained in step 9.
13. Draw a section. See the section View. (Detail Level = Fine)

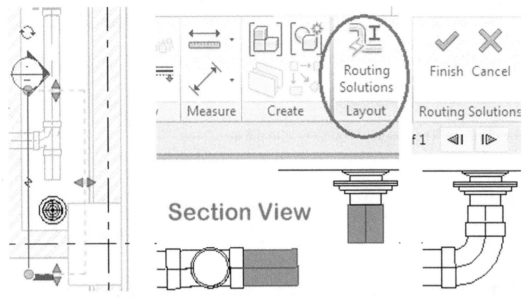

Fig. 24.11 – Connect Floor Drain with Routing Solution

14. Draw a section. See the section View. (Detail Level = Fine).
15. Draw Pipe from Floor Drain as explained in step 9.
16. On Layout panel, click on Routing Solutions.
17. On Routing Solutions panel, click on Finish.

24.2.3 Cleanouts in Restroom 104

1. On System tab → Plumbing & Piping panel → click Pipe (Fig. 24.12).

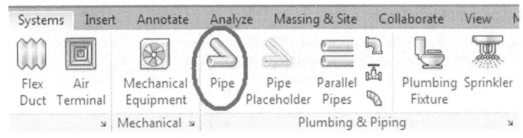

Fig. 24.12 – Draw Pipe

2. In Properties palette, select (Fig. 24.13):
   - Pipe Type = PVC Sanitary.
   - System Type = Sanitary.
3. On Option bar, select Diameter = 80.0 mm, Offset = -300.0 mm.
4. On Modify | Place Pipe contextual tab → Sloped Piping panel → select Slope Down, Slope Value = 1.000%.

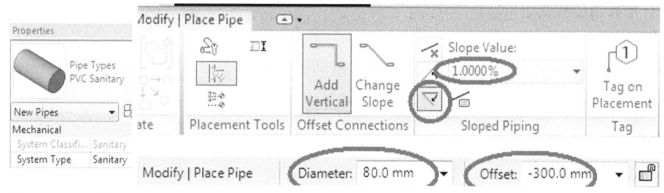

Fig. 24.13 – Pipe Properties

5. Start from center of cleanout at A and draw up to point B in line other cleanout. Then draw pipe from B to C joining the main pipe.

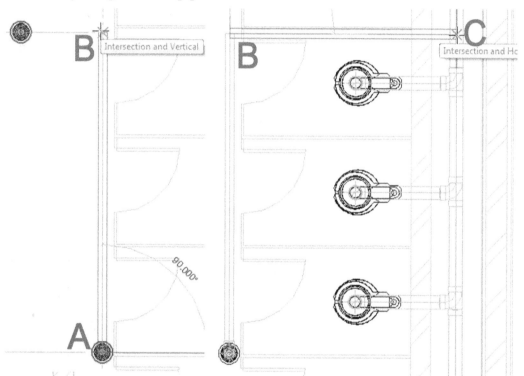

Fig. 24.14 – Draw Pipe

6. Draw a pipe joining the bend to the west side cleanout following the procedure explained in § 24.2.2.

24.2.4 Sanitary System for Sinks

You will make sanitary system for Sinks. You will attach a bottle-trap under each sink. From bottle-trap, a pipe will run into the wall behind the sinks. Pipes from two sinks will join into a multi-floor-trap (MFT). MFT's will connect to the waste pipe.

1. Project Browser → Mechanical → Plumbing → Floor Plans → 1 – Plumbing.
2. Select the sink on north side.
3. In Properties palette, click Edit Type.
4. In Type Properties dialog box, under Dimensions group, set:

    *   Sanitary Diameter = 40 mm.
    *   Cold Water Diameter = 15 mm.

- Hot Water Diameter = 15 mm.

5. On View Control bar, set:
    - Detail Level = Fine
    - Visual Style = Wireframe

6. On Quick Access Toolbar, press Thin Lines.
7. On System tab → Plumbing & Piping panel → click Plumbing Fixture.
8. From Type Selector, select Bottle_Trap.
9. Bring Bottle_Trap under the sink until it snaps to the sanitary outlet of the sink. Press space bar to turn the Bottle_Trap (Fig. 24.15).
10. Draw a section (Detail Level = Fine).
11. In the section view, select Bottle_Trap.
12. In Properties palette, set Offset = 680.
13. Select the sink. Right-click on the sanitary outlet. In the floating menu, select Draw Pipe.
14. Draw a pipe from sanitary-out of the sink to sanitary-in of the bottle_trap. (Pipe will be correct only if the bottle_trap is exactly under the sink. If it is misaligned, then draw a small pipe down under the sink and another small pipe from bottle_trap up. Align bottle_trap pipe with the sink pipe. Drag one pipe's end to the other to join both pipes).
15. Select the bottle_trap. In the floating menu, select Draw Pipe.
16. In Sloped Piping panel, Slope Down, Slope Value = 1.000%.
17. Draw pipe to the center of the wall and then vertically down.

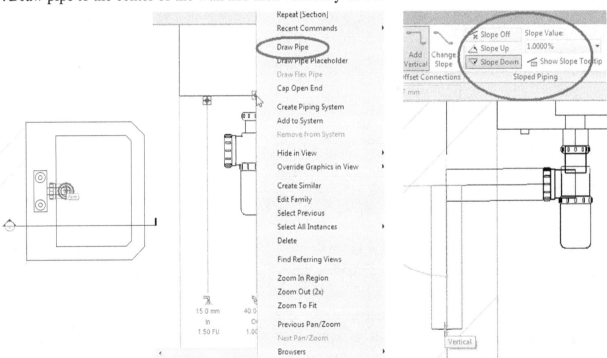

Fig. 24.15 – Sanitary Pipe under Sink

18. Select the vertical pipe. Press left or right arrows to bring the pipe near the south face of the wall.
19. Select the elbow. Click on + to convert it to tee (Fig. 24.16).

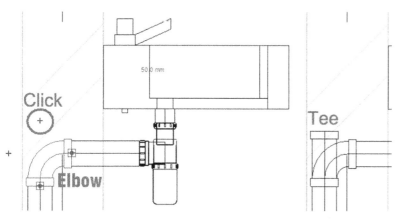

Fig. 24.16 – Elbow to Tee

20. On System tab → Plumbing & Piping panel → click Pipe.
21. In Properties palette → type selector → select type = Pipe Types: PVC Vent (Fig. 24.17).
22. System Type = Vent. Diameter = 50 mm.
23. Start from upper end of the tee and draw vertically up.

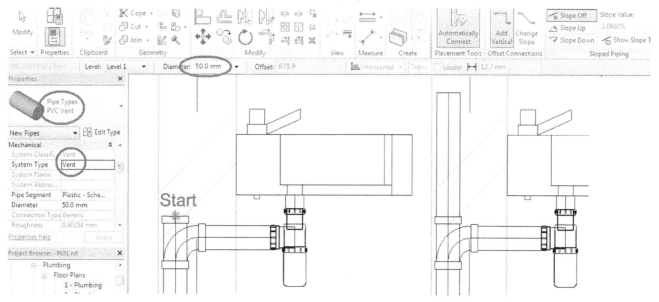

Fig. 24.17 – Vent Pipe for Sink

24. Press WT to see the plan and section views tiled. (If other views appear, close them and press WT again).
25. Select bottle_trap, pipes and pipe-fitting in the section view (Fig. 24.18).
26. Click on Control bar of the plan view to make it the active view.
27. On Modify panel, select Copy. On Option bar, select Multiple.
28. Click on the corner of the north side sink and then in the same corner of the other sinks to copy the components.

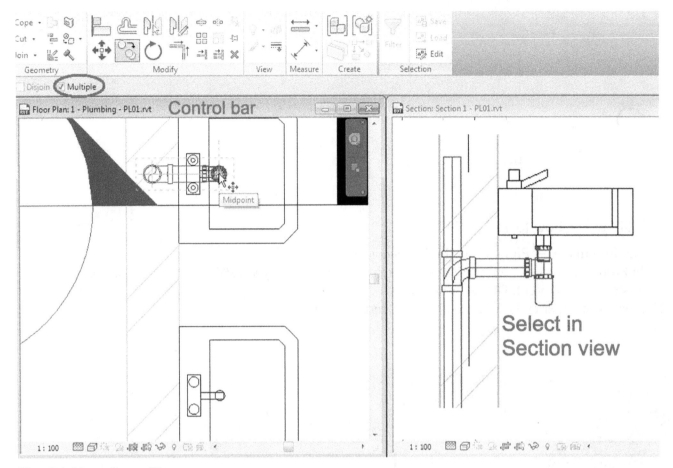

Fig. 24.18 – Copy Pipes

29. Project Browser → Mechanical → Plumbing → Floor Plans → 1 – Plumbing. (You can delete the section view).
30. On System tab → Plumbing & Piping panel → click Plumbing Fixture.
31. From Type Selector, select Multi_Floor_Trap (MFT).
32. Place Multi_Floor_Trap (MFT) between the north side sinks. Press space bar to turn the MFT.
33. Draw pipe on west side of the MFT (Slope = 1.00% Up).
34. On System tab → Plumbing & Piping panel → click Pipe Fitting.
35. Mode panel → click Load Family → Pipe → Fittings → PVC → Sch 40 → Socket-Type → DWV → M_Wye 45 Deg Double - PVC - Sch 40 - DWV.rfa.
36. Connect it to the input pipe of MFT (Fig. 24.19).
37. On System tab → Plumbing & Piping panel → click Pipe Fitting.
38. Mode panel → click Load Family → Pipe → Fittings → PVC → Sch 40 → Socket-Type → DWV → M_Cap - PVC - Sch 40 - DWV.rfa.
39. Put cap on the middle part of Double Wye and draw pipes on outer parts (Slope 1.00% Up).
40. Copy this assembly between the two south side sinks.
41. Now you will connect MFT with the outgoing pipe.
42. **Method 1**. Select MFT. On Layout panel, click on Connect Into. (Connector 80 mm).
43. Click on center line of the outgoing pipe. MFT will be connected to the outgoing pipe.
44. **Method 2**. Select MFT. Right-click on 80 mm connector. Click on Draw Pipe.
45. On Offset Connections panel, click on Change Slope (Fig. 24.20).
46. Click on center line of the outgoing pipe. A sloped pipe will be drawn from MFT to the outgoing pipe.

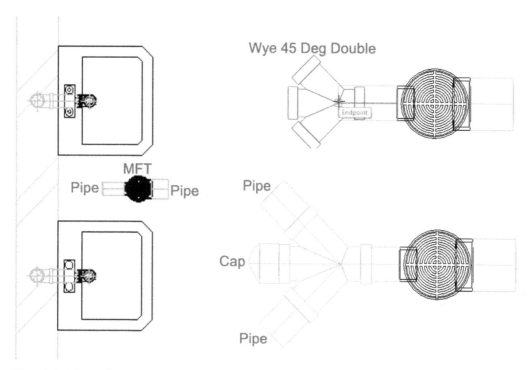

Fig. 24.19 – Connecting Wye 45 Deg Double and Cap

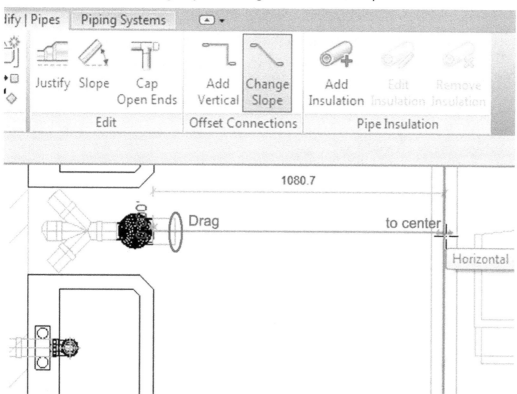

Fig. 24.20 – Draw Sloped Pipe

47. Project Browser → Mechanical → Plumbing → 3D Views → 3D Plumbing.
48. Zoom to backside of the sinks.
49. Select two pipes shown in Fig. 24.21.
50. On Layout panel, select Routing Solutions.
51. Cycle through different solutions to find the appropriate solution.
52. On Routing Solutions panel, click Finish.

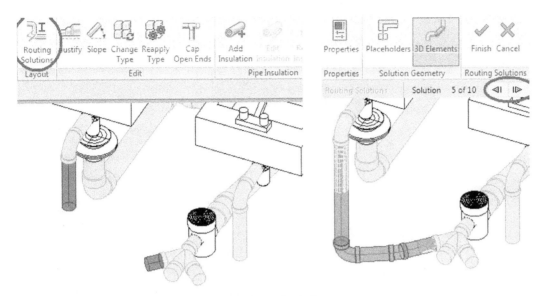

Fig. 24.21 – Select pipes for Routing Solutions

53. Do the same for other sinks.
54. The overall sanitary layout 3D view will be as shown in Fig. 24.22.

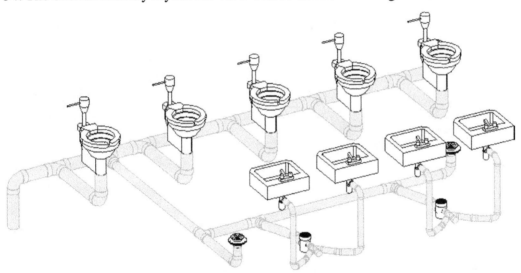

Fig. 24.22 – Overall Sanitary Layout

24.3 Vent System

You will use PVC pipes for vent system. The pipes are raised to offset = 2750 with zero slope.

24.3.1 Vent Pipes for Toilets

You will make vent system for toilets.

1. Project Browser → Mechanical → Plumbing → Floor Plans → 1 – Plumbing.
2. Draw a section near south toilet (Fig. 24.23).

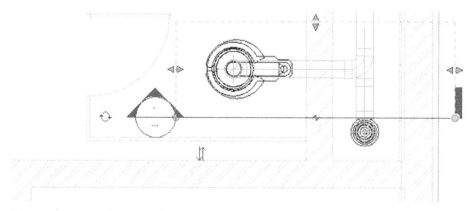

Fig. 24.23 – Draw a Section

3. Double-click on the section head. Section view will open.
4. On View Control bar, set:
   - Detail Level = Fine
   - Visual Style = Wireframe
5. On System tab → Plumbing & Piping panel → click Pipe.
6. In Properties palette → type selector → select
   - type = Pipe Types: PVC Vent.
   - System Type = Vent.
   - Diameter = 50 mm.
   - Slope Off
7. Start from the pipe under the wall and draw vertically up in the wall (Fig. 24.24).

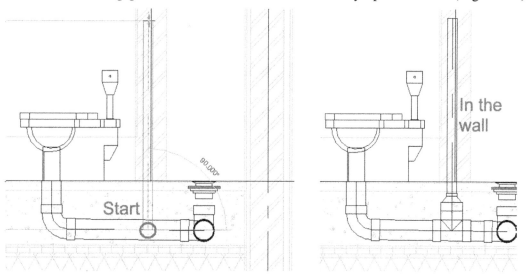

Fig. 24.24 – Draw Vent Pipe for Toilets

8. Do the same for other toilets.
9. Select all vertical vent pipes for toilets and in section view, push them away from toilets to make space for cold water pipe.

24.3.2 Vent System for Sinks

1. Project Browser → Mechanical → Plumbing → Floor Plans → 1 – Plumbing.
2. On System tab → Plumbing & Piping panel → click Pipe.

3. In Properties palette → type selector → select
   - type = Pipe Types: PVC Vent.
   - System Type = Vent
   - Diameter = 50 mm
   - Offset = 2750
   - Slope Off
4. Draw pipe starting from A → bend at B → to C in the shaft close to wall → Offset = 4000 → to D (Fig. 24.25)
5. Delete the last part from C to D (with elbow) in 3D view.
6. Draw pipe (Offset = 2750) starting from E, joining BC at F.
7. Draw pipe (Offset = 2750) starting vent pipe of sink, joining AB.
8. Draw pipe (Offset = 2750) starting vent pipe of toilet, joining EF.

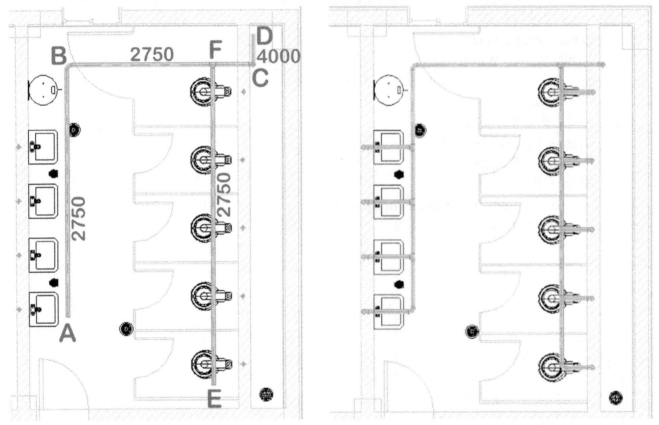

Fig. 24.25 – Draw Vent Pipe   Fig. 24.26 – Vent Pipe Layout

9. Delete extra pipe near A and E. Convert any Tee at end to Elbow (Fig. 24.26).
10. The overall sanitary and vent layout 3D view will be as shown in Fig. 24.27.

Fig. 24.27 – 3D View of Sanitary and Vent pipes

11. Click  to Save Project As **PL01**.

24.4 Cold Water System

You will use PVC pipes for cold water system. The pipes are laid at different offsets with zero slope.

24.4.1 Cold Water System for Toilets

You will make cold water system for toilets.

1. Open Project **PL01.**
2. Save Project As **PL02.**
3. Project Browser → Mechanical → Plumbing → Floor Plans → 1 – Plumbing.
4. Select all toilets.
5. On Modify | Plumbing Fixtures contextual tab → Create Systems panel → Click Piping (Fig. 24.28). (If you do not see Piping tool, try steps 9-10 in § 20.2.1).

6. On Create Piping System dialog box, set System Type = Domestic Cold Water. (Change System Name if you want to). Press OK.
7. On Modify | Piping Systems contextual tab → Layout panel → click Generate Layout (Fig. 24.29).

Fig. 24.28 – Piping

Fig. 24.29 – Generate Layout

8. On Generate Layout contextual tab → Slope panel → set Slope = 0.000%.
9. On Option bar, click Settings (Fig. 24.30). Set Offset = 355.6 for Main and Branch. (The Offset of cold water input connector for M_Water Closet - Flush Valve - Floor Mounted: Public - Flushing greater than 6.1 Lpf is 355.6. If you are using a different type of water closet, set Offset equal to the Offset of cold water input connector).

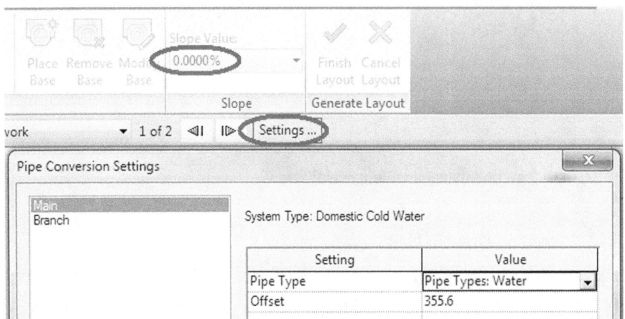

Fig. 24.30 – Cold Water Settings

10. Select solution shown in Fig.24.31.
11. On Generate Layout panel, click Finish Layout.
12. Select the cold water pipe. Using left arrow key, bring the cold water pipe inside the east wall. (Or Edit Layout → Bring pipe inside the wall → Finish) (Fig. 24.31).
13. Adjust position of pipes so that there is no conflict between the cold water and vent pipes.

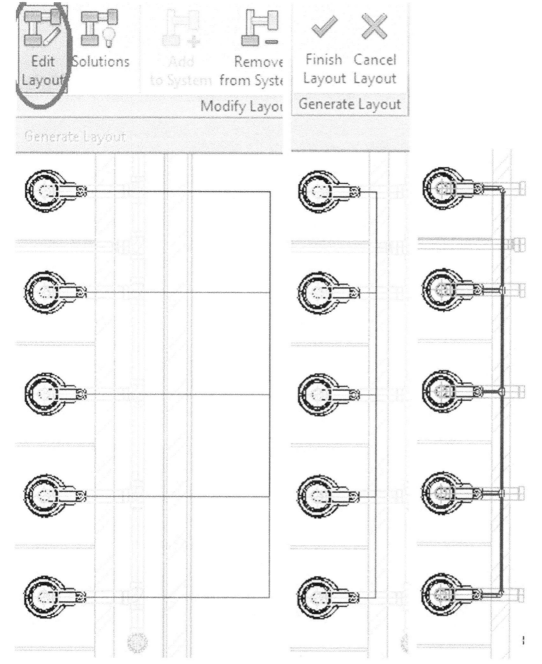

Fig. 24.31 – Cold Water Layout for Toilets

24.4.2 Cold Water System for Sinks

You will make cold water system for sinks.

1. Project Browser → Mechanical → Plumbing → Floor Plans → 1 – Plumbing.
2. Select all sinks.
3. On Modify | Plumbing Fixtures contextual tab → Create Systems panel → Click Piping (Fig. 24.32). (If you do not see Piping tool, try steps 9-10 in § 20.2.1).
4. On Create Piping System dialog box, set System Type = Domestic Cold Water. (Change System Name if you want to). Press OK.
5. On Modify | Piping Systems contextual tab → Layout panel → click Generate Layout (Fig. 24.33).

Fig. 24.32 – Piping

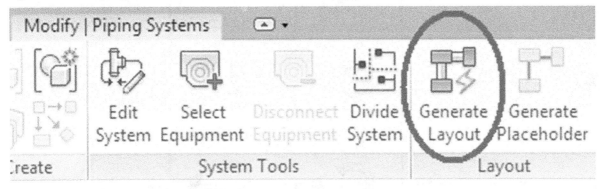

Fig. 24.33 – Generate Layout

6. On Generate Layout contextual tab → Slope panel → set Slope = 0.000%.
7. On Option bar, click Settings. Set Offset = 540.0 for Main and Branch.
8. Select a solution.
9. On Modify Layout panel, select Edit Layout.
10. Bring the cold water pipe inside the west wall (Fig. 24.34).
11. On Generate Layout panel, click Finish.
12. Adjust position of pipes so that there is no conflict between the cold water and vent pipes.

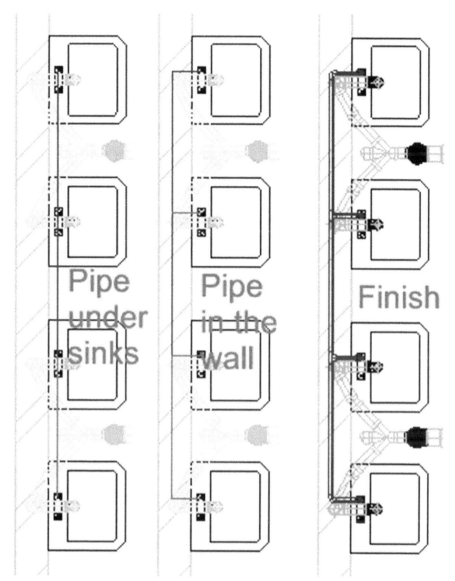

Fig. 24.34 – Cold Water Layout for Sinks

24.4.3 Cold Water Supply Connections

You will make cold water supply connections.

1. Project Browser → Mechanical → Plumbing → Floor Plans → 1 – Plumbing.
2. On System tab → Plumbing & Piping panel → click Pipe (Fig. 24.35).
3. In Properties palette, select (Fig. 24.36):
    • Pipe Type = Water.
    • System Type = Domestic Cold Water.
4. On Option bar, select Diameter = 15.0 mm, Offset = 2800.0 mm.
5. On Modify | Place Pipe contextual tab → Sloped Piping panel → select No Slope, Slope Value = 0.000%.

Fig. 24.35 – Draw Pipe   Fig. 24.36 – Water Pipe Settings

6. Start from point A (at the center of cold water pipe of sinks) and draw up to point B (at outer side of east wall in the shaft) (Fig. 24.37).

7. Change Offset = 4000 and draw pipe from B to C along the outer side of east wall.

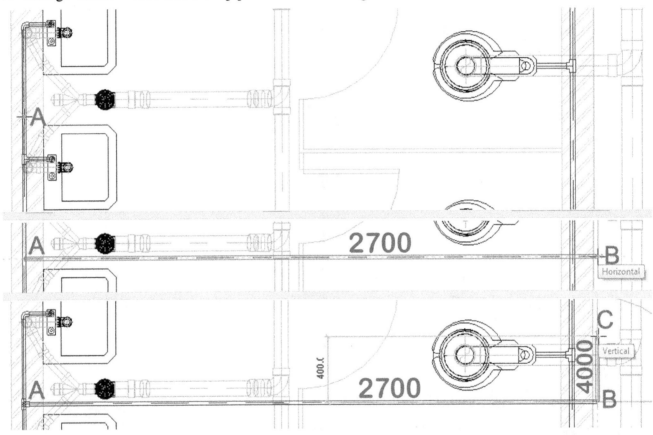

Fig. 24.37 – Cold Water pipe connections

8. Change Offset = 2800. Draw a pipe from point D (on the overhead pipe) to E. Take a bend and draw up to point F (at the center of cold water pipe of toilets) (Fig. 24.38).

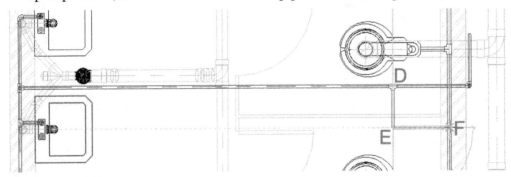

Fig. 24.38 – Cold Water supply for Toilets

9. Select the Water heater (Fig. 24.39).

10. In the Layout panel, click on Connect Into.
11. In Select Connector dialog box, select Connector 1: Domestic Cold Water : Round : 20 mm : CW Inlet.
12. Select the overhead cold water pipe.
13. The water heater is connected to cold water supply.

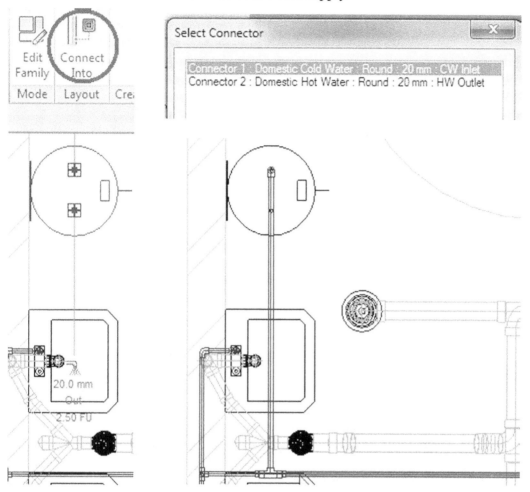

Fig. 24.39 – Cold Water supply for Water Heater

14. The overall cold water layout 3D view will be as shown in Fig. 24.40.

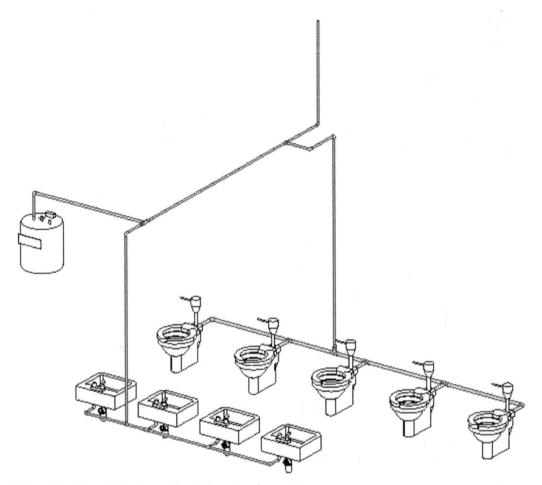

Fig. 24.40 – 3D view of cold water layout

15. Click [save icon] to Save Project As **PL02**.

24.5 Hot Water System

You will use PVC pipes for hot water system. The pipes are laid at different offsets with zero slope.

24.5.1 Hot Water System for Sinks

You will make hot water system for sinks.

1. Open Project **PL02.**
2. Save Project As **PL03.**
3. Project Browser → Mechanical → Plumbing → Floor Plans → 1 – Plumbing.
4. Select all sinks.
5. On Modify | Plumbing Fixtures contextual tab → Create Systems panel → Click Piping. (Fig. 24.41). (If you do not see Piping tool, try steps 9-10 in § 20.2.1).

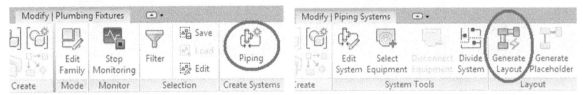

Fig. 24.41 – Piping   Fig. 24.42 – Generate Layout

6. On Create Piping System dialog box, set System Type = Domestic Hot Water. (Change System Name if you want to). Press OK.
7. On Modify | Piping Systems contextual tab → Layout panel → click Generate Layout (Fig. 24.42).
8. On Generate Layout contextual tab → Slope panel → set Slope = 0.000%.
9. On Option bar, click Settings. Set Offset = 490.0 for Main and Branch.
10. Select a solution.
11. On Modify Layout panel, select Edit Layout.
12. Move the hot water pipe inside the west wall.
13. On Generate Layout panel, click Finish (Fig. 24.43).

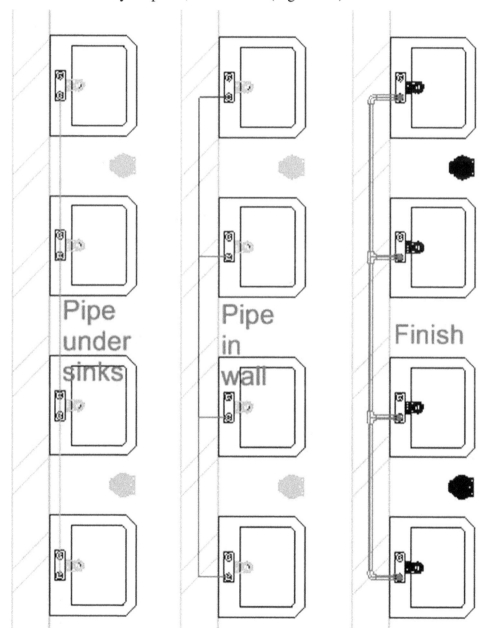

Fig. 24.43 – Hot Water Layout for Sinks

24.5.2 Hot Water Pipe Sizing

You will make Hot water supply connections.

1. Project Browser → Mechanical → Plumbing → Floor Plans → 1 – Plumbing.

2. Zoom to north side sink.
3. Click on the elbow (Fig. 24.44).
4. Click on + to convert elbow to tee.
5. Right-click on tee. On floating menu, select Draw pipe.
6. Draw pipe towards north. Press ESC.

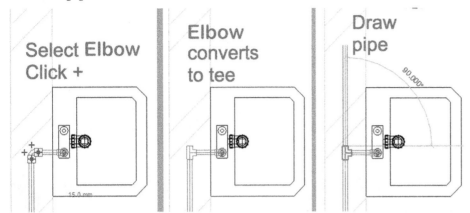

Fig. 24.44 – Hot Water Pipe

7. Bring cursor on the open end of the pipe. When it is highlighted, press Tab two times or more until all hot water pipes are highlighted. Click to select.
8. On Piping Systems contextual tab → Analysis panel → Click Duct/Pipe Sizing (Fig. 24.45).
9. In the Pipe Sizing dialog box, set:
    - Velocity = 2.5 m/s.
    - ⊙ And
    - Friction = 250.00 Pa/m
    - Branch Sizing = Match Connector Size.
10. Press OK.

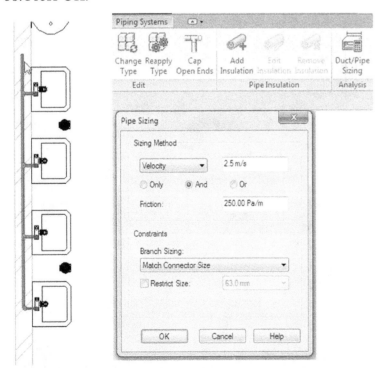

Fig. 24.45 – Pipe Sizing

11. *Sometimes there are problems in pipe sizing because enough space is not available for larger sizes. To overcome this, do the following:*
    - Select a pipe parallel to the array of fixtures (in this case sinks).
    - Pressing arrow keys, temporarily move pipe away from the fixtures.
    - Make sizing.
    - Pressing arrow keys, move pipe near again.
12. Pipe Sizing is done.
13. Click on the open end of hot water pipe.
14. On Option bar, Diameter = 32.0 mm. The connector sizes of the water heater should also be same.
15. Select the water heater.
16. In Properties palette, click Edit Type.
17. In Type Properties dialog box, under Plumbing group, set:
    - HW Outlet = 32.0 mm.
    - CW Inlet = 32.0 mm.

24.5.3 Hot Water Supply Connection with Water Heater

You will make Hot water supply connection with water heater.

18. Project Browser → Mechanical → Plumbing → Floor Plans → 1 – Plumbing.
19. Zoom to open end of hot water pipe.
20. Right-click on open end. On floating menu, select Draw pipe (Fig. 24.46).
21. Draw pipe towards north until you see intersection line with hot water connector of the water heater.
22. On Option bar, change offset to 2750.0.
23. Draw pipe connecting to hot water connector of the water heater.

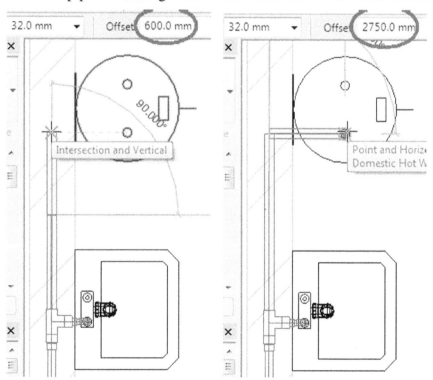

Fig. 24.46 – Hot Water supply for Water Heater

24. The overall hot water layout 3D view will be as shown in Fig. 24.47.

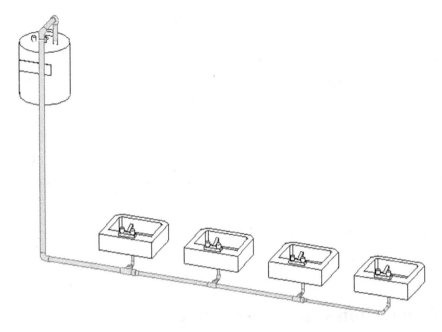

Fig. 24.47 – 3D view of hot water layout

24.6 Pipe Sizing and Valves

You will make pipe sizing for cold water pipes. Then you will connect valves. The valve size will be chosen according to the pipe size.

1. Project Browser → Mechanical → Plumbing → 3D Views → 3D Plumbing.
2. Bring cursor on the open end of the vertical pipe in Shaft 105. When it is highlighted, press Tab two times or more until all cold water pipes are highlighted. Click to select.
3. On Piping Systems contextual tab → Analysis panel → Click Duct/Pipe Sizing.
4. Follow the steps explained in § 23.4.2.
5. The valves will be connected at four places. Pips sizes are shown in Fig. 24.48.

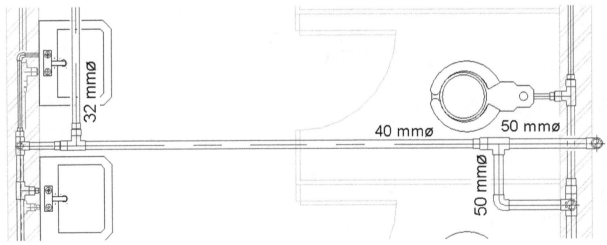

Fig. 24.48 – Check pipe sizes to install valves

6. On System tab → Plumbing & Piping panel → click Pipe Accessory.
7. Load Family → Pipe → Valves → Globe Valves → M_Globe Valve - 10-50 mm - Threaded.rfa.
8. In Properties palette → type selector → select appropriate size and click on the pipe. The valve will be connected.
9. The overall plumbing layout 3D view will be as shown in Fig. 24.49.

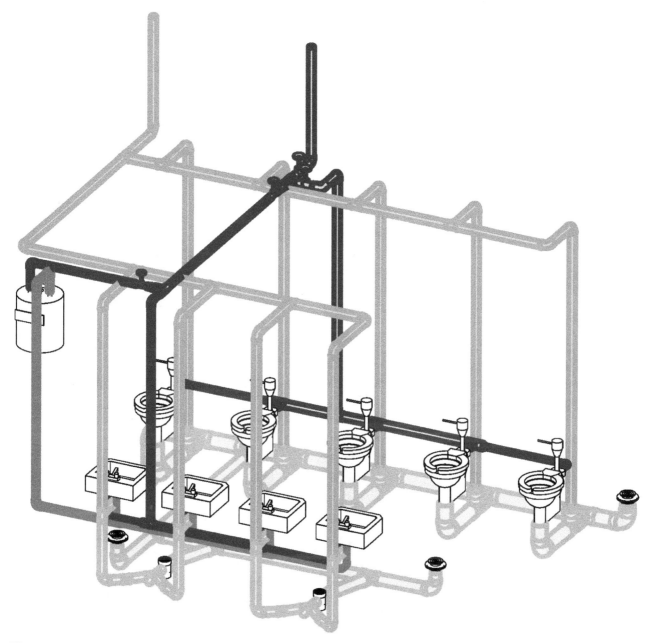

Fig. 24.49 – 3D view of plumbing layout on 01 GF level

24.7 Plumbing on Upper Levels

You will copy the same plumbing layout on level 2.

1. Project Browser → Mechanical → Plumbing → Floor Plans → 2 – Plumbing.
2. Copy plumbing fixtures from the linked model as explained in § 23.1. (Do not place water heater).
3. Project Browser → Mechanical → Plumbing → 3D Views → 3D Plumbing.
4. Select all on level 1. With Shift-click, remove sinks, toilets and cleanouts.
5. Copy – Paste to Level 2.
6. Now you will join all vertical pipes in the shaft.
7. Draw a section in the Shaft 105 (Fig. 24.50).
8. In the section view, change elbows to tees for cold water and vent pipes.
9. Draw pipes downwards and join with Level 1 pipes.

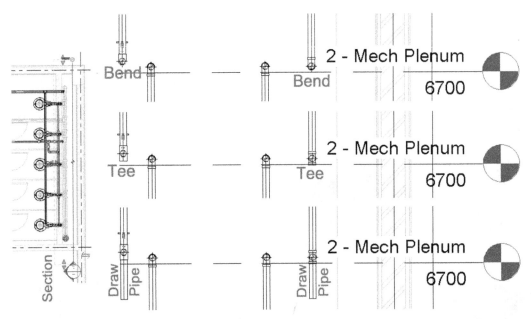

Fig. 24.50 – Section view in shaft

10. In the same way, join vertical sanitary pipes. (Convert Level 1 elbow to tee. Draw a small pipe upwards. Select two vertical pipes and make routing solutions).
11. Still some problems. In the shaft, Cold Water and Vent pipes seem to be passing through Level 2 Sanitary pipe.
12. Select the vertical Vent pipe. Press arrow keys to move it away (Fig. 24.51).
13. .Make another section view. Draw Cold Water pipe away from Level 2 Sanitary pipe.

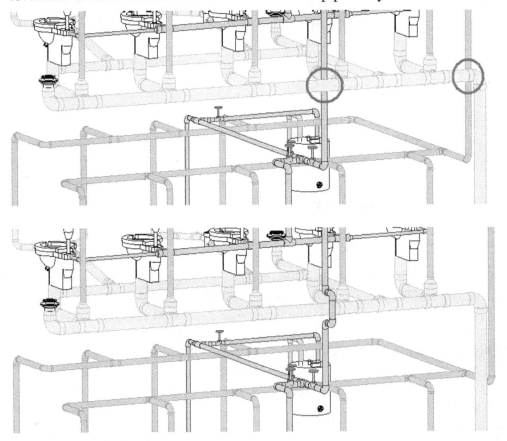

Fig. 24.51 – Move Pipes

14. The overall plumbing layout 3D view for two levels will be as shown in Fig. 24.52.

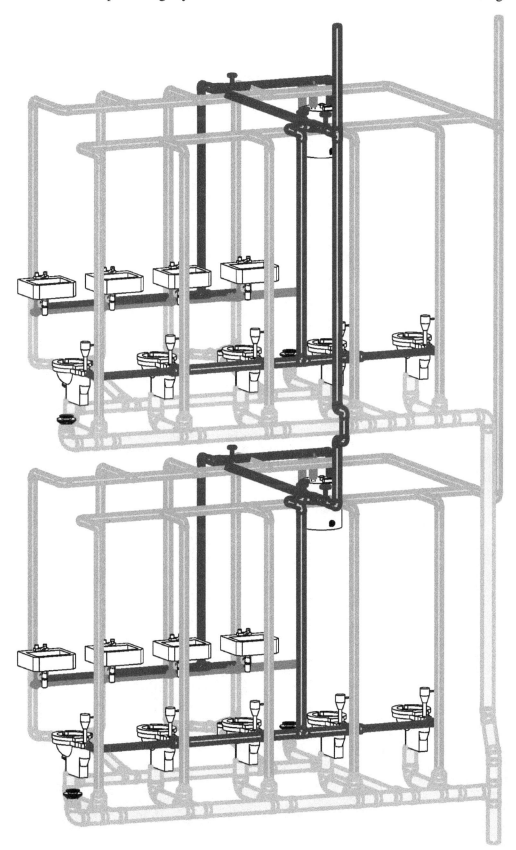

Fig. 24.52 – 3D view of plumbing layout on both levels

24.8 Presentation of Plumbing System

You will make sheets showing details about different plumbing systems.

24.8.1 Ground Floor Sanitary System

1. Project Browser → Mechanical → Plumbing → Floor Plans → 1 – Plumbing.
2. On View tab → Create panel → Callout dropdown → click Rectangle.
3. Draw a rectangular callout around the walls of the Restroom 104 (Fig. 24.53).
4. You will see a view 1 – Plumbing – Callout 1 in Project Browser under Plumbing - Floor Plans node.

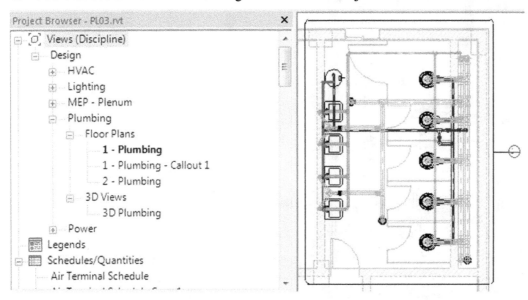

Fig. 24.53 – 1 – Plumbing – Callout 1

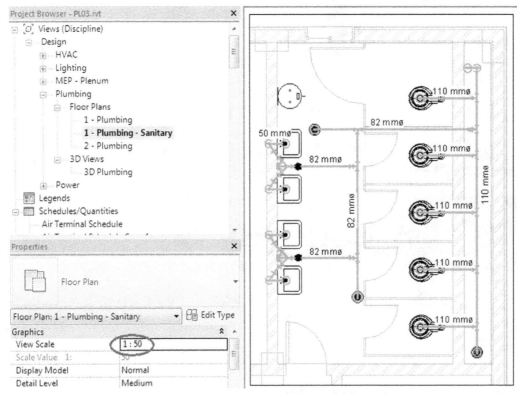

Fig. 24.54 – Sanitary Pipe Tags

5. Rename it as 1 – Plumbing – Sanitary.
6. Project Browser → Mechanical → Plumbing → Floor Plans → 1 – Plumbing – Sanitary.
7. On View Control bar, select scale = 1:20.
8. On Quick Access Toolbar, unselect Thin Lines.
9. In Properties palette → View Range → Edit → Set Top = Associated Level. Offset = 3400 → OK.
10. Press VG. On Filters tab, under Visibility column, select Sanitary only and unselect all others. OK.
11. On Annotate tab → Tag panel → click Tag by Category.
12. Add tags on pipes. Click on tags and move the away from pipes (Fig. 24.54).

24.8.2 Ground Floor Vent System

1. Project Browser → Mechanical → Plumbing → Floor Plans → 1 – Plumbing – Sanitary.
2. In Project Browser, right-click on 1 – Plumbing – Sanitary → Duplicate View → Duplicate.
3. Right-click on 1 – Plumbing – Sanitary Copy 1 → Rename as 1 – Plumbing – Vent.
4. Project Browser → Mechanical → Plumbing → Floor Plans → 1 – Plumbing – Vent.
5. Press VG. On Filters tab, under Visibility column, select Vent only and unselect all others. OK.
6. On Annotate tab → Tag panel → click Tag by Category.
7. Add tags on pipes. Click on tags and move the away from pipes (Fig. 24.55).

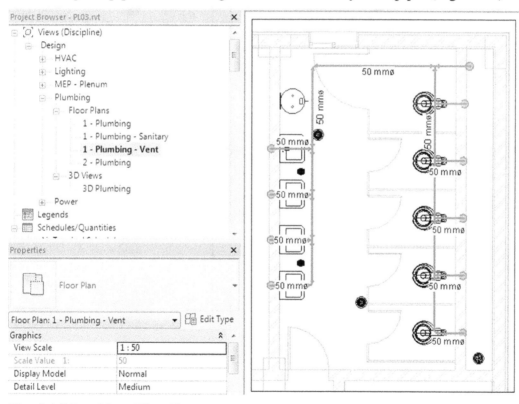

Fig. 24.55 – Vent Pipe Tags

24.8.3 Ground Floor Cold Water System

1. Project Browser → Mechanical → Plumbing → Floor Plans → 1 – Plumbing – Sanitary.
2. In Project Browser, right-click on 1 – Plumbing – Sanitary → Duplicate View → Duplicate.
3. Right-click on 1 – Plumbing – Sanitary Copy 1 → Rename as 1 – Plumbing – Cold Water.
4. Project Browser → Mechanical → Plumbing → Floor Plans → 1 – Plumbing – Cold Water.
5. Press VG. On Filters tab, under Visibility column, select Domestic Cold Water only and unselect all others. OK.

6. On Annotate tab → Tag panel → click Tag by Category.
7. Add tags on pipes. Click on tags and move the away from pipes (Fig. 24.56).
8. Use Leader with tags where needed. (Select a tag. On Option bar, select Leader. Move tag. Move Leader from its Control Point).

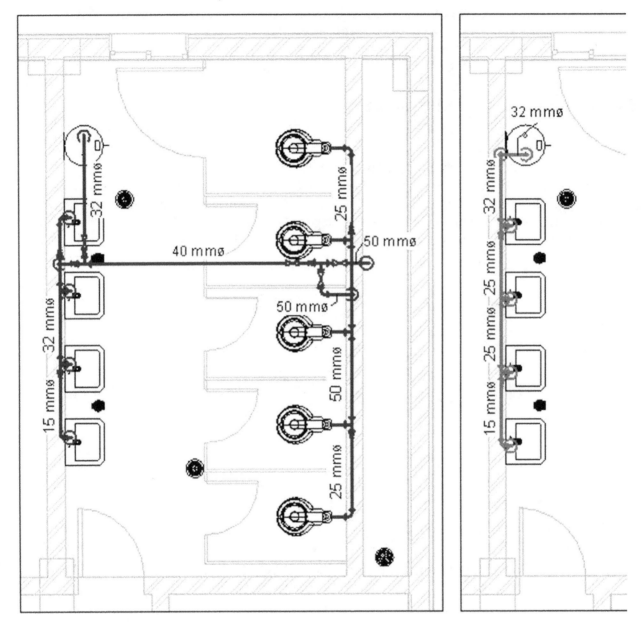

Fig. 24.56 – Cold and Hot Water Pipe Tags

24.8.4 Ground Floor Hot Water System

1. Project Browser → Mechanical → Plumbing → Floor Plans → 1 – Plumbing – Sanitary.
2. In Project Browser, right-click on 1 – Plumbing – Sanitary → Duplicate View → Duplicate.
3. Right-click on 1 – Plumbing – Sanitary Copy 1 → Rename as 1 – Plumbing – Hot Water.
4. Project Browser → Mechanical → Plumbing → Floor Plans → 1 – Plumbing – Hot Water.
5. Press VG. On Filters tab, under Visibility column, select Domestic Hot Water only and unselect all others. OK.
6. On Annotate tab → Tag panel → click Tag by Category.
7. Add tags on pipes. Click on tags and move the away from pipes.

24.8.5 Ground Floor Plumbing System Sheets

1. Project Browser → Sheets → Right-click → New Sheet → Select titleblock Arch A1 → OK.
2. Select the Titleblock. In Properties palette, make:
   - Sheet Number = Plumbing 101.
   - Sheet Name = Hot and Cold Water Pipe Layout.
3. Drag the views 1 – Plumbing – Cold Water and 1 – Plumbing – Hot Water on the sheet.
4. The sheet looks as shown in Fig. 24.57.

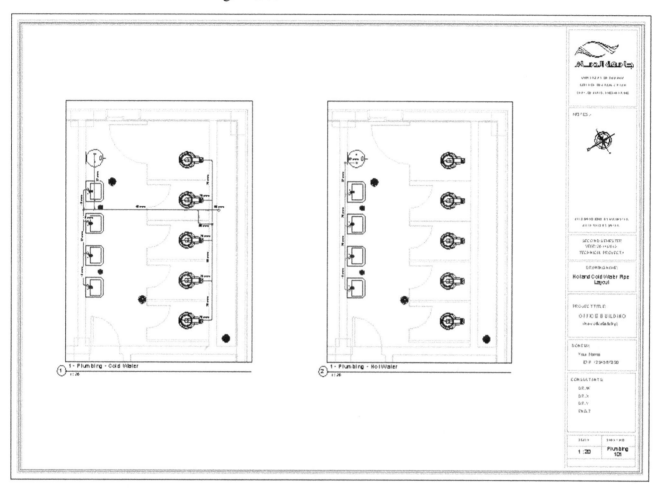

Fig. 24.57 – Sheet for Hot and Cold Water System

5. Project Browser → Sheets → Right-click → New Sheet → Select titleblock Arch A1 → OK.
6. Select the Titleblock. In Properties palette, make:
   - Sheet Number = Plumbing 102.
   - Sheet Name = Sanitary and Vent Pipe Layout.
7. Drag the views 1 – Plumbing – Sanitary and 1 – Plumbing – Vent on the sheet.
8. The sheet looks as shown in Fig. 24.58.

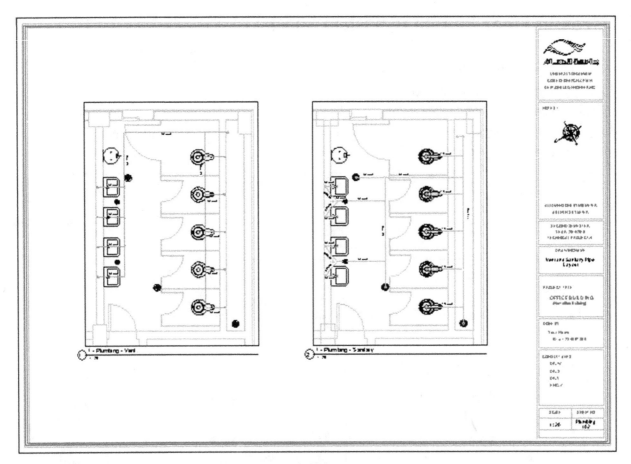

Fig. 24.58 – Sheet for Vent and Sanitary Systems

24.8.6 Ground Floor 3D View of Plumbing System

1. Project Browser → Mechanical → Plumbing → 3D Views → 3D Plumbing.
2. In Project Browser, right-click on 3D Plumbing → Duplicate View → Duplicate.
3. Right-click on 3D Plumbing Copy 1 → Rename as 3D Plumbing S V.
4. Project Browser → Mechanical → Plumbing → 3D Views → 3D Plumbing S V.
5. Adjust the section box to view only the Ground Floor plumbing only. (Follow the steps explained in § 9.7).
6. Using the View Cube, set a certain orientation of the 3D view (Fig. 24.59).
7. On View Control bar, click on Save Orientation and Lock View. (Once the view is locked, you cannot change its orientation. If you want to change the orientation, you will unlock the view again).

Fig. 24.59 – Lock 3D View

8. On View Control bar, click on Show Crop Region.
9. Click on the crop region boundary. Bring the four boundaries close to the layout.
10. On View Control bar, click on Hide Crop Region.
11. On View Control bar, select a scale of 1:25.

12. Press VG. On Filters tab, under Visibility column, select Sanitary and Vent only and unselect all others. OK.

13. On Annotate tab → Tag panel → click Tag by Category.

14. Add tags on pipes. Click on tags and move the away from pipes.

15. Project Browser → Mechanical → Plumbing → 3D Views → 3D Plumbing S V.

16. In Project Browser, right-click on 3D Plumbing → Duplicate View → Duplicate.

17. Right-click on 3D Plumbing Copy 1 → Rename as 3D Plumbing C H.

18. Project Browser → Mechanical → Plumbing → 3D Views → 3D Plumbing C H.

19. Press VG. On Filters tab, under Visibility column, select Domestic Cold Water and Domestic Hot Water only and unselect all others. OK.

20. On Annotate tab → Tag panel → click Tag by Category.

21. Add tags on pipes. Click on tags and move the away from pipes.

22. Project Browser → Sheets → Right-click → New Sheet → Select titleblock Arch A1 → OK.

23. Select the Titleblock. In Properties palette, make:

   • Sheet Number = Plumbing 103.
   • Sheet Name = 3D Plumbing Layout.

24. Drag the views 3D Plumbing S V and 3D Plumbing S V on the sheet.

25. The sheet looks as shown in Fig. 24.60.

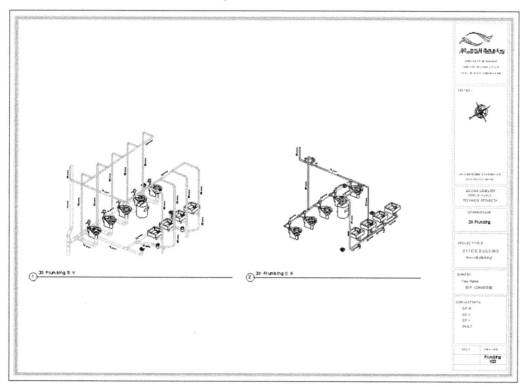

Fig. 24.60 – Sheet for 3D Views of Vent and Sanitary Systems

26. Click [save icon] to Save Project As **PL03**.